The Gazelle

The Gazelle

Medieval Hebrew Poems on God, Israel, and the Soul

Raymond P. Scheindlin

OXFORD UNIVERSITY PRESS
New York   Oxford

Oxford University Press

Oxford   New York
Athens   Auckland   Bangkok   Bogotá   Buenos Aires   Calcutta
Cape Town   Chennai   Dar es Salaam   Delhi   Florence   Hong Kong   Istanbul
Karachi   Kuala Lumpur   Madrid   Melbourne   Mexico City   Mumbai
Nairobi   Paris   São Paulo   Singapore   Taipei   Tokyo   Toronto   Warsaw

and associated companies in
Berlin   Ibadan

Copyright © 1991 by Raymond P. Scheindlin

First published by The Jewish Publication Society, 1991
Philadelphia   New York

First issued as an Oxford University Press paperback, 1999

Oxford is a registered trademark of Oxford University Press, Inc.

Library of Congress Cataloging-in-Publication Data
The gazelle : medieval Hebrew poems on God, Israel. and the soul /
[compiled and translated by] Raymond P. Scheindlin.
p.   cm.
Hebrew poems and English translation on opposite pages; commentary
and notes in English
Companion vol. to: Wine, women, and death.
Originally published: Philadelphia : Jewish Publication Society, 1991.
Includes bibliographical references and index.
ISBN 0-19-512988-1 (paper)
1. Hebrew poetry, Medieval—Translations into English.   2. Jewish
religious poetry, Hebrew—Translations into English.   3. Hebrew
poetry. Medieval—History and criticism.   4. Jewish religious
poetry, Hebrew—History and criticism.   I. Scheindlin, Raymond P.
PJ5059.E3G3913   1999
892.4'1208—dc21   99-11841
                                                                    CIP

1 3 5 7 9 8 6 4 2

Printed in the United States of America
on acid-free paper

To Gerson D. Cohen

Contents

Foreword

In the early eleventh century, Jewish synagogue poets in Arabic-speaking Spain began to compose poetry addressed to God, using themes and imagery derived from secular love poetry. In my earlier book, *Wine, Women, and Death: Medieval Hebrew Poems on the Good Life*, I attempted to describe and explain this secular poetry, the appearence of which was a surprising innovation in the history of Hebrew literature. The present book attempts to complement that study of Hebrew literature in medieval Spain with a discussion of the religious poetry composed in the same circles by the same poets.

The title, *The Gazelle*, alludes to the nexus between the two bodies of Hebrew literature. In love poetry, the gazelle is one of several animals frequently used as a simile or epithet for the beloved. Along with many other conventions of secular poetry, this image was taken over into liturgical poetry, where it represents God or the Messiah, depicted as Israel's lovers, or Israel itself, represented as God's beloved.

The Gazelle is thus a companion to *Wine, Women, and Death*. The earlier work made the case for the worldliness of Golden Age courtier-rabbis. Yet, for all their worldliness, and despite the sensuousness that they celebrated in life and poetry, the courtier-rabbis managed to be spiritual people as well; and for all the universalism of their outlook, they continued to be Jews. A description of the rich and complex culture of the Hebrew poets of Arabic-speaking Spain would be incomplete and misleading if it did not account for religious attitudes and religious poetry. In order to understand their age it is important to study both sides of their activity.

The Gazelle is a complete and independent work, but it is best read in conjunction with *Wine, Women, and Death*. The fact that both types of poetry coexisted in the medieval Jewish community is more interesting than the existence of either type taken separately. Furthermore, much about the liturgical poetry is not fully intelligible without an acquaintance with secular love poetry. Accordingly, in the course of the exposition I have taken every possible opportunity to refer the reader to the earlier work.

The history of Hebrew religious poetry is far more complex than that of secular poetry. The latter began in the tenth century, but liturgical poetry had its origins in the Talmudic period, and by the tenth century had grown and spread to every part of the world reached by the Jews. Thus the introduction to this book must reach far back into Jewish history and literature. Furthermore, while the secular poetry was but little influenced by the liturgical poetry, the latter was heavily influenced by the former. The secular background has been sketched in *The Gazelle* so that it can be read independently of *Wine, Women, and Death*.

The Gazelle was written during a leave of absence made possible by a grant from the Guggenheim Foundation. The preparation of the manuscript was accomplished during an additional leave supported by the Abbell Research and Publication Fund of the Jewish Theological Seminary. In this connection I wish to thank most particularly Chancellor Ismar Schorsch of the Jewish Theological Seminary for his continual encouragement, understanding, and friendship.

Thanks are due also to the Hochschule für Jüdische Studien in Heidelberg and to the Oxford Centre for Postgraduate Hebrew Studies for their hospitality while the work was in progress.

I have learned much about verse translation through discussions with Evan Zimroth, who critiqued a draft of the translations; about medieval philosophy from my teacher and colleague Fritz Rothschild; and about the poems themselves from my colleague Menahem Schmelzer, who read a draft of the entire work and made numerous enlightening comments. Sheila Segal, Diane W. Zuckerman, and Ilene Cohen, editors and consultants of the Jewish Publication Society, provided invaluable guidance and advice. Naomi Lewin and my wife, Janice Meyerson, assisted with the technical preparation of the manuscript.

Finally, I wish to thank the editors of Prooftexts for permitting republication of the parts of Chapter I that appeared in an earlier form in that journal.

The Gazelle

Introduction

THE JUDEO-ARABIC DUALITY

Rabbi Moses Ibn Ezra was a sober and distinguished leader of the Jewish community of Granada at the height of the Golden Age of Spanish Jewry. A former student at the renowned rabbinical academy of Lucena, he was also a poet who specialized in composing penitential liturgy for the synagogue. Among his many compositions of this type we find the following lines, part of a poem included in the services of the penitential month preceding the Jewish New Year:

> Her name is "Earth"
> > And of no worth
> > > Are all her ways.
> A garden green,
> > But in her trees
> > > Are poisoned leaves.
> . . . .
> And if she speaks
> > Smooth words and sweet
> > > Into your ears,

Pay her no heed!
     Her words sound true,
          But false her deeds,
And when she sings,
     Her words are mixed
          With poison fell.
Resist her beauty;
     None but fools
          Thrill to her charms.
Suck not the sap
     Her nipples drip;
          Press not her breast.
How I have come
     To hate this life!
          How bad its ways now seem![1]

The world here is said to resemble a beautiful woman singing in a garden; but the woman is a whore, her song a lie, and the garden abundant with poisoned fruit.

The language and the imagery of this poem are by no means original with Ibn Ezra but are drawn from an age-old tradition of wisdom literature.[2] It is ironic, however, that Moses Ibn Ezra should be the bearer of this literary tradition, for elsewhere in his poetry he champions the very way of life that he here decries. In fact, his secular verse employs the very same imagery with exactly the opposite intent, depicting gardens and dancing girls as emblems of a world of poignant beauty meant for society's elite and deriding those who do not share this taste. This attitude was not a personal idiosyncrasy but was shared by his entire social class.

Another example shows how intimately Ibn Ezra knew the sensuous world that his penitential poem so bitterly rejects. Here he uses language derived from the Torah to bid his reader celebrate the rebirth of the garden in spring, and imagery resembling that of our penitential poem to advocate a life of pleasure and sensuality:

Caress a lovely woman's breast by night,
And kiss some beauty's lips by morning light.

Silence those who criticize you, those
Officious talkers. Take advice from me:
With beauty's children only can we live.

....
Immerse your heart in pleasure and in joy,
And by the bank a bottle drink of wine
Enjoy the swallow's chirp and viol's whine.[3]
....

Living as he did in two different ideological systems at once, combining sincere piety with a sincere commitment to earthly beauty and pleasure, Moses Ibn Ezra was the product of the peculiar Jewish culture of Arabic-speaking Andalusia. From the mid-tenth to the mid-twelfth centuries there existed in Muslim Spain an elite class of Jewish courtiers and officials who were as polished in Arabic language, literature, and culture as they were learned in the Hebrew language and the Jewish religious tradition. With the gradual reconquest of Spain by Christianity from the mid-twelfth century on,[4] this class continued to exist under the altered cultural and social conditions. This later period, which lasted until the expulsion in 1492, also had its great poets, philosophers, and scientists; but the two centuries from the reign of ʿAbd al-Raḥmān III (912–961) to the collapse of Almoravid rule over Spain (1145) were the high-water mark of Jewish culture in Spain and the age of its greatest successes.[5]

During this period, the Jewish elite had access to positions of power in the Muslim courts of Spain. They were exposed to a brilliant and proud culture, and they absorbed as much of it as they could accommodate to their Jewish loyalties. The problem of how much non-Jewish culture one could in conscience adopt was resolved in different ways by different persons. There is evidence that on one end of the continuum were religious extremists for whom any amount of foreign culture was too much. On the other end were Jews who became so integrated into Arabic culture that they converted to Islam, contributing their skills to a host people who welcomed their conversion and did not discriminate against them on account of their Jewish origins. Between the extremes were those who created the Golden Age of Hebrew letters in medieval Andalusia by attempting to balance the two cultures. As happens whenever cultures are allowed to come together, rather than being kept apart by ideological rigidity and fear of contamination, the result was complex and eclectic, with occasional signs of strain. Here and there, the works of each of the great figures of the Golden Age betray the author's unease.[6]

The literary, religious, and philosophical worlds in which the courtier-rabbis moved all included elements conducive to symbiosis.

POETRY AND RELIGION

Poetry, the most prestigious literary category and the chief cultural institution of the Arabic-speaking world, was religiously neutral, for it was rooted in the period before Muhammad and Islam, known to Muslims as the Age of Ignorance. Though rejected by Islam, the traditions of this period lived on in poetry and, to some extent, in life.

From pre-Islamic times the Arabs had inherited such values of Bedouin desert culture as courage and skill in war, endurance, tribal loyalty, generosity, and hospitality. Also associated with Bedouin life were the worldly pleasures of drinking, games, and sex, as well as certain personal attitudes such as pride and dignity. Though the forms in which these values and attitudes found expression had been modified by urbanization and by the influence of the vast populations conquered and absorbed in the course of the seventh and eighth centuries, they remained a substratum of Arabic culture. Their chief medium, in the Age of Islam as in the Age of Ignorance, was poetry. Poetry had served as the archive of the tribes' traditions and values and as the record of their battles; it was a source of pride, a tool of war, a form of competition, and a means of entertainment. The conquering Arabs carried this poetic heritage along with their language and religion to the new territories, where it was adopted by the native populations. Persians, Egyptians, Berbers, and Jews were soon memorizing the ancient Arabian classics and composing new poems in the same language and spirit.

Against this heritage stood the new religion, Islam, demanding loyalty to a community of believers rather than to a tribe and holding up before its adherents lofty ideals of spirituality, asceticism, humble submission to God, and religious scholarship. The

Bedouin at first resisted these ideals as contrary to their way of life. Muhammad in turn denounced Arabic poetry as the embodiment of paganism, and its ideals as the antithesis of religion:

> As for the poets, the erring follow them. Hast thou not seen how they stray in every valley, and how they say that which they do not?[7]

But even Muhammad was said to have enjoyed poetry and to have encouraged certain poets in his entourage.

After his death Islam made an uneasy peace with poetry, which flourished as an Arabic, rather than an Islamic, element within the Muslim world. As Islam evolved into a world empire, the tribe was replaced by the court, and its warrior-nomads by caliphs, statesmen, public officials, and members of the state bureaucracy. Within these circles a new ideal type now flourished: the *adīb*, a kind of Muslim humanist who understood statecraft and commanded the social graces; who knew something about everything, but a lot about the Arabic language and its poetry. Though such persons took religion seriously, their main concern was public life and the skills connected with it. The elegance that they cultivated in both life and language was something that could be acquired by anyone—even a non-Muslim—who possessed the means and the wit. Thus, literary and social culture, known as *adab*, was a door through which some Jews and Christians could pass to prominence in the medieval Muslim world. Muslim religious authorities made their peace with the new cultural ideal: sometimes they even embraced it. But the poetry cultivated by the *adīb* continued the old, pre-Islamic literary traditions. It was accommodated, if uneasily, by official Islam.

When Arabic poetry eventually did find a place in the religion of Islam, it was for limited purposes. The early ninth century saw the emergence in Arabic of a poetry of asceticism (*zuhdiyāt*), in which elements of Islam and of the older Middle Eastern culture mated, producing versified exhortations to live in awareness of death and to renounce the vanities of material pleasures. The immediate impulse behind this denunciation of worldly pleasures for a life dedicated to contemplation of death and service to God was the eschatological message of the Quran. But the Quran itself had inherited many of these ideas from Christianity and the monks of the Byzantine Middle East.[8] Furthermore, much of the contents of the ascetic poetry derives not from revelation or from any particular religious tradition but from a pessimistic attitude toward life that was widespread in the ancient cultures of the region. Even within the predominantly moderate and optimistic attitudes of the rabbis of the Talmud, this strand of pessimism and rejection of the world may be seen to thread its way. Thus, the ascetic poetry cultivated by early Muslim pietists was a gnomic literature that could speak to adherents of any of the three monotheistic religions. One example is the following poem, in which the "abode" is of course the world:

> An abode whose love has afflicted me—
> A woman who deceives her lovers.
> All men are consumed, afflicted,
> With what she gives and what she snatches,
> Her charm and her deceit,
> Her distance and her intimacy
> Her praise and her blame,
> Her love and her abuse . . . [9]

The ideology of this Arabic poem is no different from that of the Hebrew poem by Moses Ibn Ezra with which this chapter began. Here then is a literary manifestation of Islam that crosses the boundaries of religion on the path of international gnomic verse.[10]

Poetry and religion also converged in Sufism. The greatest literary by-products of their partnership came later than the period of the great Hebrew poets. But Sufism made a contribution to Islam that did affect the Hebrew writing of the Golden Age, for it offered an approach to religious experience that could transcend the detailed precepts of revealed religion. This tendency should not be exaggerated, for most Sufis were not antinomians but pious Muslims, and socially they were usually to be counted among the conservative element in Islamic society. But for many Sufis, observance of religious law was only the first step toward full religious development, which leads from religious law to "the Way," that is, to perfect, existential confession of the unity of God.[11]

Since in Sufism the specific details of the Islamic religious tradition are transcended by a larger spiritual vision, many of its characteristic ideas and even much of its spiritual language could be and were easily adopted by like-minded adherents of other religions. Jews are known to have studied works of Muslim mystics and religious thinkers of a spiritual bent, and even to have translated them into Hebrew. The influence of these works has been traced in the writings of the eleventh-century Jewish pietist Baḥya Ibn Paquda and of the thirteenth-century mystic Abraham Maimonides. When Abraham Ibn Ḥasdai, in the twelfth century, translated into Hebrew the inspirational treatise *The Balance of Religious Practice* by the renowned Muslim religious thinker abū Ḥāmid al-Ghazzālī, he needed to make only minor alterations, substituting passages from the Bible and the Oral Law for Ghazzālī's quotations from the Quran and the Muslim tradition. The great bulk of the treatise was perfectly suitable for the religious guidance of Jews. This commonality went so far that the Jew Baḥya and the Muslim al-Ghazzālī could *both* adopt and incorporate into their own works with only slight changes a treatise by a Christian Arab writer.[12]

Arabic literature and Islamic religion were thus two discrete native elements of the civilization inhabited by the Jewish courtier-rabbis, elements sometimes contradictory and sometimes complementary. Yet another component entered this civilization when the Muslim conquests brought the Arabs into contact with Greek science and philosophy. The Muslim world of the tenth century was a far more complex world than that of the desert tribesmen who had been won over from tribal values to monotheism through Muhammad's efforts. The conquerors in turn had won virtually the entire Middle East for the religion of Islam and the Arabic language. In so doing they absorbed, or at least acquired sovereignty over, a vast non-Arab population, including Greek- and Syriac-speaking scholars versed in the scientific and philosophical writings of late classical antiquity. The eighth century saw the intensive translation of Greek writings into Arabic, both directly and mediated by Syriac, with profound effect on Islamic religious thought and Middle Eastern intellectual life. The translations made available a body of scientific learning that was not attached to any people's covenant with God. The Byzantine emperor could, in 949, send a Greek medical text as a gift to the Spanish caliph, knowing that it would be an object of intense interest to him and his courtiers, but also that it would not be religiously offensive. In Cordoba it was a Jewish court-doctor together with a Byzantine monk who translated the work into Arabic for the benefit of the local scholars and to the admiration of the Caliph and the court.[13] Here was a common world of discourse that united intellectuals of the different religions and mitigated the divisive effect of religious competition.

Even in the sensitive area of religious thought, the Greek philosophical systems provided the Jewish, Muslim, and Christian intellectuals who inhabited the Muslim world with a common language and a common set of problems. Logic became the shared basic tool, the foundation of the philosophical study of revelation and the first field of study for those seeking higher education. In Islam, the early fruit of this application of Greek systematic thinking to religion was *kalām*, scholastic theology, which was paralleled in Judaism by the writings of Saadia Gaon (d. 942) and others. Specific doctrines of the Greek scientific and philosophical schools, particularly Neoplatonism and Pythagoreanism, underlie the writings of the Brethren of Purity, apparently a tenth-century fraternity of philosophical-minded Muslim religious thinkers. Their vast philosophical encyclopedia hardly refers at all to Islamic religious doctrines, and their work was studied and cited extensively by Jews. Neoplatonic writings translated into Arabic had powerful influence on sophisticated Muslim thinkers in the tenth and eleventh centuries, and this influence spilled over to Jewish thinkers, so that a Muslim writer like Avicenna and a Jewish writer like Abraham Ibn Ezra—for all the differences in their historical outlooks, religious practices, and details of their philosophical views—can be said to inhabit the same intellectual world.[14] Later, when Aristotelianism prevailed, such thinkers as the Muslim Averroës and the Jewish Maimonides again reflected on similar problems in a similar way, sharing an intellectual life that transcended the particular religious traditions that they had inherited.[15]

Living as a tolerated minority in the Muslim world, the Jews absorbed as much of the dominant culture as they could. Remarkably, recent research has shown that even some aspects of the Islamic religious tradition were adopted into Jewish religious practice. The legal theory and practice of the geonim, the Talmudic scholars of Iraq whose teaching dominated world Jewry until the eleventh century, were influenced by Islamic legal thought. Not even liturgy, that most intimately Jewish religious institution, escaped the influence of Islam.[16]

Naturally enough, the external forms of social life current among the Arabs, including the social setting in which poetry was recited, were also adopted by Jews. Thus, Arabic poetry had a profound effect on Hebrew literature and related literary activities.

Adopting these Arabic cultural institutions, literary tendencies, and ways of thinking sometimes led to conflict with Jewish traditions. But as our sketch of the contradictory elements in Islam has shown, the Jews were not alone in experiencing such conflicts. Wine drinking was prohibited to Muslims no less than was pork to Jews; yet wine parties and wine poetry were an indispensable part of Arabic culture. And 'ulamā' disapproved of licentiousness no less than the rabbis. Greek philosophy posed exactly the same threats to Islamic theology as it did to Judaism.

Arab-Islamic society did not respond uniformly to these cultural contradictions. Over this society's enormous geographical expanse and throughout the three centuries of Islam that preceded the Hebrew Golden Age, Islam displayed a range of responses, from bigoted fanaticism to religious indifference combined with libertine excess. At its best, however, and notably in Spain, Islam produced a cultured elite with a broad cosmopolitan outlook, and individuals who lived with both piety and worldliness, spirituality and pleasure, prayer and poetry. The Jews learned from them not only the specific details of their Arabic-Islamic culture but also how to live with its contradictions. It was this skill, characteristic of tenth-century Andalusia, that allowed the courtier-rabbis to flourish.

The Jews, as a subject people, faced one conflict that the Muslims did not. For the Jewish elite, participation in the culture of the non-Jewish majority was religiously problematic, not simply because it might lead to specific transgressions of religious law, but because it constituted a breach with the traditions of the community and could be construed as an act of identification with the overlord. The question of loyalty arises repeatedly in the writings of the very leaders and creators of Judeo-Arabic culture. In one form or another the reproach echoes that of the Psalms against the ancient Israelites: "They mingled among the nations and learned their ways"—punning with the first word, as if it meant, "They Arabicized themselves."[17] But for the most part, the courtier-rabbis managed to overcome their reservations and embrace a dual life, experiencing only slightly more conflict than did many Muslims.

Of all the specific things that the Jews learned from the Spanish Arabs—science, grammar, philosophy, poetry, forms of social organization—perhaps the one with the most sweeping effect was this ability to maintain two opposing sets of ideals: to cultivate both *dīn* and *dunyā*, religion and the world, to belong to both Israel and to the international class of intellectuals. Of course, the medieval courtier-rabbis were not modern people. Like Muslims and Christians, they were tied to their own community and their particular religious tradition, and they were on the whole subject to the intellectual limitations and the narrowness of view typical of their age. They shared with their host people the assumption that only one of the three claimants to revelation could possess the truth, and that the others must be impostors. But the intellectual and social currents sketched above mitigated the harshness of this logic, especially in Spain during the brief flourishing of Golden Age culture. At their best, the courtier-rabbis held to a cosmopolitan outlook that reflected their membership in an international intellectual class based on Greek philosophy and Arabic language and literature.

These courtier-rabbis were capable of a universalism that is inspiring to this day, an ideal that found its most beautiful expression in a passage from Ibn Gabirol's great philosophical meditation, *The Kingly Crown*.[18] The first part of the poem is an elaborate hymn to the transcendent Being from Whom emanated the Will, from which in turn emanated form and matter, intelligence, and the soul. Although the worshiper speaks in awe of the majesty and intellectual perfection of God in His various attributes, he does not refer to any special relationship between God and Israel or to revealed religion at all. Instead, he stresses that all who sincerely seek God are engaged in an equally legitimate pursuit:

> Thou art God:
> Every creature is Thy servant and Thy devotee.
> Thy glory never can diminished be
> Because to others some men bend their knee,
> For none intends but to come near to Thee.

THE PIYYUT TRADITION

The Arabs did not teach the Jews how to write poetry. For all the importance of Arabic culture in the history and development of Hebrew poetry, that history was already an ancient one by the time it was touched by Arabic influence. Although we cannot yet date the origins of Hebrew synagogue poetry, we know that by the beginning of the Golden Age, in the mid-tenth century, it was at least five hundred years old. It is the only native Jewish art form: whatever outside influences have colored it and shaped its development, it is the only art rooted in the indisputably Jewish soil of the Hebrew language, the Jewish Scriptures, and a liturgy of prayers.

The origins of Hebrew liturgical poetry, or *piyyuṭ*, are bound up in the development of the public liturgy, a process still not clearly understood and stubbornly resistant to absolute dating. The outlines of the three daily services are already visible in the Mishna, composed toward the end of the second century, but the extent to which the actual texts of the prayers were fixed by that time cannot be determined. Although some standard prayer texts were in circulation by the time of the Mishna, they do not seem as yet to have been completely obligatory. In the period after the Mishna, Palestinian Jews were encouraged to vary the wording of their prayers—as long as they kept to the statutory outline and pre-scribed themes and formulas and avoided certain proscribed themes and turns of phrase. Not until the period of the geonim, in eighth- and ninth-century Iraq, was there an attempt to can-onize the text of the prayers.

Between the second and the ninth centuries two contrary ten-dencies affected the liturgy. On the one hand, a more or less stan-dard text, refined and codified by the geonim, gradually emerged. On the other hand, the process of free composition of prayers con-tinued within the framework authorized by the Mishna, yielding numerous versions of the individual prayers. Often these versions were not simply variant wordings of a common text but completely different texts that were considered ritually interchangeable since they covered the same themes and ended with a more or less identical concluding formula. Increasingly, the freely composed versions of the prayers, in contrast to the more standardized versions, were composed in verse. The verses could be quite elaborate and often ranged quite far from the subject before returning at the end to the prescribed theme. Cantors who were also scholars and poets composed the whole Sabbath service anew each week in poetic cycles covering the entire liturgical year. Others recited the same simple prose prayers week after week, occasionally varying them by inserting simple verses. During the Talmudic period and for some time thereafter, prayer leaders could use either prose or poetic versions of the prayers, whether of their own composition or the work of others.

During the process of the canonization of the liturgy, the status of liturgical poetry became problematic. The Babylonian geonim, bent on standardizing the liturgy and religious institutions generally, tended to suppress it as a centrifugal force. They succeeded in establishing a fixed prose liturgy that was to endure universally for a millennium. While they did not succeed in halting the use of existing liturgical poetry and the free composition of new poetry, they did manage to change its status. Whereas liturgical poetry had formerly been seen as a completely acceptable independent version of the prayers, having equal status with the standard prose texts, it now came to be seen as an optional elaboration, or decoration, of the fixed prayers. The many communities that refused to bow to geonic pressure to eliminate the poetry inserted it into the now-standardized prose prayer texts fixed by the geonim.[19]

While a detailed description of the liturgy is not needed here, an outline of the main features of the morning public liturgy permits discussion of the intended function of the poems included in this book. It also enables us to view the achievement of the Spanish liturgical poets against the background of the tradition that they inherited.

After some preparatory prayers and psalms that originated as private devotions, the core of the Morning Service is introduced by a formal call to prayer. This core consists of: a benediction (*b*ᵉ*rakha*) praising God for the creation of the world and its daily renewal; another, praising God for His covenant with Israel; the *Sh*ᵉ*ma*ᶜ, the communal confession of faith, which consists of a selection of three biblical passages;[20] and a benediction praising God for the redemption from Egypt. There follows a complex prayer known as the *Tᵉfila* (Prayer), or *ᶜAmida* (Standing), which is composed of a number of benedictions that fluctuates from seven on Sabbaths and festivals to nineteen on weekdays. Following the *ᶜAmida*—on weekdays, but not on Sabbaths and festivals—the worshipers in some communities, at least up to Maimonides' time, used to prostrate themselves to utter spontaneous private petitions. Subsequently the prostration was discontinued and the petitions acquired a fixed text, which came to be known as *Taḥanun*.

The core of the service is thus understood to consist of two sets of benedictions, one set grouped around the *Shᵉmaᶜ* and the other constituting the *ᶜAmida*. These benedictions were originally, and ordinarily still are, short prayers, mostly of praise. Each is summarized at the end by a concise eulogy such as "Blessed are You, Lord, Creator of the luminaries." Sometimes a benediction also begins with the eulogy formula "Blessed are You . . . " The precise wording of the eulogies appears to have been more or less fixed by the time of the Mishna, but the texts that introduced them remained fluid for a long time. The wording might be one of several standard versions, or it might be freely composed in prose or verse. Early liturgical poetry was thus functionally equivalent to the prose text; when the prose text came to be fixed, the poetry was inserted between it and the concluding eulogy. One example is the first benediction of the Morning Service, known as the "Creator" benediction (*yoṣer*). The simplest known prose version of this prayer reads:

> Blessed are You, Lord our God, King of the world, who forms light and creates darkness, makes peace and creates everything, *who gives light to the world and those who inhabit it, and in whose great mercy and beneficence renews the act of creation each day.* Blessed are You, Lord, Creator of the luminaries.

Originally the italicized section could be freely replaced or expanded, whether in prose or in verse. Since geonic times it has been canonical, in a considerably expanded form that includes fragments of other versions of the prayer. Some of these fragments are ancient *piyyuṭim*, vestiges of a huge literature of poems that was available for this purpose.[21]

In antiquity the cantor was often free to compose his own poems. He would usually try to connect the prayer for which the poem was intended with the occasion—Sabbath, festival, fast day, or other community event—on which the prayer was recited. Part of the poet's artistry consisted in demonstrating a relationship between the prayer and the occasion. Such is the origin of the following poem, of unknown authorship, which is inserted into the above benediction on the Day of Atonement:

> On the Day of Atonement You taught how to gain pardon;
> Light and forgiveness for the people You made Yours . . .
> Sin took control while I was asleep,
> Until a certain day of the year arrived . . .
> Make sweet the light of my forgiveness
> By speaking today the words "I forgive."
> Make our eyes shine when You pass over our sins . . .
> Guide us with Your light.

Since the prayer must deal with the daily renewal of light, the poet has used light as a symbol for God's forgiveness and pleasure, thus bringing together the theme of the fixed daily prayer and that of the special occasion. Such poems were composed for every festival and for every benediction of the service. Over time the weekly scriptural reading became the variable theme, so that eventually every Sabbath of the annual and triennial cycles had its own set of liturgical poems.

The artistic principle of liturgical poetry resembles that of another body of sacred literature, midrash. Midrash, originally simply the exegesis of Scripture, evolved into a homiletical technique in which a relationship is demonstrated between two apparently unrelated verses of the Bible, yielding some moral or halakhic instruction. The connection is usually established by pointing to a rhetorical linkage. Regularly used as the framework for sermons, midrash also came to play a central role in liturgical poetry, which sometimes became a kind of versified midrash and at other times, a concatenation of allusions to specific midrashim. With its verbal allusions to the text of Scripture and to rabbinic interpretations, with its special poetic dialect, its dense texture, and its opaque diction, the *piyyuṭ* made considerable demands on the erudition of the congregants who listened to its recitation. It also reflected a completely different conception of liturgy from that represented by the standard prayers. It turned the few simple benedictions expressing gratitude or petition, grouped around unadorned scriptural readings, into an elaborate, even arcane text, permutating and combining the words of Scripture and the traditions of the rabbis into a recondite web. *Piyyuṭ* is difficult to understand not because the poets did not know Hebrew or because they lacked aesthetic sensibility, as is sometimes charged. It is difficult because the poets were aiming for a particular kind of liturgical experience, in which Torah, understood as meaning the entirety of rabbinic exegesis of Scripture, is turned into prayer. But when the poets felt like writing simple Hebrew they did so, as attested even by Kallir, despite his reputation as the avatar of opaque style.

The work of the liturgical poets was not intended as self-expression but as communal expression, not as art but as liturgy. It is functional, even didactic. Its collective character makes the works of one poet indistinguishable from those of another, despite the common practice of weaving the author's name into the poem by means of acrostics. But *piyyuṭ* is expressive, not merely didactic. It is often artistic; the techniques that make it so can be appreciated when they are understood. Many *piyyuṭim*, though not all, can be read as poems. The larger question of how this literature is to be understood has not yet received systematic attention.[22]

The bulk of the work of the great Golden Age poets is in a direct line with the poetic tradition of the geonic period and reflects the gradual evolution of the poetic forms and liturgical practices. While their poems are not identical in form and style with those of their predecessors, the filiation can be traced with some clarity.[23] The older type of poetry did not die in Spain. The diction of the Spanish poets tends to be clearer and closer to that of the Bible, and the texture of their works thins out so that the poems no longer resemble riddles; but vestiges of the *piyyuṭ*-dialect remain, and midrash continues to provide much of the poems' content. For all the limpidity and polish of their best works, the Golden Age poets were still capable of producing lengthy and tedious versifications that must have been intended to evoke the same kind of mysterious verbal spell as the ancient *piyyuṭ*. Even though the words are more comprehensible, and the grammar more biblical,[24] the intellectual content of these poems also tends to stay close to the world of rabbinic thinking.

THE NEW SYNAGOGUE POETRY

Alongside this body of liturgical poetry stands a smaller one that is radically different from anything the synagogue had previously known. This new synagogue poetry came into being thanks to the influence of Arabic literary culture on the Hebrew poets and the Jewish tradition. Arabic secular poetry and Hebrew secular poetry, its offspring, provided the formal materials for the new Hebrew liturgical poetry; Greek philosophy, acquired through participation in Arabic intellectual life and through reading Arabic books, provided the new content.

Like Arabic poems, the new poetry is constructed mostly in quantitative meter. The rhythm is not based on stress patterns, as in English; on parallelism, as in the Bible; or on stress count, as in earlier Hebrew liturgical poetry. Rather, it is based on vowel length. Certain patterns of long and short vowels were canonical, and each poem employs one such pattern consistently in every verse. The verse is divided into two identical or very nearly identical hemistichs; one rhyme is employed throughout the poem, at the end of the verses. Often the first verse of a poem has the rhyme in the first hemistich as well. From traditional Jewish liturgical poetry the poets adopted the name-acrostic and grafted it on to this Arabic form. Their poems are usually short, containing the same number of verses as the number of letters in the poet's personal name (e.g., Judah, Solomon, Moses), often with one additional verse. But the acrostic is not invariably present. The form of these liturgical poems most resembles the Arabic *qit'a*, a short poem in classical meter dealing with a single theme.

By the eleventh century Arabic had also acquired a strophic verse form, known as *muwashshah*, which was adopted by Hebrew poets for their secular verse alongside the classical monorhymed, nonstrophic type just described. Secular strophic poems were sung to instrumental accompaniment. Each strophe consists of two parts: in the first, the rhyme changes from strophe to strophe, whereas in the second, it remains unchanged throughout the poem. The two parts of the strophe may differ in meter as well as rhyme. The first strophe may be preceded by a leading-verse, which gives the constant rhyme and may have served as a refrain; the second part of the final strophe, called the *kharja*, is in vernacular Arabic or Romance. The prosodic patterns of these poems were adopted by the synagogue poets as well, together with the melodies to which the poems were sung.[25] Strophic forms combining a changing and a constant rhyme had already appeared in Hebrew liturgical poetry in the East even before the Jews came into contact with the secular Arabic *muwashshah*; but it was the popularity of the Arabic form that induced the extraordinary flourishing of this type of strophic poetry in the Jewish liturgy of eleventh-century Spain.

The introduction of these new forms, particularly the *muwashshah*, was a far more striking innovation to medieval Jews than might be imagined by modern readers, whose ears are not so finely tuned to the niceties of medieval Hebrew prosody. Arabic prosody had distinctly profane associations, and the tunes of the strophic poems could often be recognized as those of specific Arabic love or wine poems. Importing the rhythms and melodies of Arabic poetry into the synagogue was as jarring to medieval traditionalists as would be the introduction of the practice of the nineteenth-century concert hall into the German synagogue. Though these forms were respectable in the outside world, there was something daring about using them in the service of God. For some, this was a source of religious uplift and pride; for others, it was pandering to the culture of prestige and a desecration of the liturgy.

The Golden Age liturgical poets took the same approach to the diction of liturgical poetry as to the diction of secular poetry. They consciously eliminated rabbinic vocabulary and syntax and broke with the artificial dialect of synagogue poetry often referred to as Kallirian style, attempting instead to write pure biblical Hebrew.[26] Although they restricted their vocabulary to roots found in the Bible and strove to limit word formation from these roots to patterns authorized by biblical usage, these efforts did not protect their

Hebrew from the influence of their native Arabic. This influence is especially noticeable in roots common to both languages, where the meaning of the Hebrew word has been contaminated by the meaning of its Arabic cognate. It is also evident in loan-translations, idiomatic usages, and syntax. But if the poets did not manage to write pure biblical Hebrew, they did simplify their language and differentiate it from that of traditional synagogue poetry.

Liturgical poems composed in classical, monorhymed Arabic patterns always employ the new diction, as do most strophic poems of the *muwashshah* type. In both types the status of midrash is drastically reduced. A poem may still be based on a particular midrash, or it may use Hebrew words or biblical quotations to recall a particular midrash,[27] but the density of such allusions is much thinner. The new poems are never built out of the heaping together of several versified midrashim; unlike much of the older synagogue poetry, they are always intelligible without knowledge of their midrashic sources.

Biblical quotations and allusions remain however an important stylistic feature of this poetry. Since Hebrew was learned mostly by memorizing the Bible, the poet could count on the learned in his audience being able to recognize allusions and to recall the biblical context of any word. Thanks to the poets' pursuit of simplicity and clarity, the poems are usually intelligible, on some level at least, even to present-day readers who cannot automatically make these connections. But the poems almost never reveal all of their meaning without meticulous study of the biblical passages to which they refer and of the history of interpretation of these passages. The biblical contexts from which a word was taken and the word's traditional rabbinic interpretation were all part of its semantic range; to neglect them is to miss the effect.

The changes in poetic forms and diction are matched by thematic changes. All the Golden Age poets wrote love poetry in Hebrew modeled on Arabic love poetry. Most of them also incorporated themes from Arabic love poetry into their religious verse, treating them as an extension of the traditional love imagery of the Song of Songs. The original erotic character of the Song of Songs was hardly perceptible any longer, for the exegesis of that book in accordance with the theme of the covenant between God and Israel was by now taken for granted. As a living genre identified with real-life sensuality, the new secular love poetry had the power to revive this erotic element in the religious tradition. We will explore this topic more fully in Chapter I.

One new theme that the synagogue poets of the Golden Age adopted from the religious and quasi-religious literature of Islam is that of asceticism and renunciation of the world, the theme of Arabic *zuhd* poetry. This genre, as we have noted, rests upon common Near Eastern traditions, for all its identification with Islam, and its overall message and tone is in harmony with the strand of pessimism and rejection of the world found here and there within rabbinic preaching. Whether the Hebrew poets drew directly on Muslim moralists and poets or whether they got their ideas indirectly through Jewish adaptations like Bahya's, they made extensive use of them, especially in the *tokheha*, an ancient genre of poetic sermon associated with the liturgy for fast days.

More important, however, were the thematic innovations due to the poets' exposure to a broader intellectual life. The ancient liturgical poets apparently were educated exclusively in rabbinic texts, but such texts represented only a part of the curriculum of their counterparts in the Golden Age. When writing in a hymnic vein, for example, a poet of the old type would draw on the stores of imagery and ideas available in the Bible, Talmud, midrash, and the earlier liturgical poetry. But a poet who had mastered not only Jewish lore but also Greco-Arabic science and philosophy—and who had been trained to view the latter not merely as sources of useful information but as sources of truth alongside the Jewish tradition—would automatically synthesize the Jewish and the scientific material in his work, just as they were synthesized in his mind. The scientific data were seen not as undermining the religious purpose of the liturgy but as enhancing it.

This process had already begun early in tenth-century Iraq, when Saadia Gaon introduced philosophical materials into his poetry, not for didactic purposes but simply as part of his hymnic theme.[28] Several Golden Age poets made use of information derived from their philosophical studies, especially in astronomy and cosmology. The best-known example today is Ibn Gabirol's long penitential prose-poem, *The Kingly Crown*, cited above. Part I of this monumental work is a philosophical-poetic meditation on God's attributes and on the creation. Part II is an extended hymn to God as creator of the universe, which is described sphere by sphere in consecutive stanzas, as the poet attempts to build a cumulative impression of God's infinitude out of astronomical data on the dimensions of the celestial spheres and the duration of their periodic motions.[29]

The inclusion of technical data in liturgical poetry might seem to us awkward and stylistically confusing; it was in fact criticized even by intellectuals like Moses Ibn Ezra.[30] But it was not really a stylistic innovation, for technical data from the realm of halakha were regularly incorporated into the traditional liturgical poetry. What was new was that this technical material came from outside the Jewish tradition. Furthermore, this innovation occurred not within a radical movement at the fringe of the Jewish community, but in the community's very center. The political, social, and religious leadership had become so much at home with their worldly learning that they instinctively merged it with their traditional Jewish culture. Moses Ibn Ezra criticized this poetry as being stylistically inappropriate, for the Golden Age poets aimed for clarity and simplicity. He did not challenge it for its scientific content.

The most profound effect of the new learning resulted from the medieval preoccupation with metaphysics—the study of the nature of God—and psychology—the study of the nature of the soul. The new ideas forced a rethinking of the older, less rigorous rabbinic theology that had been the intellectual background of the standard prayers and the earlier *piyyuṭ*. Through the influence of Arabic Neoplatonism, the soul of the individual came to be the focus of much religious thought. Reinforced by Sufi pietism and the ascetic tradition of *zuhd* poetry, this trend brought about a shift in creative liturgical activity, from the concerns of the community toward the inner religious experience of the individual. This shift, which Chapter II treats in detail, was strong enough to dictate a change in the actual liturgical practice: the addition of poetry to the readings originally intended for private devotion, the part of the service *preceding* the formal call to public prayer ("Bless the Lord who is blessed"). This change is an indication that the Golden Age poets were sufficiently conscious of the innovative character of their enterprise to feel the need for a new liturgical context in which to make their innovative statements.

Even when the poems are attached to traditional liturgical sites, they often seem to be reinterpreting the prayers, as if their purpose were to shift the meaning of the old liturgy onto the track of contemporary religious thought. With the new stress on the cultivation and purification of the soul, the idea of redemption tended to turn inward, becoming more an individual than a collective concern. Philosophy, emphasizing the powers of human reason and grounded in logic, fostered a new consciousness of the commonality of mankind. This universalizing tendency led to a reinterpretation of the themes of Israel's covenant with God, an important element in the liturgy. The very nature of prayer came to be problematic: the intellectual elite now thought of God in an abstract and rigorously nonanthropomorphic way; at the same time they saw a continuity between God and the soul of man that was completely new to rabbinic Judaism. In this environment the nature of prayer itself became a theme of liturgical poetry.

Had the innovations in Golden Age religious poetry been limited to the introduction of themes and forms absorbed from Arabic culture, the poetry would have been historically interesting but not necessarily the more appealing. Alongside these innovations in form and content, two other qualities distinguish it from traditional synagogue poetry and account for its appeal to modern readers: its individuality and its intimacy.

From its origins, synagogue poetry was recited not by the congregation but by the precentor, who was often also the poet. In theory the precentor was the congregation's spokesman. Accordingly, the speaker in traditional *piyyuṭ* is ordinarily anonymous and usually speaks in the first person plural. Even when he speaks in the first person singular, he enunciates collective ideas, wishes, and aspirations, and most of what he says can be traced to authoritative sources in rabbinic classics. It is an index of the extent to which the synagogue poets masked their own personalities behind that of catholic Israel that there is ordinarily no way to distinguish the authors of the poems by their contents.

The speaker in the new poetry usually calls himself "I," not "we," and he addresses God repeatedly, so that the pronouns "I" and "You" constantly alternate. Without alluding to personal biographical experiences, and though occasionally alluding to the presence of a congregation, he manages to convince us that we are listening in on a private conversation between himself and God. The same intimacy is suggested by the same means in poems in which the speaker addresses his own soul. Both types contrast with the tone of the classical *piyyuṭ*, in which the congregation seems to be standing behind a spokesman who is addressing God on its behalf. The speaker in the new poetry may expose thoughts and beliefs that are not those of the standard Jewish repertoire but that instead reflect his own synthesis of the tradition with contemporary thought. Sometimes these thoughts are doctrinally daring and are expressed indirectly. Often they can be compared with the religious ideas expressed by the writer in other works of poetry or prose. For the first time we are able to see how a poet's reflections on a prayer bespeak a distinctive religious personality, and we can distinguish one poet's work from that of another.

There is also a blurring of the distinction between public and private prayer. Sometimes poems known to be private prayers of a particular poet resemble liturgical poems in form and content. Conversely, a liturgical poem sometimes seems so individualistic that we have trouble imagining that it was actually used in public worship.

As the voice of the precentor resolves into a new, individual voice, there occurs of necessity a certain distancing of the precentor from the congregation. Their relationship takes on some of the quality of the relationship between audience and artist, and thus the poetry begins to function more like Western poetry than does the older *piyyuṭ*. Now, for the first time, liturgical poetry becomes less an artful reshaping of canonical materials than a new art form in its own right. Its range may never have become as wide as that of Western poetry, but it experienced a breakthrough nevertheless, a breakthrough analogous to that of Giotto against the iconic tradition in painting.

The warmth of tone and the immediacy of the poet's inner life enable the modern reader, for all the differences of culture, to glimpse the underlying religious spirit. These poems hold particular appeal for our age of the individual, for they show how even a medieval community could make room for the individual spirit within the framework of the community's ritual life. They also show how a new, more sophisticated, and more complex intellectual life could be harmonized with forms that had arisen in an older and simpler intellectual climate. We can only admire these communities that allowed the poet's individuality and the philosopher's intellect to modify the ancient traditions, instead of stifling the one and closing its eyes to the other.

SELECTIONS FOR THE GAZELLE

The poems in this book were chosen to illustrate two central themes of Golden Age religious poetry: the love between God and Israel and the relationship between God and the individual soul. These themes are both representative of the period and closely related to each other. In the Golden Age both found new poetic forms, derived from Arabic and having close affinities with secular poetry of the type presented in *Wine, Women, and Death*. The very title of this companion volume, *The Gazelle*, is meant to suggest the affinity: In the secular poetry "gazelle" is a code word for the lover; in religious poetry, for God or the Messiah.

The poems selected trace a broad arc from the particularly Jewish to the most broadly universal. Chapter I begins with poems about God and Israel, the covenant, and the problem of exile, and then moves on to consider how these themes were modified and softened by the universalizing tendencies of philosophy. Poetry on the soul follows in Chapter II. Here the traditions and history of Judaism play but a negligible role as the poems represent man confronting a God who exists inside himself. Our selection ends with a reprise of the more particularistic theme.

Most of the poems were intended for use in the synagogue, but since the line between the new liturgical poetry and private religious meditation is not always clear, I have taken the liberty of including a few that probably belong to the latter class. The liturgical slot for which a specific poem was intended is not always identified: for while many of the poems allude to their liturgical context, others indicate it only ambiguously or not at all. Nor is the actual usage of the congregations a reliable guide, for the liturgical function of any given poem has often changed during the long centuries since composition. For the most part, the poems are capable of standing free of any liturgical context.

The poems presented here are all of the "new" type. Most are short poems in quantitative meters, but a few are of the *muwashshaḥ* type. Most are by poets whose secular verse appears in *Wine, Women, and Death*. One notable absence is Samuel the Nagid: though his nonliturgical poetry reveals a developed religious sensibility, he does not seem to have made an important contribution to liturgical poetry. The following poets are represented in this collection:

Solomon Ibn Gabirol (c. 1020–c. 1057) was apparently the first of the Golden Age poets to write synagogue poetry of the new type. His philosophical treatise has already been mentioned. A very distinctive personality emerges from his secular poetry—passionately devoted to metaphysical speculations, contemptuous of those whose intellectual aspirations were less lofty than his own, yet thirsty for their acclaim. Unlike Moses Ibn Ezra and Judah Halevi, he did not write much poetry on love and wine, though he did not neglect those subjects.

Isaac Ibn Ghiyath (1038–1089) was the chief Spanish authority on religious law in his time and head of the academy of Lucena. One of the most prolific of the Golden Age liturgical poets, he also wrote a small quantity of secular verse as well as halakhic treatises, responsa, and a commentary on Ecclesiastes in Arabic.

Moses Ibn Ezra (c. 1055–after 1135) was an important official in the kingdom of Granada until its fall to the Berbers in 1090; sometime thereafter he became an exile in the Christian north of Spain. Moses Ibn Ezra wrote an important treatise on Hebrew poetry and another on poetic imagery, both in Arabic. His own voluminous secular Hebrew poetry hews even more closely than that of the other Golden Age poets to the ornate style of Andalusian Arabic poetry. In the sphere of liturgical poetry he is particularly famous for his penitential poems.

Levi Ibn al-Tabban (late eleventh century) was a grammarian and poet in Saragossa who wrote mostly liturgical verse.

Judah Halevi (before 1075–1141) was apparently a prosperous doctor, businessman, and courtier, as well as an enormously popular secular and liturgical poet. In middle age he wrote an apologetic philosophical treatise generally known as the *Kuzari*, in which he evinces discontent with the worldly values of the courtier-rabbis. In 1140, to the dismay of his friends, he went on pilgrimage to Palestine, abandoning his family forever and expressly rejecting the world in which he had grown up and flourished.

Abraham Ibn Ezra (1089–1164), like his friend Judah Halevi, was born in Tudela and left Spain in 1140. Unlike Halevi, though, he became a vagabond scholar, traveling to various places in Italy, France, and England, where he probably died. Abraham Ibn Ezra wrote treatises on many scientific and religious subjects and is best known today as the author of much-studied commentaries on the Bible. These commentaries, laconic and opaque in style, reflect his wide interest in grammar, science, and philosophy. He wrote a very large number of liturgical poems as well as secular verse.

For each of the poems in *The Gazelle*, the Hebrew text is provided, and the metrical scansion is indicated above the first line. I hope in this way to encourage the metrical reading of the poems, since that is often an important key to the craft in the poem's construction.

There is no one way to translate a poem. Each translator must decide what aspects of the poem he most wants to convey. Generally, this means deciding to what degree he wishes to stress the semantic as against the formal properties of the poem. In translating the poems for this volume, my priority has been to suggest the distinctive tone and texture of each. This means that meter and at least some rhyme are indispensable, as are wordplays, self-conscious rhetorical effects, and a noncolloquial, sometimes even an archaic, diction. I have also tried to give the formal properties their due, within the limits of philological responsibility, and have provided explanations of important features of the poem that are perforce left untranslated. But even the formal properties of the poem are of less interest to me than the tone and texture that they help to create through their interplay with the poem's content. Since it is the poem's effect, and not form for its own sake, that I am trying to re-create, it would be pointless to try to "translate" the acrostics that are a standard feature of much liturgical verse; being inaudible, they have no bearing on the poem's effect.

Given these objectives, a strict literal translation would be impossible. It may even be asked whether there is such a thing as a literal translation. In the notes the reader is referred to existing translations that stress the semantic level of interpretation, as well as to other attempts to re-create the poems in English verse; comparisons with other translations may yield a more rounded picture of the poems.

In the discussions of the individual poems, I try to evoke their spirit and cultural background, focusing on what they reveal about the religiosity of the Golden Age. Wherever possible, I call attention to the nexus between secular and religious poetry, referring to *Wine, Women, and Death* for parallels. Finally, I attempt to explain the poetic effects that the poet was trying to achieve and the means that he employed, so that the non-Hebraist, or the Hebraist not experienced in this literature, can see how the poems work. This sometimes necessitates discussion of the poems' formal properties.

The interpretation of the poems often calls for a consideration of the the biblical allusions embedded in them, for these play an even more prominent part in religious poetry than in secular poetry. The biblical verses in turn frequently send one delving into the rabbinic and medieval exegetical traditions as well, for the poets quote the Bible as they understood it, not as it is understood by the modern biblical scholarship that underlies present-day translations. For Golden Age biblical exegesis we are fortunate to have an eyewitness, Abraham Ibn Ezra, whose commentary on the Bible quotes the opinions of Solomon Ibn Gabirol and Judah Halevi, among others. Accordingly, he is frequently cited in the discussions. I have tried to limit discussion of biblical references to the essentials, for to call attention to every quotation or allusion would result in an impenetrable intertextual tangle. Sufficient Hebrew commentaries on these poems exist to guide the reader to allusions of secondary importance.

In the notes, I have cited the recent sources for each poem, especially the classic anthology by Ḥ. Schirmann, *Hashira ha'ivrit bis'farad uv'provans*, through which earlier editions may easily be traced. I also cite other English translations of which I am aware.[31] Since the secondary literature on liturgical poetry is far more extensive than that on secular medieval poetry, I cite only those studies that I have found particularly helpful or stimulating.

1

God and Israel

LOVE AND THE COVENANT

While the Golden Age of Spanish Jewry was at its height, the Holy Land, embroiled in the Crusades, was torn between Christians and Muslims. World Jewry looked on helplessly as strangers battled over the shrines they regarded as their own:

> The bride who yearned for You went out to greet You
>   Sick at heart ever since she could not visit Your Temple.
> Ascending the Holy Mountain she was struck with sorrow,
>   For she saw strangers going up while she did not.
> So she stood afar off, bowing in the direction of
>   Your Temple from the places of her exile . . . [1]

These lines by Halevi evoke the Jews' poignant feeling of being left out by history, passive spectators of the great events being orchestrated by Christian and Muslim empires and determining their fate. The lines also evoke the rivalry that was the consequence of the intimate connection within medieval monotheism between religion and politics. For all their disagreements on specific matters of doctrine, Christians, Muslims, and Jews all concurred that sovereignty is bestowed by God: to have it was evidence of divine approval and satisfaction, whereas to lose it was a sign of divine disfavor. Christians and Muslims saw the Jews' loss of sovereignty as proof that God had passed over them and their version of the truth, and they saw the Crusades as an episode in their historic duel to determine which was the favored child. On the sidelines were the Jews—divested of independent sovereignty, not even contenders.

Those Jews who rejected this reasoning and refused to convert to Christianity or to Islam needed an explanation for their subservient condition, for in principle they accepted the same premise as their overlords. The problem was not a new one; they had been dealing with it since long before the rise of Islam, in fact even before Christianity became a serious rival. By Halevi's time the answers elaborated in the first and second centuries—the period of the fall of Jerusalem to Rome in 70 and of the disastrous uprising of Bar Kokhba in 132–135—were firmly rooted in official Judaism. The Jews had been chosen by God out of all mankind to live under the laws of the Torah. They had disobeyed these laws and were being punished by temporary loss of sovereignty. But their kingdom would be restored, with a descendant of their original dynasty, a scion of the house of David, as sovereign. The Jews, now chastened, would be restored to their land, and the nations that had tormented them, now humbled, would acknowledge the truth of their claims and submit in turn to their domination. Though none of these ideas was completely new—they were all largely inherited from the prophets—they were much on the minds of the rabbis in the late first and early second centuries.

This period was a formative one for the liturgy, as it was for many other enduring institutions of Jewish life. The theological issues that concerned the rabbis of the age became embedded in liturgical texts. Accordingly, the themes of divine sovereignty, the election of Israel, and messianism came to be featured very prominently in the prayer book and liturgical poetry. With the passing of centuries and the continued dispersion of the Jews, the problem to which these ideas were a response and the sorrow for which they were intended to provide comfort endured and continued to shape the Jewish self-image. In order to understand the role in the liturgy of the poems discussed in this chapter, we must examine two passages in the daily Morning Service in which this complex of ideas is paramount.

The general outline of this service, already sketched in the Introduction, is essentially identical on weekdays, Sabbaths, and festivals. We have seen how poetry came to be attached to the "Creator" benediction, and that such poems were the first of a cycle attached to the three benedictions of the Shᵉmaᶜ.

We now turn to the second benediction in this cycle, the purpose of which is to praise God for His covenant with Israel, as embodied in the idea of the Torah. Known in ancient times as the Benediction of the Torah, this prayer came early in its development to describe the giving of the Torah as God's act of love toward Israel and Israel's study and observance of the Torah as its act of love toward God. The Talmud debates which words should open the benediction: "With great love" or "With eternal love," and versions with both openings have been incorporated into the canonical prayer books. Likewise the eulogy that concludes the prayer reads, in current versions, "Blessed are You, Lord, who chooses His people Israel in love" or, in the wording used in the analogous benediction of the Evening Service, "Blessed are You, Lord, who loves His people Israel." Like "Creator" and the other prayers and benedictions surrounding the Shᵉmaᶜ, this benediction became a node to which liturgical poetry could be attached. Such poems are called ahᵃva (love), after the contents of the benediction. In the Golden Age the ahᵃva was singled out from the other poems of the cycle, acquiring new and distinctive forms. These new Golden Age ahᵃvot were short poems, often in quantitative metrics, that drew much of their imagery from secular love poetry. In connection with these new poems, the technical term ahᵃva could now actually be rendered with some justice as "love poem." Many of the poems in this chapter are ahᵃvot.

Another traditional node for liturgical poetry in the Morning Service was the benediction following the Shᵉmaᶜ, known as gᵉʾula, the Benediction of Redemption. The concluding formula, "Blessed are You, Lord, who redeemed Israel," sums up a prayer, linked to the third part of the Shᵉmaᶜ, that expresses gratitude for Israel's redemption from Egypt. Many rabbinic authorities tried to keep the expression of gratitude in this prayer limited to the one-time event in the past; but it inevitably attracted prayers for the longed-for future redemption, especially since the prophets and the ancient rabbis were already thinking of the Exodus from Egypt as an archetype and guarantee of Israel's future expectations. Thus, in the classical period of liturgical poetry, poems called *g^e'ula*, or redemption poems, were composed as part of the cycle of poems around the *Sh^ema^c*. In the Golden Age these poems tended to be composed in strophic forms, often in patterns resembling the secular *muwashshah*. Whereas earlier poets generally seem to have composed only complete cycles, they now began to compose independent *ah^avot*, *g^e'ulot*, and other poems that were originally components of the cycle.[2]

There is a potential thematic link between the *ah^ava* and the *g^e'ula*: the certainty of God's love for Israel, which is the object of the benediction in the former, is both the consolation for Israel's tribulations and the guarantee of its future redemption.[3] Thus the poems *ah^ava* and *g^e'ula*, composed to expand and develop these two benedictions, could both draw on the great tradition of rabbinic exegesis of the Song of Songs, which seems to have emerged at about the same time as the outline of the prayers was taking shape.[4] In second-century Palestine—when Jewish sovereignty was being definitively crushed, when the messianic dreams of a speedy restoration were being dashed by Roman troops, and when the liturgy that was to be universally in force throughout the Middle Ages until modern times was being formulated—Rabbi Akiba defended the claim that the Song of Songs is part of Holy Scripture. Rabbi Akiba and his fellows taught that the Song of Songs was more than a collection of charming, yet trivial love songs, completely worldly in its themes and imagery; it was rather the key to the resolution of the paradox of Israel's subjugation, a coded message of mutual, eternal love between God and Israel, guaranteeing their ultimate union.

ARABIC LOVE POETRY IN THE SYNAGOGUE

Soon after the Jews began imitating the Arabic love lyric in Hebrew, they began to amalgamate its themes, images, and conventions with the themes and imagery of the Song of Songs as it was used in the synagogue. In the *thematic* sense, this development was an extension of the allegorization of the Song of Songs into an allegorization of the secular love poetry; in this regard it was not a dramatic break with tradition. Still, it was a noticeable departure from the *style* of tradition. The first poet definitely known to have adapted themes from Arabic love poetry to the synagogue was Solomon Ibn Gabirol.[5]

Arabic love poetry suited the synagogue because it had so much in common with the Song of Songs. We may begin the list of correspondences with the simple example of terms of endearment. Arabic poets ordinarily referred to the beloved not by name but by an animal epithet, such as *ghazāl* or *ẓaby*, that is, gazelle. The Song of Songs uses the equivalent Hebrew word, *ṣᵉvi* or the feminine *ṣᵉviya* (cognate with the Arabic *ẓaby*), as a simile in descriptions of the lover or the beloved. Thus, images and associations connected to the gazelle of secular love poetry were transferred to liturgical poetry, where they came to symbolize God or, when the feminine form was used, Israel. Other words denoting similar animals, like *ayala* (deer) or *ᶜofer* and its feminine *ᶜofra* (fawn), play the same roles. For the purposes of this book, I usually use gazelle, or occasionally fawn or stag, for all of these emblematic animals.[6]

In secular love poetry the lover's companions play an important role as a foil to the lover. They criticize him for his excessive devotion to the beloved, urge him to behave more prudently, and generally discourage him in his quest. To medieval Hebrew poets, these companions seemed to correspond to the "daughters of Jerusalem" in the Song of Songs, who mock the beloved for her swarthiness and who demand that she explain the reasons for her devotion to this particular lover. In rabbinic allegory, the "daughters of Jerusalem" had been identified with the nations of the world, who seek to dissuade Israel from her loyalty to her God. Now the obstructionists of the love poetry joined the "daughters of Jerusalem" in the role of Israel's detractors, and they even extend the role to that of rivals.

The springtime setting of the Song of Songs and the prominence in it of gardens, birds, and outdoor fragrances all had their parallels in Arabic love poetry, which was familiar to Jewish writers and imitated by them in Hebrew. Gardens in spring were a central image in the literary imagination of both Arabs and Jews in Andalusia.

Beyond the individual conventions that were adopted by the Hebrew poets, there is a larger parallelism of spirit between Arabic love poetry and the allegory of the Song of Songs. Conventional Arabic love poetry does not merely celebrate a love; its true theme is the celebration of the personality of the lover, a personality defined by its passion for an unfulfilled love. Arabic love poetry is not merely about passion, but about frustrated passion, passion in the face of or even intensified by separation. It was the frustration typically described by Arabic love poetry that made it such a fruitful source for the Jewish liturgical poets.

More than the conventions for describing the beloved it was typically the theme of frustration that the liturgy adopted from love poetry. As descriptive materials from the Song of Songs had been used in the earlier liturgical poetry in describing and praising God, it would have been an easy matter for the poets to amalgamate the analogous descriptive material from the secular love poetry with the descriptive material of the Song of Songs. But the love theme was important to them mainly as a vehicle for dealing with the problem of exile.

As we have seen, even in the comfortable Spain of the courtier-rabbis and the great Hebrew poets, the communal status of the Jews was defined by the reality of exile, subjugation, and the feeling of separation from God. God's love for Israel and Israel's for God were ancient themes of rabbinic doctrine and liturgy, in use for centuries before the Andalusian rabbis discovered Arabic love poetry. What was new in Arabic poetry was the habitual idealization of a love that endures the lovers' separation and the hostility of the environment, a love nurtured by dreams of the past and expressing itself in prayers for satisfaction in the future. For Jews brought up on Arabic literature and sharing its outlook, there must have been considerable comfort in the analogy it provided with their national status, an analogy that enabled them to express their national tragedy in terms that made sense in their own—Arabic—culture.

Finally, the Hebrew poets adopted from Arabic love poetry its tone of intimacy and intense feeling. For all the stylization of the secular love poetry, it draws on a well of primary experiences shared by most people. Medieval love poetry controls our vulnerability to love and beauty by stylizing the response to it in predictable ways; but the underlying, delicious agony is experienced by most people at one time or another in their lives. Some may have felt that the lofty idea of divine love was diminished by being expressed in terms of flesh and blood; but for the Hebrew poets any such diminution was well compensated by the intensity gained from the emotional associations of a living literary genre. The familiar quotations from the Song of Songs, worn to clichés by long use, were given new life by their identification with the living love poetry of the courtiers.

The erotic note of some of these poems can be quite overpowering. A poem by Ibn Gabirol evoking the ecstatic submission of the beloved to the mastery of a powerful lover begins as follows:

> The lover who towers over all lovers
> Will bring to his room
> The friend in a faint, head whirling
> To think of him and his love.[7]

It is not far in spirit from one by St. John of the Cross:

> O living flame of love,
> how tenderly you wound
> my soul in her profoundest core!
> You are no longer shy.
> Do it now, I ask you:
> break the membrane of our sweet union.[8]

Since Ibn Gabirol's poem was read by the precentor as part of a synagogue service, the medieval auditor did not need a literary critic to tell him that "the lover who towers over all lovers" is God, not a flesh-and-blood swain so manly that his beloved's knees go weak with sexual arousal at the thought of him. But we who read the poem out of context might have to get as far as verse 15, where the text pleads for "the troops of Jacob," that is, the Jewish people, before being absolutely sure of the poem's true nature.

This intentional overlapping of secular and sacred love, this pretended confusion of the boundaries, has led at least one reader to claim that some of Ibn Gabirol's liturgical poems were originally secular poems later misappropriated by the prayer book.[9] As we shall see below, one liturgical poem by Halevi (poem 5) has actually been identified as a translation of a secular Arabic love poem that was converted into a synagogue poem by the addition of a single line. The ambiguity is not unique to Jewish poetry. Ibn al-'Arabī, the thirteenth-century Muslim mystic, composed a large body of poems that can be seen to be sacred only with the help of a commentary,[10] and the same difficulty exists with much of the intensely erotic sacred poetry of St. John of the Cross, as evidenced by the brief quotation above. Jewish tradition has nothing as extreme in this regard as Persian and Turkish Sufi poetry.

It is important to be aware that the sacred and the secular themes do not cancel each other out. When a poem that reads like a love poem reveals—in the last verse or somewhere along the way—that its object is God, that revelation does not annul its eroticism. The poem continues to be colored by a sensuousness that clashes with the religious content even as it intensifies it. Moreover, by convincing us that he has known human passion, the poet makes his experience of divine passion psychologically more plausible. To claim to love God without having experienced, or at least longed for, human passion is pretense. It should occasion no surprise that piety and sensuality occur together, since they have in common an intense desire for intimacy and self-abandon. Examples abound in many cultures.

Thus, the door had been opened to the influence of secular Arabic poetry on the liturgical poetry of medieval Spanish Jewry by the traditional exegesis of the Song of Songs and by the older liturgical poetry. We shall follow the interaction of these two influences on every page of this book. We should also consider whether any trends in Islamic religious literature might have created a climate favorable to the adoption of erotic materials for religious purposes.

Although Islam does not have a tradition of poetry attached to the public liturgy, it does have a tradition of devotional poetry dating back to about 800. At that time individual Sufis began using the short love, wine, and descriptive poems as models for religious verse. This trend reached its full flowering only in the thirteenth century with Ibn al-Fāriḍ in Egypt and Ibn al-ʿArabī in Spain. But by the beginning of the Hebrew Golden Age, in the mid-tenth century, a large number of miscellaneous verses by individual mystics had already accumulated. There was also a substantial body of devotional poetry by the renowned mystic and martyr al-Ḥallāj, who was executed in Baghdad in 922, during the time of Saadia Gaon.[11] Much of this verse draws heavily on the love poetry tradition. In it, as later in Hebrew poetry of the Golden Age, longing for union with God is a very prominent theme. It therefore seems reasonable to seek the inspiration of the Golden Age poets in these works. But their interest in the soul is better explained by the currency of Neoplatonism, which was the dominant philosophical school, and there are significant differences between the two literatures that argue against much direct influence of Sufi poetry on Golden Age religious poetry.

Sufi poetry deals exclusively with the religious experience of the individual, whereas Hebrew liturgical poetry, historically part of the public liturgy, generally speaks from a national perspective. Although Hebrew liturgical poetry was always recited by the precentor, never by congregants, the "I" was traditionally collective, representing the prayers and aspirations of the community as a whole. One of the most characteristic and interesting developments in the Golden Age was the emergence of the individual voice in religious poetry,[12] a development that led to a personalizing of the national symbolism of the language of love in the *piyyuṭ* tradition. There is a remote possibility that these developments reflect the influence of Islamic mysticism. But the synagogue poetry, even at its most daring, lacks the extremes of Sufi poetry. Such commonplace ideas of Sufism as the annihilation of the devotee in God, much less the extreme identification with God characteristic of a Ḥallāj, seem to be wholly absent from Golden Age poetry. This question, however, is due for systematic study.[13]

LOVE AND THE SOUL

Ibn Gabirol, as noted, seems to have been the first of the Golden Age poets to employ the imagery, diction, and prosody of Arabic secular love poetry to describe the love between God and Israel. But he was not only a synagogue poet. He was also a philosopher who produced a substantial treatise on metaphysics that is totally independent of the Jewish tradition. His *Source of Life*[14] is neither a work of philosophical apologetics like Halevi's *Kuzari*, nor an attempt to define the Jewish revelation in terms of Islamic scholasticism like Saadia's *Beliefs and Opinions*, nor an exploration of the relationship between the Bible and Aristotelian thought like Maimonides' *Guide of the Perplexed*. More than any other extant philosophical work of medieval Jewry it belongs to the supraconfessional project of Arabic humanism—the continuation of the Greek philosophers' attempt to understand the world in light of human reason. Yet for all the book's labored definitions, arguments, and proofs, its purpose is ultimately a spiritual one: to guide the reader in developing his soul to the highest degree possible in this life so that it will be prepared to rejoin the source of life from which it originally emanated. The book is nominally in the form of a dialogue between a master and his disciple. On its last page, the master sums up his doctrine: "The purpose for which every existing thing exists . . . [is] to know the divine world, which is the greatest, most comprehensive one; everything below it is puny in comparison."[15] To the disciple's question as to what fruit is to be attained from this study, the master replies, "Freedom from death and union with the Source of Life." Earlier in the dialogue, the master had described the quest as follows:

> You must raise your intelligence to the supreme intelligible, strip it and purify it of every stain of the sensible, deliver it from the prison of nature, and attain by the virtue of the intelligence to the highest knowledge that you can achieve of the truth of the intelligible substance, until you are as it were divested of the sensible substance and are in this respect so to speak in a state of ignorance.[16]

This image of the body as a prison is a Neoplatonic commonplace. The soul of man is actually a part of the divine world, lodged by God in the body and ever yearning to return to its source. The captivity of the soul in the body is often described as exile; its yearning to return to its source, as love. These conceptions are not at all unique to Ibn Gabirol; in one form or another, they were shared by all the major thinkers of the period.[17]

It was perhaps inevitable that the two themes of exile and redemption should merge: the national theme of Israel's captivity among the nations and its yearning for restoration with the philosophical theme of the soul's captivity in the body and its yearning for union with the divine world. The literary prerequisites for the merger were already present in the synagogue's traditional image of God and Israel as separated lovers on the one hand and in the Neoplatonic image of the soul's longing for union with the object of its love on the other. Ibn Gabirol, the first to use themes from secular love poetry as a model for poetry of Israel's redemption, was also the first to use language associated with the theme of Israel's exile and redemption in his poetry of the soul.[18] One of his *ahᵃvot* has the following as its leading-strophe:

> To You, O living God, my Only One yearns
> And my spirit and soul long [for You].[19]

"My Only One," which sounds like a term of endearment, is actually a standard epithet for the soul in medieval Hebrew poetry;[20] like the other terms for the soul, it is grammatically feminine. The diction from the very beginning of the poem is that of a woman who longs to be united with her lover. In the older synagogue poetry such a pair would automatically have been understood as representing Israel and God, but here the lover separated from God is the soul. The poem goes on with four stanzas describing the soul's residence in the body, the last of which reads:

> Can anyone praise her all her due?
> Who can deny her beauty and perfection?
> Answer quickly, Lord, a girl sick with love!
> "Gently, my daughter! From the waters of my salvation
> You will surely drink, for you are my Awesome One.[20]

The images used in this stanza are all derived from the traditional language of national redemption. "Sick with love" echoes the words of the beloved in Song of Songs 2:5 and 15:8, hence of Israel in exile; "the waters of salvation" are drawn from the prophecy of consolation in Isaiah 12:3; but most telling is the startling epithet "Awesome One," a phrase from Song of Songs 6:4, used regularly for Israel in the *piyyuṭ* tradition. The various commentaries on Ibn Gabirol's poem have innocently glossed these lines as if they were about national salvation, having been distracted from the poem's true contents by the traditional usage of all these expressions.

In the four stanzas on the soul preceding the one just discussed, there is a single word that might cause a reader to hesitate about adopting this spiritual interpretation and that might confirm him in the impression that the poem is about national aspirations. That word, in line 5 of the poem, is *sᵉgulatᵉkha* (your treasure); *sᵉgula* is the Hebrew word often rendered by the expression "chosen people":

> Your presence dwells in the hearts
> *Of Your treasured ones*, sons and fathers,
> And [of] the beasts attached to [Your] chariots.

The language of these lines is that of the familiar liturgical theme that God dwells with Israel as He does with the angels. But to a philosopher, God's *sᵉgula* is mankind, the possessors of the rational soul, as opposed to the lower forms of life. Daring as is this appropriation of Israel's cherished epithet, it is not unique to Ibn Gabirol. In one of his penitential poems Ibn Ezra writes:

> He distinguished with intellect and wisdom
> His *treasured creatures* in the world;
> He was their salvation,
> And they were his portion.[21]

Though nearly every word of this passage derives from the literary tradition of God's relationship to Israel, the poem has nothing to do with the covenant. The "treasured creatures" are mankind in general, who alone of the inhabitants of the lower world (*tevel*) have been chosen to receive the gift of the intellect.

In a passage from Ibn Gabirol's *The Kingly Crown*, partly quoted earlier, the place of Israel as God's elect is occupied not by mankind in general but by those who have cultivated the intellectual potential that resides in mankind:

Thou art God:
> Every creature is Thy servant and Thy devotee.
> Thy glory never can diminished be
> Because to others some men bend their knee,
> For none intends but to come near to Thee.

> But they are like blind men,
> Who set their faces toward the royal way,
> But go astray.
> One falls into a pit, another into a ditch;
> Every one thinks he has found what he sought,
> But they labored for naught.
> Only Your servants have eyes in their heads.
> They walk straight ahead,
> Not turning aside right or left from the way,
> Until they reach the realm where the King holds sway.[22]

If the errant ones in the second half of the quotation were meant to represent non-Jews, the stirring, even immortal words of the first half would be retroactively vitiated. Ibn Gabirol must intend those who have failed to strive to purify their intellect, as urged by the master in the *Source of Life*.[23]

To return to the language of redemption, let us consider a long penitential poem by Moses Ibn Ezra. It is a strophic poem in which each strophe ends with a biblical verse containing the word "night":

> My soul longs for the place of her rest,
> And pines for the site of her root,
> And yearns for her holy home,
> "Going day and night."[24]

Stanza 13 continues this theme of the misery experienced by the soul as a result of her being separated from her source. Here again the language is that of national redemption, only this time the words are borrowed not from the Song of Songs but from Lamentations. This book's famous opening image of Israel as a widow continues the theme of God and Israel as lovers ordinarily associated with the Song of Songs, only now the lovers are separated as if by death. Though not explicitly quoted in the poem, the image is close to the consciousness of the reader who is alert to this stanza's allusions to the first chapter of Lamentations:

> She goes in darkness during her exile,
> She lowers her ornaments down to the ground
> She shakes her head, with tears on her cheek,
> "She weeps bitterly at night." [25]

Like the poem by Ibn Gabirol, that of Moses Ibn Ezra also ends with words of consolation by God:

> Good tidings, my girl! I will yet grant you my favor.
> Gently I will lead you and bring you to my habitation,
> For you have no kinsman closer than I:
> "Stay the night."

Verse 2 alludes to Song of Songs 8:2, where it is the beloved who speaks; according to rabbinic exegesis Israel is addressing the Messiah, offering to go with him to the restored Temple. The word "habitation" used in our poem has distinct associations with secular love poetry.[26] Lines 3 and 4 introduce into our vocabulary of redemption a new pair of biblical lovers, Ruth and Boaz. Boaz's words in Ruth 3:12–13 have been used elsewhere with reference to Israel's patient endurance of exile;[27] the word translated "kinsman" is *go'el*, which means both "kinsman" and "redeemer." If this stanza were encountered in isolation, the reader would have no reason to think that it refers to anything but Israel's expectation of redemption at a time of God's choosing. But after seventeen stanzas on the soul, we cannot assume that the theme suddenly shifts to Israel. The stanza can be meant to refer only to the soul's salvation.

Similarly, Judah Halevi ends a poem on the soul with a stanza that sounds very much like a national petition:

> Kindle the light that has dimmed
> With the kindness of Your right hand.
> Long enough has the cloud
> Pitched a tent for Your anger.
> A cloud of sin is stretched
> Between me and You.
> Split with the light of Your favor's star
> The night of Your anger.
> Look down from Your dwelling
> And attend to this vine.[28]

The vine is a classic image of exiled Israel as a ruined vineyard, derived from Psalm 80:16; but the poem has nothing to do with the aspirations of Israel. It is entirely about the longings of the individual soul.[29]

Clearly the interpretation of any given line is completely dependent on its context. If we were to encounter in isolation Ibn Gabirol's line:

> Restore the bereaved one to the home
> Of the land of beauty, the inheritance.[30]

we would have no doubt that it is about Israel's restoration to the land. But the three lines that precede it completely alter the meaning of its national vocabulary:

> At dawn I awaken, I
> Look for Your grace, and I hope.
> My soul longs for You: she is very
> Weak, very despairing.
> I am anxious because of my many sins and my crime
> Of unjust gain.

As hard as it is to read line 4 ("Restore the bereaved . . . ") in isolation as being about anything but Israel, so it is hard to read the poem's opening as being about anything but the individual soul. Line 4 would be a non sequitur if we did not have as one of our interpretive tools the knowledge that Israel's exile is often a symbol of the exile of the soul.

Sometimes the poet seems consciously to play with the possible overlapping of the two themes in the congregation's mind. A poem beginning "Dear are Your kindnesses, O my shelter and shade; / With the best of my praises and my songs I thank You"[31] continues for five lines speaking in the first person to God. Only a single word clouds the poem's completely personal character: a reference to Amalek as the "chief of the clan of rebellion." Amalek, according to Exodus 17:14–16 and Deuteronomy 25:17–19, is the hereditary enemy of Israel; the reference probably means that the poem was intended for recitation on the Sabbath before Purim, when the passage in Deuteronomy is the prescribed scriptural reading. But in the Zohar (end of the thirteenth century), Amalek is interpreted allegorically as representing Samael, the embodiment of death or of the "Evil Inclination."[32] Though admittedly this emblematic interpretation of Amalek is not found in Golden Age poetry, it is tempting to read it back into Halevi's poem. The overwhelmingly personal tone of the poem makes it hard to resist, and, as we have seen, this type of exegesis is not foreign to Golden Age thinkers. For medieval Jewish intellectuals, the old rabbinic notion of the Evil Inclination may simply have been tradition's way of speaking of the body, the impediment to the purification of the soul. If this poem was in fact originally composed for the Sabbath before Purim, it would have served as a kind of reinterpretation of the entire service for that day, suggesting gently to the congregation that they look inward to find the real, spiritual enemy.

We may conclude with two quotations from Ibn Gabirol in which the language of the Song of Songs is used in passages that unambiguously refer to the soul and God. Addressing the soul, Ibn Gabirol says:

> Learn to do His will,
>   Follow His paths;
> [Then] you will be saved from the fire of His wrath,
>   And you will be saved from the heat of His spheres;
> *You will come and feed in His garden,*
>   You and all who hope and wait for Him.
> When you return to your source
>   Then all will be well with me for your sake.[33]

And addressing God:

> *Bring me to Your hidden room*
>   And from my room to Your room
> Bring my soul to Your hidden place
>   When it sings "Blessed be the blessed God."[34]

The same shift from national to personal salvation that we have seen in the poetry and especially in the poetic references to the Song of Songs led, not surprisingly, to a new exegesis of the Song of Songs itself. The first extant commentary on Song of Songs in this philosophical vein seems to be that of Ibn 'Aqnin in the second half of the twelfth century. Around the same time there appear in

Spain and elsewhere in the Near East allegorical stories in rhymed prose that deal with philosophical themes under the cover of love stories.[35] But such interpretation can probably be traced back to the period of our poets. The first explicit reference to commentaries interpreting the Song of Songs as an allegory of the relationship between the world-soul and the individual is in the introduction to Abraham Ibn Ezra's commentary on that book. Ibn Ezra himself professes to reject this approach as "vanity and empty breath," insisting that the only view of the book acceptable to the rabbinic authorities is that of national allegory. However, philosophical allegory would have been consonant with his approach to other biblical books, such as Genesis or Psalms.[36] Perhaps we should not take his protestations too seriously in view of his well-known penchant for obscuring his true opinion about the esoteric meaning of a text. It would seem that in this case poetry led the way; in any case, an interesting commentary on the Song of Songs could easily be derived from the use he makes of it in his poetry.

COSMIC LOVE

In addition to the two types of love that are the dominant subject of this chapter—love between the nation and God, and love between the individual and God—a third type also played an important part in the thinking of the philosopher-poets: the philosophical notion of cosmic love. The idea is a part of the heritage of Aristotelian and Neoplatonic thought that was current among Arab philosophers and frequently echoed in the medieval Hebrew poetry as well. According to Ibn Gabirol, all matter is in motion, a motion that arises because of its desire to receive form. "Everything that exists desires to move in order to obtain some of the good of the First Cause."[37] This motion is seen as desire and love, words that are actually used in this connection in philosophical texts. In the hierarchical view of the relationship of the parts of the universe that underlay all then-current systems of thought, it was commonly accepted that each element of the system had a natural inclination to rejoin its source. Thus in his commentary Ibn Ghiyath explains Ecclesiastes 1:5–7:

> Just as the (heavenly) bodies yearn ardently toward their origins
> and seek to ascend and attain the substance out of which they
> were separated, so everything that is brought into being out of the
> four elements seeks only to join its origin. . . . Thus as they revolve,
> ascend, and incline, the fiery, airy, and earthy forms seek only to
> attain that source from which they were formed, in accordance
> with the desire and longing that God imprinted in them.[38]

In light of this general upward yearning, the desire of the soul to
return to its source was viewed as merely a particular case of a
universal phenomenon.

The theme of love and desire is sometimes used in describing
the motion of the heavens. In a verse that makes use of the lan-
guage of Psalms and Proverbs to express this philosophical con-
ception, Ibn Gabirol says:

> (The heavens) hewn[39] by the din of troops love You,
> They love Your might with their voice and thoughts,
> With their thoughts and voice they utter hymns of song.[40]

In our final two examples, both by Abraham Ibn Ezra, the
biblical language is provided by the Song of Songs. The allusion
might pass by the uninitiated reader unnoticed:

> (The heavens are) supported by His right hand,
> And drawn by His love.
> For their mouth and voice is their motion, their praise.
> This is their desire, but no stranger can move their bounds.[41]

"Drawn" is the key word, because it reminds us of Song of
Songs 1:4, where, combining motion with love, the beloved ad-
dresses her royal lover saying, "Draw me after you, let us run."

Finally, in a remarkable use of our now-familiar image of the
gazelle, Abraham Ibn Ezra describes the origin of the heavens as
follows:

> When God stretched forth His splendid sky
> Lifted it above the earth's head,
> It was drawn and lifted up to His light
> Just as the Fair Gazelle brought up His flocks.[42]

The "Fair Gazelle" is God, and His flocks are Israel. But the poem is not about Israel; it is about the sky. The poet mentions God bringing His flocks up out of Egypt only as a simile for His lifting of the heavens above the earth. Here is yet another example of the allegorical use of Scripture in liturgical poetry. It was not a big step from such readings to the composition of commentaries on the biblical books in an allegorical and philosophical vein.

The tendency of the imagery of love to move in the direction of a philosophical allegory of the relationship of the soul or of the cosmos itself to God goes together with a weakening of the national theme that was the original occasion for liturgical poetry of love. This does not, however, mean that the poets represented in this book repudiated the traditional ideas of Israel's chosenness or that they ceased to lament the exile and to pray for Israel's redemption. It only means that their intellectual life embraced other problems as well, problems arising not out of the religious tradition but out of the intellectual life they shared with non-Jews. These two sets of problems merged in their minds, so that rather than canceling each other, they complement each other, just as do the themes of secular and profane love.[43] The poems in Chapter I all revolve around the national theme. In the course of the chapter we shall observe the blending of the spiritual themes into the older national theme. In Chapter II, the national theme is nearly absent.

The gazelle of our title turns up with several different identities, sometimes representing Israel, sometimes God, and sometimes the messianic redeemer. Because the themes of the poetry on God and Israel are close to the themes of love poetry, the gazelle appears more frequently in Chapter I. We begin our selection of poems in the desert, the habitation of this elegant creature and the site of Israel's original covenant with God.

–◡–|–◡–|–◡–//–◡–|–◡–|–◡–

יַעֲלַת חֵן מִמְּעוֹנָה רָחֲקָה, / אוֹהֲבָהּ כּוֹעֵס וְלָמָּה צָחֲקָה?

צָחֲקָה עַל בַּת אֱדוֹם וּבְנוֹת עָרָב / הַמְבַקְשׁוֹת לַחֲשֹׁק דּוֹד חָשְׁקָה?

הֵן פְּרָאִים הֵם—וְאֵיךְ יִדְמוּ אֵלַי / יַעֲלָה עַל הַצְּבִי הִתְרַפְּקָה?

אֵי נְבוּאָה, אֵי מְנוֹרָה, אֵי אֲרוֹן / הַבְּרִית, אֵי הַשְּׁכִינָה דָּבְקָה?

אַל מְשַׂנְאַי, אַל תְּכַבּוּ אַהֲבָה. / כִּי תְכַבּוּהָ—וְהִיא אֵשׁ נִשָּׁקָה!

יהודה הלוי

·1·

Beautiful gazelle, so far from camp—
    Her love is angry with her; why her smile.
She smiles just thinking of those Edom girls,
    And Hagar's daughters too,
Who want to win him for themselves,
    Those desert-asses!
                Can they vie with her
Who once was road-companion to the stag?
Did they have prophets? Did they have
    The lamp, the Ark
        Of Covenant?
Where did His presence lie?

Oh no, my rivals, you will never
Put out love; its raging flame can never die.

Judah Halevi

The gazelle and her stag, the desert encampment, the anger be-
tween lovers, the jealousy of rivals—all are standard motifs of
Arabic love poetry that were imitated in secular Hebrew love po-
etry and adapted to the poetry of the synagogue.[1] The theme of
the rivals' jealousy in verse 2 may also call to mind the harems of
Middle Eastern cities; but it was the desert ambience of pre-Islamic
Arabic love poetry that best suited the needs of the synagogue
poets, for here they found an analogue to the traditional image of
God and Israel as young lovers in the desert. "Who is it that comes
up from the desert, like columns of smoke, in clouds of myrrh and
frankincense, of all the powders of the merchant?" asks the Song
of Songs. The Targum answers that it is Israel. And again the Song
of Songs asks, "Who is she that comes up from the desert in com-
pany with her lover?" It is this last phrase that was borrowed by
our poet for verse 3.[2]

This rabbinic tradition of Israel's desert romance with God com-
bined in the imagination of Arabic-educated Jews with the desert
of secular love poetry, the desert in which the Arabic poet Majnūn
died mad for his love of Lailā, the desert evoked by countless other
poets when recalling the loves of their youth.

Israel's rivals for God's love, the nations of the world, are also
connected with the desert through the word $p^e ra^{\circ}im$ (desert-asses).
The source of this deprecating image is the biblical story of the
angel who appeared to Hagar when, cast out of Abraham's home,
she wandered with her child in the desert. With the words "He
shall be a wild ass of a man," the angel prophesied that Ishmael
would grow up to be a free man of the desert, ever embroiled in
conflicts with his neighbors. Since the Arabs were commonly be-
lieved to be descended from Ishmael, the expression "wild ass" is
regularly used in liturgical poetry to refer to them and to Islam.
Here it is extended to refer to the nations of the world in general.[3]

The rivalry and hostility in the opening verses are reinforced
by sounds that mimic the speaker's feelings. Verse 2, where the
gazelle laughs at her rivals, so exploits the sounds of the Hebrew
root *ṣḥq* (to laugh) that its second hemistich fairly resolves into a

cackle. Plaited in and out of this series of alliterations is the vowel *o*, which seems to derive from Edom, a syncopating element that lends this passage a more complex texture than the merely decorative, mechanical repetition of the gutturals.

Very different is verse 4, where long vowels and soft consonants express the soothing experienced by the beloved when she reminisces about the gifts she has received from her lover. As separated lovers may find comfort in fondling old gifts and rereading old letters, the gazelle reviews these tokens. The wit and craft of the analogy between secular and divine love so carefully constructed in verses 1–3 vanishes, for the tokens come frankly from the world of the cult, not from the traditions of love poetry. With a religious imagination habitually attracted to the concrete and the tangible, it was natural for Halevi to depict Israel assuring herself of God's love in this way. But though the list of tokens is meant to assure, the form in which they appear, a series of rhetorical questions, "where . . . where . . . where," lends the verse an undertone of insecurity. This pattern is an ancient one associated with loss and mourning in Arabic and medieval Hebrew, as well as in earlier Mediterranean literatures.[4] But for the last word, the verse could very well convey a discouraging message: "Where is prophecy now? Where is the lamp now?" implying the answer "They are gone." Even if we were not aware of the history of the rhetorical pattern, we would not miss the tone of insecurity implied by the enumeration. This tone is reinforced by the inevitable return of the guttural rhyme syllable: clashing with the soft sounds of the rest of the verse, it recalls the acoustic harshness of verse 2, and partially neutralizes the consolatory purpose of the list of love tokens.

Partially, but not completely. If we think as concretely as Halevi habitually did, we are justified in imagining the spatial relationship of the four items in the list. They turn out to be arranged in ascending order: first come the prophets, outside the desert tabernacle; then comes the lamp, which stood within; next, the ark, secluded in the inner room; and finally the divine presence dwelling above the ark between the cherubim. This motion towards the presence of God has a climactic effect that overbalances all political and rhetorical uncertainty.

The concluding verse reverts to the language of love poetry and uses a theme that again ties together the language of secular poetry and the Bible. The comparison of love to fire is common in secular love poetry; Samuel the Nagid used almost the same words to begin an erotic poem:

> Burnt by passion's flame—
> How can I refrain?[5]

On the religious side, the Song of Songs says, "Passion is mighty as Sheol; its darts are darts of fire."[6]

Whose love are the enemies charged with trying to extinguish: Israel's for God or God's for Israel? Ostensibly the latter: verses 2 and 3 are about rivalry over God's favor, and it is to prove God's fidelity that the list of gifts is cited in verse 3. But because it is centered on love itself and not on the lovers, the last verse hangs strangely loose from the rest of the poem. That the enemy should try to divert God's love is not unexpected, because that is how the warfare of love is normally waged. Truly sinister is the idea that the enemy should try to undermine Israel's own devotion. Surrounded by temptations to join the dominant society, Israel could very well need to assure herself of her own steadfast love for God. It may not be farfetched to see the wording of the last verse as being intended in part to address this internal anxiety.

—–|–◡–|–|–◡–//–|–◡–|–|–◡––

מַה לָּאֲהוּבִי כִּי יִקְצֹף וְיִתְגָּאֶה / עָלַי וְלִבִּי לוֹ יָנוּד כְּמוֹ קָנֶה?

שָׁכַח זְמָן לֶכְתִּי אַחֲרָיו בְּעִי מִדְבָּר / תָּאֵב וְאֵיךְ אֶקְרָא הַיּוֹם וְלֹא יַעֲנֶה?

הֵן יִקְטְלֵנִי לוֹ אוֹחִיל, וְאִם יַסְתִּיר / פָּנָיו וְאֶל טוּבוֹ אַבִּיט וְגַם אֶפְנֶה!

לֹא יְשַׁנּוּ חַסְדֵי אָדוֹן אֱלֵי עֶבֶד / כִּי אֵיךְ נְעִים כְּחֶם יוֹעַם וְאֵיךְ יִשְׁגֶּא?

משה אבן עזרא

·2·

Why does my lover rage and tyrannize me,
    While my heart
        Bends like a reed to him?

Has he forgotten how I followed him in lust
    Through desert wastes?
        But now I call and he is still.

And though he kill me, yet in him I hope,
    And though he hide,
        I turn my face to him.

The master loves his slave for evermore.
    That cannot change,
        For how can gold go dim?

Moses Ibn Ezra

·2·

The emotional ambience is again the desert, with its Arabic resonance of lost love and its biblical resonance of Israel's long-ago marriage to God at Mount Sinai. The two themes are brought together by the allusion, in verse 2, to Jeremiah 2:2:

> I accounted to your favor the devotion of your youth,
> Your love as a bride,
> How you followed me in the wilderness
> In a land not sown.

But the use of a biblical quotation would not in itself mark this as a religious poem, for such quotations often appear in secular love poems.[1] In fact, this poem contains very little to indicate that it was written for the liturgy. Even verse 3, with its almost verbatim quotation of Job 13:15, would be perfectly at home in love poetry, in which the speaker often complains—or even expresses satisfaction—that the beloved is killing him.

> You can bestow on me life if you will,
> Or use the power of your beauty to kill.[2]

Until verse 4 every word of this poem would be at home in a wine party held in a garden in spring, and it is not hard to imagine some medieval congregants finding it out of place in a synagogue.

The identity of the lovers is given away only in verse 4, where the speaker expresses confidence that the beloved's feelings will never change. Such confidence would be completely contrary to convention and out of place in secular love poetry, because in this genre the beloved is typically characterized as capricious and fickle. It is precisely her inconstancy that causes the lover's heartache and occasions the poem. Compare the complaint of Samuel the Nagid: "He betrayed; so all gazelles betray."[3] Here the speaker's certainty of the beloved's continued affection necessarily implies a different order of beloved. Their philosophical training predisposed the medieval poets to associate mutability with the mundane world, and permanence with God.

Even taking into consideration the influence of secular love poetry, the degree of passivity attributed to the speaker here is noteworthy. Like the preceding and the following poems, but in contrast to many of the later poems in this book, it is not even addressed to God, a trait that might seem strange in a prayer. In verse 1 the speaker describes his submissiveness; in verse 2, his frustration; in verse 3a, his patient and loving acceptance of God's cruelty and neglect. The whole relationship is summarized in verse 4, where he speaks of God as master and of himself as slave, another comparison not lacking in secular love poetry.[4]

This imbalance in the status of the two figures of the poem is gently imitated in its rhythm. Poems composed in classical Arabic meters are made up of verses divided into two hemistichs of equal length. Ordinarily each hemistich corresponds to a syntactic unit, so that the two halves of the verse feel balanced. Occasionally a verse will deviate from this regular division, sometimes out of necessity, sometimes to create a particular effect. Our poem is unusual in that of its four verses, only the last exhibits the balanced construction. In both verses 1 and 2, the sentence with which the verse begins, and which speaks of God, spills over into the second hemistich. Crowded into the remaining space in each of the two verses is the sentence describing the actions of the speaker; the rhythmic imbalance may be meant to suggest the speaker's weakness and passivity. Verse 3 is also asymmetrical, but the imbalance is in the opposite direction. The verse is built of two "if . . . then" sentences: (1) If God kills me / I shall hope. (2) If He hides His face / I shall turn and look to His goodness. Instead of disposing these four clauses two to a hemistich, he has squeezed three of them into a little more than half the line, as follows:

If He kills me, I shall hope; if He hides
His face, I shall turn and look to His goodness.

Because the first three clauses are so compressed, there is room for two verbs in the last clause. As a result, this clause feels stretched beyond any reasonable length, and its vision of God's goodness enjoys extra emphasis.

The poem has thus adopted an attitude typical of lovers in

secular poetry to describe a specific religious posture, submissive trust, known in the language of Arabic pietism as *tawakkul*.[5] This passive reliance on God is usually recommended for individual piety; here it is extended to the personified nation. As we shall see, *tawakkul* is one of the characteristic strands of the religiosity of the age; having an analogy in the behavior of frustrated lovers, it was also one that made it possible for the synagogue to adopt the conventions of love poetry.

·3·

—–∪|–∪–|—–∪–//—–∪–|–|–∪–|—–

מַהֲרוּ נָא אֱלֵי מְעוֹנֵי אֲהוּבִים / פֻּזְּרָם הַזְּמָן, וְנוֹתְרוּ חֲרֵבִים.
לָעֲפָרִים אֲזַי מְעוֹנִים—וְהִנָּם / לַכְּפִירִים מְעוֹן וְגַם לַזְּאֵבִים.
אֶשְׁמְעָה נַאֲקַת צְבִיָּה תְּיֵלִיל / מִכְּלוּאֵי אָדוֹם וּמַאֲסַר עֲרָבִים.
עַל אֲהוּבָה תֵּבְךְ וְאַלּוּף נְעוּרִים, / גַּם תְּעַנֶּה בְּמַאֲמָרִים עֲרֵבִים:
"סַמְּכוּנִי כְּבַאֲשִׁישׁוֹת יְדִידוֹת / רַפְּדוּנִי בְּמִגְדְּנֵי הָאֲהָבִים!"

משה אבן עזרא

·3·

Hurry to the lovers' camp,
　　Dispersed by Time, a ruin now;
Once the haunt of love's gazelles,
　　Wolves' and lions' lair today.

From far away I hear Gazelle,
　　From Edom's keep and Arab's cell,
Mourning the lover of her youth,
　　Sounding lovely, ancient words:
"Fortify me with lovers' flasks,
　　Strengthen me with sweets of love."

Moses Ibn Ezra

·3·

The motif of the desert camp, alluded to in verse 1, is here used in a way reminiscent of the long Bedouin odes of the pre-Islamic period, the *qaṣīda*s, which for centuries served as the foundation of an Arabic literary education. Such poems often begin with the following stock situation: A rider bids his two companions halt in their journey through the desert because he recognizes the traces of a ruined camp where the tribe of his beloved had once sojourned. Though years have passed since their rendezvous, he still feels the nostalgic tug of the spot, now a ruin. The following passage from a Bedouin ode displays a number of features that are found also in Moses Ibn Ezra's poem:

> The tent-marks in Mina are worn away
>   Where she encamped
> and where she alighted,
>   Ghawl and Riján left to the wild . . .
>
> Dung-stained ground
>   That tells the years passed
> since human presence, months of peace
>   Gone by, and months of war . . .
>
> The white pondcress has shot upward,
>   And on the wadi slopes,
> gazelles among their newborn
>   And ostriches, . . .
>
> I stopped to question them.
>   How is one to question
> Deaf, immutable,
>   Inarticulate stones?[1]

This stylized *qaṣīda*-opening gradually fell out of use during the eighth and ninth centuries, with the shifting of the centers of Arabic culture from desert to city. But the older poems continued to be studied, and the image retained its hold on the imagination, experiencing revivals and remaining a subject of controversy. In tenth- and eleventh-century Spain it was not much used in original poetry, but the classical odes were still memorized, anthologized, and revered. Moses Ibn Ezra was the first Hebrew poet to incorporate such openings into his secular odes in the Arabic manner.[2]

As with so many other motifs from Arabic literature, the ruined camp motif may have seemed to the medieval courtier-rabbis to have been simply a variation on a traditional Jewish one. The following anecdote appears several times in rabbinic literature:

> . . . Rabban Gamaliel, R. Eleazar b. Azariah, R. Joshua, and R. Akiba . . . were once going up to Jerusalem . . . .When they reached the Temple Mount they saw a fox leaving the area of the Holy of Holies. They began to weep, but R. Akiba laughed. They asked, "Why are you laughing?" He asked, "Why are you weeping?" They answered, "The place of which Scripture says, 'Any outsider who encroaches shall be put to death' [Numbers 1:51], now foxes are walking on it—should we not weep?" He said to them, "For that very reason I laugh. In Uriah's prophecy it is written ' . . . Zion shall be plowed as a field, and Jerusalem shall become heaps of ruins, and the Temple Mount a shrine in the woods' [Micah 3:12; see also Jeremiah 26:18]. In Zechariah it is written, 'There shall yet be old men and women in the squares of Jerusalem' [Zechariah 8:4]. As long as Uriah's prophecy was unfulfilled I feared that Zechariah's would never be. Now that Uriah's has been fulfilled, it is certain that Zechariah's will be." They said to him as follows: "You have comforted us, Akiba, you have comforted us."[3]

Like the riders in the Arabic poems, the rabbis in this anecdote halt and urge each other to weep over the site of a past intimacy. That site is now a ruin, haunted by scavengers of the wilderness. The similarity of the two images of lamentation could hardly have been lost on Moses Ibn Ezra and his contemporaries. In light of the rabbinic anecdote, the Arabic motif must have seemed to them a misappropriation of their own literary heritage, which they were eager to reclaim in the new Hebrew poetry.

The word *ma῾on* used in our poem and in poem 1 to designate the beloved's ruined camp is another link between the Temple and the Arabic motif. Its fundamental meaning is "habitation," and it is used in the Bible of God's dwelling place, whether celestial or mundane. It is also used for the lair of a wild beast.[4] With these three usages in the background, the word is well suited to serve as the link in this perfect syncretism of rabbinic and Arabic literary motifs.

Consideration of the Arabic model suggests that the speaker is probably not calling on his auditors to return to Palestine[5] but rather to share his imaginary vision of Zion in ruins. The wild beasts that now inhabit the Holy Land are Christians and Arabs. We shall encounter more examples of the designation of the nations of the world by animal names in subsequent poems.[6]

In verse 3, the image shifts from the ruined camp to its exiled inhabitants, leading us to imagine that the camp was broken up by an enemy and that its people, representing Israel, are now in captivity. Christians and Muslims are not portrayed as rivals for God's love, as in poem 1, but as captors. And how does Israel pass her time in captivity while awaiting redemption? She reminisces about the happy times of her love, singing a love song taken from the Song of Songs:

> Sustain me with raisin cakes,
> Refresh me with apples,
> For I am faint with love.[7]

In the source, the beloved recalls a happy time spent with her lover in a tavern; after having worn herself out with excesses of pleasure, she had called for refreshment so that she could return to carousing. Here, using the same words, she calls for sustenance to enable her to endure captivity and the absence of her lover. It may be helpful in this connection to know that in his commentary on the Song of Songs, Abraham Ibn Ezra interpreted the flasks and sweets as representing the consolatory message of the prophets.[8]

Each of the last two poems ends with a paraphrase of a biblical verse, and this one ends with a nearly exact quotation. This is a fairly common closure device. Its braking effect is a bit more firm in the present poem than in poem 2, since here it is not diluted by other references to the Bible in the preceding verses. But there is another association between quotations and poem endings that may be even more significant. It was a convention of early Romance love poetry that in the last strophe the speaker, who is always a woman, turns to her mother or a confidante and com-

plains of her frustration occasioned by separation from her lover
and of her lovesickness. Her complaint is introduced by the words
"she said" or "she sang," and the last line of the poem purports
to be a quotation from her song, the same technique as in verses
3 and 4 of our poem. Although examples of such Romance poems
are not preserved from before the end of the twelfth century, they
must already have existed a century earlier, since verses of such
poems are quoted—in the original Romance language—in Arabic
and Hebrew *muwashshahāt* even from before the time of Moses
Ibn Ezra.[9] It is entirely possible that the convention, which was
well known to Moses Ibn Ezra, underlies the structure of the last
two lines of our poem, though it is not a strophic one like the
muwashshahāt.

−∪−|−∪−|−∪−−//−∪−|−∪−|−∪−−

יוֹנַת רְחוֹקִים נָדְדָה יַעֲרָה / כָּשְׁלָה וְלֹא יָכְלָה לְהִתְנַעֲרָה.

הִתְעוֹפְפָה הִתְנוֹפֵפָה חוֹפֵפָה / סָבִיב לְדוֹדָהּ סוֹחֲרָה סוֹעֲרָה,

וַתַּחֲשֹׁב אֶלֶף לְקֵץ מוֹעֲדָהּ / אַךְ חָפְרָה מִכֹּל אֲשֶׁר שָׂעֲרָה.

דּוֹדָהּ—אֲשֶׁר עִנָּהּ בְּאֹרֶךְ נְדוֹד / שָׁנִים, וְנַפְשָׁהּ אֶל שְׁאוֹל הֶעֱרָה—

הֵן אָמְרָה "לֹא אֶזְכְּרָה עוֹד שְׁמוֹ!" / וַיְהִי בְתוֹךְ לִבָּהּ כְּאֵשׁ בּוֹעֲרָה.

לָמָּה כְאוֹיֵב תִּהְיֶה לָהּ? וְהִיא / פִּיהָ לְמַלְקוֹשׁ יֶשְׁעֲךָ פָּעֲרָה.

וַתַּאֲמִין נַפְשָׁהּ וְלֹא נוֹאֲשָׁה / אִם כָּבְדָה בִּשְׁמוֹ וְאִם צָעֲרָה.

יָבוֹא אֱלֹהֵינוּ וְאַל יֶחֱרַשׁ—/ עַל כָּל סְבִיבָיו אֵשׁ מְאֹד נִשְׂעֲרָה!

יהודה הלוי

·4·

Far-flown dove wandered to a wood,
    Stumbled there and lay lame,
Flitted, flailed, and flustered
    Storming, circling round her love's head.
A thousand years she thought would bring her time,
    But all her calculations failed.
Her lover hurt her heart by leaving her
    For years; she might have died.
She swore she'd never say his name again,
    But in her heart it burned like fire.

Why so hostile to her?
    Her mouth is open always to your rain.
She keeps her faith, does not despair,
    Whether in your name her lot is pain or fame.
Let God come now, and not come quietly,
    But round him raging storms and wild flame.

Judah Halevi

·4·

Though not a standard epithet for the beloved in Arabic poetry, the dove is associated with gardens, spring, and love in a general way, as may be judged from the title of the most famous Arabic book on love, Ibn Ḥazm's *The Dove's Neck Ring*.[1] The return of doves and other birds in spring occasions the Arab poet's call to celebrate the reawakening of nature and to reflect on the gradual dissolution of all things through the action of the unending cycle of time.[2]

In Hebrew, however, the word "dove" was an epithet for the beloved in the Song of Songs[3] and so served the same function in the secular love poetry of the Golden Age. Like all the other designations, descriptions, and epithets of the beloved in the Song of Songs, the dove had been from earliest times an emblem of Israel in synagogue poetry. This usage was reinforced by other biblical passages: the dove's mournful cooing is an image of suffering in Isaiah; the Psalmist longs for a dove's wings so that he might fly far from his enemies; Hosea and Isaiah use the dove's flight as an image for return from exile; Noah's dove, like the Jews of a later age, "could not find a resting place for its foot." As the smallest living creature deemed ritually fit for sacrifice in the Temple cult, the dove was the preferred offering of those who could not afford a bull, sheep, or goat. All of these associations coalesced in the rabbinic imagination to connect the dove with Israel's suffering in exile: "Just as the dove stretches out its neck to be slaughtered, so does Israel."[4]

The dove of our poem comes from Psalm 56, which bears the enigmatic heading "The Silent Dove of the Distance,"[5] combined with Psalm 55:7–8, "O that I had the wings of a dove! I would fly away and find rest; surely I would flee far off; I would lodge in the wilderness."

The word *n^edod* (wander), the root of which appears in verse 1 of our poem, rhymes with *dod* (lover), permitting a pun often used in speaking of separated lovers. Here the lover is God, who appears in verses 2 and 4. But Halevi downplays this easy sound effect in favor of a more complicated and original one, the remarkable onomatopoetic passage in verse 2. This verse opens with a series of verbs with similar morphological patterns and roots alliterating in *f,* as if to imitate the frantic fluttering of the dove's wings. This sound effect is followed by another group of words beginning with *s.* The last two of these words contain guttural consonants and *r;* these sounds have an afterlife in verse 3, where the repeated gutturals and *r*-sounds recall the actual sound made by doves—with a reprise of *f.* It is an acoustically dense, distinctively Halevian passage.[6]

The first purpose of the dove's struggle is to draw the lover's attention to her plight so that he will bring her back to him from the forest of the nations. Her desperation is an image of the powerlessness of a community in exile in seeking to control its own destiny in a hostile world. But the poem speaks of another struggle as well, one that takes place within the dove's own self.

Some of the preceding poems have alluded to the anguish of medieval Jews who believed that God had abandoned them, leaving them isolated among hostile nations, perhaps even superseded in God's love by the oppressor. This thought has its own parallel in secular love poetry, in which well-meaning friends advise the unrequited lover to give up his frustrated hopes, and in which the poet himself sometimes seems tempted to put an end to his own misery by abandoning his suit. On such advice, there exists a whimsical reflection:

> I've had enough of friends who criticize,
> They bother me; we never can agree.
> They think that love's a yoke about my neck;
> A medal on my chest it seems to me.[7]

Considering the ease with which a Jew in the Muslim world could convert to Islam and the social advantages of such conversion, it is not surprising that those who kept faith did so at the cost of some inner struggle. It was not only the nations of the world that enticed the Jew away from his people; a voice within also urged him to extract himself from his painful love.

Here the medieval poet combined the conflicts of the love poetry with those acknowledged by the prophet Jeremiah. He too confessed that the prophetic call set him apart from other men, consigning him to loneliness and a hostile world; he too longed to join mankind and reject God's painful summons. But his desire for freedom was not so strong as to prevail against his own passion for God.[8] One of the attractions of Golden Age poetry for a modern reader is that, unlike the classic poetry of the synagogue liturgy, it occasionally affords a glimpse of such ambivalences and inner uncertainties of the religious life.

The poem's last line seems to signify a change to a mood that at first seems not to match the rest of the poem. We have seen that poems often conclude with a verbatim or a near-verbatim quotation from the Bible. Here the source is Psalm 50:3, an apocalyptic call for a final reckoning—perhaps only a God of fire could satisfy the burning heart. But this verse is also a call for vengeance against the nations.[9] The theme is common enough in medieval religious poetry, but it is unexpected here, coming after the inwardness of the preceding verses.

Unexpected, but not inexplicable. The emotional background of the entire poem is the nation's helplessness, so musically evoked in lines 1–2. Unable to control the outside circumstances, Israel, the dove, is reduced to such passive behavior as calculating the date of redemption,[10] opening her mouth to receive water, trusting, and not flagging. But beneath the passivity rages a fire of love and frustration. The redirection of these feelings outward is hinted at here. It will be taken up again in this chapter, but not until we have explored the inward direction a bit further.

———|ᵕ—|ᵕ—ᵕ—//———|ᵕ—|ᵕ——

מֵאָז מְעוֹן הָאַהֲבָה הָיִיתָ. / חָנוּ אֲהָבַי בַּאֲשֶׁר חָנִיתָ.

תּוֹכְחוֹת מְרִיבֵי צָרְבוּ לִי עַל שְׁמֶךָ, / עָזְבֵם—יְעַנּוּ אֶת אֲשֶׁר עִנִּיתָ.

לָמְדוּ חֲרוֹנְךָ אוֹיְבַי וָאֹהֲבֵם / כִּי רָדְפוּ חָלָל אֲשֶׁר הִכִּיתָ.

מִיּוֹם בְּזִיתַנִי בְּזִיתִינִי אֲנִי / כִּי לֹא אֲכַבֵּד אֶת אֲשֶׁר בָּזִיתָ—

עַד יַעֲבָר־זַעַם וְתִשְׁלַח עוֹד פְּדוּת / אֶל נַחֲלָתְךָ זֹאת אֲשֶׁר פָּדִיתָ.

יהודה הלוי

·5·

From time's beginning, You were love's abode:
    My love encamped wherever it was You tented.
The taunts of foes for Your name's sake are sweet,
    So let them torture one whom You tormented.

I love my foes, for they learned wrath from You,
    For they pursue a body You have slain.
The day You hated me I loathed myself,
    For I will honor none whom You disdain.

Until Your anger pass, and You restore
    This people whom You rescued once before.

Judah Halevi

Nothing in the tranquil tone of this poem prepares us for the contained agony of its theme. The now-familiar abandoned campsite of love with which it opens lulls us into anticipating another sentimental evocation of the ancient romance between Israel and God. Even the taunting foes are a comfortably routine convention of secular love poetry. In love poetry they are either friends of the lover who counsel him to behave more prudently, as we saw in poem 4, or they are meddlers who disapprove of the relationship altogether and want to break it up. According to Ibn Ḥazm, the Hispano-Arabic theoretician of love, true lovers rejoice at being berated for their infatuation: this allows them to display their defiance, and also gives them the opportunity to hear the name of the beloved repeatedly mentioned, as our poet says in verse 2.[1]

Into this conventional framework, employing disarmingly understated diction, Halevi has set a statement of the Jewish condition so radical that it may even be said to court ugliness. The Israel who speaks in this poem goes so far in identifying her own will with that of God that she has stopped longing actively for redemption. She embraces the punishment, yes, the very hatred of herself that is the punishment's cause. She loves the enemy who does God's will by punishing her.

In a note on our poem, Ḥayim Schirmann points to a passage in Halevi's *Kuzari* in which this very attitude is held to be the appropriate one for the exiled folk. In the fictional dialogue between a rabbi and the king of the Khazars, the rabbi attempts to prove that the fact of Israel's subjugation to the nations is actually proof that Israel is closer to God than her subjugators: For, the rabbi argues, Christians and Muslims are in agreement that poverty and humility are religiously preferable to riches and sovereignty. The Khazar king replies that the rabbi's claim would be stronger if the Jews accepted their lot voluntarily and gladly, like the martyrs and ascetics of Christianity and Islam. To the reader's surprise, the rabbi in Halevi's dialogue concedes that only a small number of Jews accept Israel's subjugation in the true spirit of submission to God's will. He points out, however, that even if their attitude falls short of the ideal, their loyalty is still meritorious, given the ease with which they could escape their subjugation through conversion to Islam.[2]

But our poem goes even further than merely embracing subjugation; it internalizes the very attitude of the oppressor toward the oppressed and posits that the ideal mood for hated and rejected Israel is self-hatred and self-rejection.

Just how radical Halevi's poem is may be brought out by contrasting it with other poems close to it in theme. Isaac Ibn Ghiyath, for example, had written:

> I bear my separation; I rejoice in my exile.
> I serve my enslavers; I remain hopeful in my illness.
> ....
> I rejoice in my disaster; I am happy in my poverty.
> My illness and oppression—they are my pride.[3]

And Abraham Ibn Ezra, Halevi's younger contemporary, was to write:

> I listen to the contentions of the foes—
> And how sweet they are![4]

Striking as are these passages, neither takes the idea beyond expressing Israel's pride in her suffering for the sake of her loyalty to God—the pride of the martyr. Halevi's statement advances the idea to the next level, the pride of the mystic. Here Israel's identification with God is so complete that she adopts even His anger toward herself, even the contempt of her enemies, whom God has temporarily chosen to favor. Nowhere else in the medieval Hebrew literature on the national problem do we encounter this extreme, paradoxical degree of self-denial and identification with God.

There is an additional, implicit paradox. The faith so radical as to find expression in self-contempt constitutes the very grounds for Israel's claim to being God's elect. The words are words of self-loathing, but the message is one of comfort, of reassurance as radical as the idea of identification with the enemy. The poet's tranquil tone reflects this implied message. And this, not the agony behind the poem's premise, is the point of the poem.[5]

That a lover should identify so strongly with his beloved as to adopt her rejection of himself has a certain psychological truth that has not been lost even on Western poets. Petrarch, writing in the same vein in a turbulent sonnet, depicts himself as a lover tormented by contrary feelings:

> . . . I desire to perish, and yet I ask for health;
> I love another, and thus I hate myself;
> I feed me in sorrow, and laugh in all my pain.
> Likewise displeaseth me both death and life,
> And my delight is causer of this strife.
> In this state am I, Lady, on account of you.[6]

He comes close to Halevi's idea—in almost the very words—when he says in another sonnet that his heart can never again be his own because he disdains whatever displeases his love. In yet another sonnet he applies to his beloved the same verse from Job that Moses Ibn Ezra applied to God:

> Though she kill me a thousand times a day,
> I shall still love her and hope in her.[7]

In Hebrew secular love poetry the theme is attested in a verse by Halevi himself:

> Intensify your battle against the corpse of one who died
>   For love of you . . .
> You despise me; therefore you hurl your lance at me.
> So I despise myself; hurl away![8]

and in the verse by Ibn Ṣadiq:

> Since he hates me, I also hate myself;
> False wisdom it is to love what the fawn despises.[9]

The Hebrew poets, of course, derived the theme from Arabic love poetry. Ibn Zaidūn, one of the greatest Hispano-Arabic poets of this period, said of his Wallāda, "I love my enemies because you are one of them," and "If you were to say to me 'die' I would not say 'no.'" Furthermore, we now know that our poem was not actually composed by Halevi but translated by him. The first four verses were originally a secular Arabic love poem that Halevi translated into Hebrew: By adding the fifth line, he converted it from a secular to a religious poem. Our poem is thus a twofold translation, as remarkable in its origins as in its content.[10]

The theme of our poem, therefore, is at home in secular love poetry. But in Islam, as in Judaism, the idea that the lover subjugates his own will to that of the beloved did not remain restricted to the realm of secular love. Along with other motifs of love poetry, it was adopted by the mystics. Al-Ḥallāj, for example, wrote:

> I desire that which pleases you—my death,
> O You who kills me; and what You choose, I choose.[11]

Another mystic, Ruwaim Ibn Aḥmad, when asked about the meaning of love, defined it as "agreement under every circumstance," and recited:

> If you should say to me "die" I would die in servile
>   obedience,
> And I would say to the one who calls me to death,
>   "welcome," "greetings."[12]

Had our poem employed the hyperbolic, violent language of some of the poetry of frustrated secular love, it might have been too grotesque to be convincing. In its calm and even tone there is a mitigating factor that makes it possible to listen with sympathy to its uncomfortable message. Poetic imagery, though present, plays but a small part, and there are no outcries or high-flown language.[13] Instead of mimetic evocations of mood there are plain statements of the central emotional facts: that the speaker loves God and therefore loves his enemies. In the context of the craft of medieval Hebrew poetry, with its penchant for imagery and rhetorical decoration, these unadorned statements might have come across as understated, almost unpoetic. Even the logically climactic statement "The day You hated me I loathed myself" is rhetorically undermined by the negative reasoning of the complementary clause "For I will honor none whom You disdain." The words are words of self-loathing, but the tone is one of passive acceptance of God's will. Such cultivated passivity is Halevi's characteristic religious posture; its expression here is so effective because of what at first appears as a discrepancy between tone and content.

This discrepancy may also be observed in a semantic pattern common to all five verses of the poem; that is, a potentially violent emotion in each first hemistich is dissipated on a grammatically vague object in the second. The focus of the speaker's love in verse 1 is "wherever" God chose to encamp; the rebukes and torments of the enemy in verse 2 are directed against "the one whom" God tormented; the enemy's rage in verse 3 is leveled against "the body You have slain";[14] and in verse 4 the speaker reflects that he cannot give honor to "anyone" whom God despises. Though the referent in each individual verse is clear enough, the accumulated impression of the repeated vagueness seems to end each verse with a resigned "whatever you want." Such a construction might have no significance in a single verse, but repeated in four successive verses it cannot help but cushion a message that, expressed more directly, might be too painful to bear. Only in verse 5 does the vagueness vanish, as the same grammatical construction changes meaning to achieve the exact opposite—grammatical certainty, with the word "this" pointing clearly and unambiguously to Israel. The relative clause that follows is a concrete, historical reason for the speaker's confidence: the fact that God has already come to Israel's rescue in the past.

Unexpected as is Halevi's idea of Israel's self-denial and self-contempt, it fits in a way the emotional reality of a tolerated minority. Loss of a feeling of worth can be the fate even of minorities that enjoy sufficient toleration to be able to create a "Golden Age" for themselves, not just of those that suffer economic misery and cultural deprivation. Once we become accustomed to the thought, it may even seem surprising that Hebrew literature does not offer more examples of the despised people adopting the oppressor's attitude toward itself.

·6·

—|—◡—|—|—◡——

יָשֵׁן וְלִבּוֹ עֵר / בּוֹעֵר וּמִשְׁתָּעֵר:

צֵא נָא וְהִנָּעֵר / וּלְכָה בְאוֹר פָּנָי.

קוּמָה, צְלַח וּרְכַב! / דַּרְךָּ לְךָ כּוֹכָב,

וַאֲשֶׁר בְּבוֹר שָׁכַב / עָלָה לְרֹאשׁ סִינָי.

אַל תַּעֲלֹז נַפְשָׁם / הָאוֹמְרִים "תֵּאֹשַׁם

צִיּוֹן!" וְהִנֵּה שָׁם / לִבִּי וְשָׁם עֵינָי.

אָגֵל וְאֶסְתָּר, / אֶקְצֹף וְאֶעְתָּר;

מִי יַחֲמֹל יוֹתֵר / מִנִּי עֲלֵי בָנָי?

יהודה הלוי

·6·

O you who sleep with waking heart,
Burning, storming, in dismay,
Go forth, shake slumber off, and let
The light of my countenance light your way.

Get up, mount, and ride—
See your star shooting across the sky.
Behold the folk that lay in the pit
Already ascending Mount Sinai.

May no joy come to those who jeer
That guilty Zion in ruins must lie.
Not so! Her innocence I know!
She always will have my heart and eye.

Sometimes I hide, then show my face,
I rage sometimes and then subside;
But who is there who would have more care
For these my little ones than I?

Judah Halevi

By making God Himself the speaker in this poem, Halevi boldly indulges his penchant for prophetic speech, already noted in connection with his dream-vision in poem 4.

The precentor in Jewish prayer ordinarily addresses God on behalf of the congregation, but there are exceptions. Sometimes he addresses the congregation as a prayer leader, exhorting its members to some liturgical activity. In *tokheḥot* he takes the role of community elder, admonishing the congregation.[1] In poems composed as imaginary dialogues, he may even speak in God's name and also take the role of Israel as God's interlocutor. But it is most rare for the precentor to represent God directly to the congregation in a poem with only one speaker who takes the role of neither precentor nor admonisher, but of prophet.[2]

The prophetic character of this poem is reinforced by the density of its biblical quotations, especially in its first half, where nearly every clause seems to come from one biblical prophecy or another. The one who "sleeps with waking heart" is the beloved of the Song of Songs 5:2, changed, for the purposes of the poem, from feminine to masculine. Halevi himself interpreted this verse in his *Kuzari* as an allegory of Israel's condition: "asleep" in exile, but "with waking heart"—having never lost the power of prophecy.[3] "Let the light of my countenance light your way" alludes to Isaiah 2:5, where similar words are addressed to the house of Israel in a vision of a time in the future when all nations will march to Zion to learn God's ways. It is the king of Israel (David himself, according to Abraham Ibn Ezra), who is bidden to "Get up, mount, and ride" in Psalm 45:5. And the star that traverses the sky comes from the fourth poem of Balaam, where it has always been understood as representing the Messiah.[4] Even the call here translated "Go forth, shake slumber off" is taken from a biblical source, though the associations of the passage from which it is taken are rather at odds with the poem's mood.[5] Thick with biblical quotations, this poem is no less a tour de force for the reader—who must rapidly comb his memory for the sources of the quotations and undercurrents of meaning—than it was for the author. But more important to the poem's interpretation than even the specific allusions is their overall effect of making the poem feel like an extension of biblical prophecy, in which the poet/prophet proclaims to Israel the advent of the new age.[6]

The locus of the redemption, according to our poem, is Mount Sinai, to which the captive folk, now released by God, are streaming, to the fury of the nations of the world, who want to see Palestine reduced to a wasteland. To a Jew like Halevi, a contemporary of the First Crusade and its aftermath, it must have seemed that this was in fact their intention. But God had promised the land His eternal protection, and the poem opposes the nations' intention with an allusion to this promise in verse 3.

That the ultimate redemption should involve Mount Sinai is not traditional; rabbinic eschatology focuses on Mount Zion and the other mountains around Jerusalem. But in view of the centrality of the Sinaitic revelation in Halevi's religious thought, it was natural for him to feature Sinai so prominently. He is at pains to demonstrate in the *Kuzari*[7] that Sinai is part of Palestine, the only possible site of authentic revelation in his system. He seems originally to have planned his own journey to Palestine so as to enter the Holy Land overland from Egypt, following the route of Christian pilgrims who visited Mount Sinai along the way. In any case, Sinai figures importantly in the poetry he composed around his pilgrimage.[8]

There is another way to read this poem. The masculine sleeper addressed at the beginning may be understood as representing not Israel but the Messiah, whom God rouses to his work of salvation at the dawning of the new age. This folkloric figure of the Messiah as a sleeping king is not, as far as I know, associated with the Messiah in the Jewish literary tradition, which more typically pictures him as a leper sitting at the gate of Rome while awaiting the time for his appearance.[9] But Abraham Ibn Ezra's allegorical interpretation of the Song of Songs presupposes the sleeping king motif. And this interpretation of our poem is tempting because the biblical verses quoted in lines 5 and 6 of the translation are traditionally associated with the Messiah, as mentioned above. The Psalmist urges God Himself to wake from sleep to save Israel.[10]

And Ibn Gabirol, in a brilliant pun on Psalm 68:28, asks God to "waken the sleeping youth."[11]

But it is Ibn Gabirol, not Halevi, who lays great stress on the Messiah and surrounds his figure with colorful imagery. In Halevi's poetry the Messiah plays no role at all. I therefore regretfully commend the first interpretation as the only historically justifiable one and mention the second interpretation only because it is subjectively so compelling.

·7·

—|—|—◡—|—|—◡—

"שַׁעַר אֲשֶׁר נִסְגַּר—קוּמָה פְּתָחֵהוּ,
וּצְבִי אֲשֶׁר בָּרַח—אֵלַי שְׁלָחֵהוּ!
לְיוֹם בּוֹאֲךָ עָדַי לָלִין בְּבֵין שָׁדַי
שָׁם רֵיחֲךָ הַטּוֹב עָלַי תְּנִיחֵהוּ".
"מַה זֶּה דְמוּת דּוֹדֵךְ, כַּלָּה יְפֵה-פִיָּה,
כִּי תֹאמְרִי אֵלַי: שִׁלְחָה וְקָחֵהוּ?
הַהוּא יְפֵה עַיִן אָדֹם וְטוֹב רֹאִי?"
"רֵעִי וְדוֹדִי זֶה—קוּמָה מְשָׁחֵהוּ!"

שלמה אבן גבירול

·7·

"The gate long shut—
    Get up and throw it wide;
The stag long fled—
    Send him to my side.

When one day you come
    To lie between my breasts,
That day your scent
    Will cling to me like wine."

"How shall I know his face, O lovely bride,
    The lover you are asking me to send?
A ruddy face, and lovely eyes?
    A handsome man to see?"

"Aye, that's my love! Aye, that's my friend!
Anoint that one for me!"

Solomon Ibn Gabirol

·7·

This puzzling poem is one of thirteen by Ibn Gabirol in which God and Israel address each other on the theme of redemption. Some of these poems are dialogues; all but two are in the same meter. Several, including this one, pose a serious interpretative problem: it is very difficult to determine exactly who the speakers in the dialogue are. All thirteen poems are erotic to a degree.[1]

In the opening of the present poem it seems fairly clear that Israel is addressing God, asking Him to send back to her the stag, who we assume represents the Messiah. But in verse 2 Israel dreams of an erotic reunion with whomever she is addressing; she now seems to envision the redemption as a reunion not with the stag but with God. It seems unlikely that with the words "when one day you come . . ." she is changing the object of her address from her interlocutor (God) to the dreamed-of lover (the Messiah), because the shift is abrupt and unexplained. The upshot is that we have a dialogue in which it is tantalizingly unclear who is who.

However the poet meant us to understand the identity of the speakers, the overall picture is clear enough. Israel here appears as an abandoned bride, longing for the return of her lover, the stag, so that she can receive him in a wedding chamber. Her vision of their union is frankly erotic, but it owes nothing to the Arabic literary tradition. It is so closely modeled on the Song of Songs that it might be considered a variation or a fantasy on that book. As such, it is also a contribution to the book's exegesis.

Our poem is modeled on Song of Songs 5. Here the beloved, frustrated at her lover's disappearance just when she had made up her mind to receive him in her bedroom, asks her companions to help her search for him. They in turn ask for a description for purposes of identification; their query is the model for the one in verse 3 of our poem. The beloved replies with a kind of aria in which she describes her lover limb by limb, beginning with "My beloved is clear-skinned and ruddy." Prior to Ibn Gabirol, this passage had been interpreted throughout the history of Jewish exegesis as being about God. The Targum, for example, paraphrases it as follows:

Then the ecclesia of Israel began to speak about the praise of the Lord of the World, saying, "It is God I desire to worship, for by day He wears a robe white as snow . . . and His face is radiant as fire from the greatness of His wisdom."

But Ibn Gabirol gives the passage an original twist by seizing on the similarities between its opening words and the biblical description of the youthful David. The latter passage describes how the prophet Samuel, after rejecting Jesse's older sons for the office of king of Israel, ordered Jesse to send for the youngest:

"Send someone to bring him." . . . So they sent and brought him. He was *ruddy-cheeked, bright-eyed,* and handsome. . . . And the Lord said, *"This is the one."*[2]

In identifying the ruddy lover of the Song of Songs with the ruddy-cheeked David, Ibn Gabirol suggests a whole new exegesis of the Song of Songs, the effect of which seems to be that Israel's redemption is figured as a union not between Israel and God but between Israel and the Davidic king, the Messiah.

Nevertheless, Ibn Gabirol insists on the lover's divine character. This image in verse 2 of the lover lying between the beloved's breasts like a sachet of myrrh rests on well-established exegesis of Song of Songs 1:13. The beloved's breasts in this verse were traditionally understood to represent the two golden cherubim that stood on the ark in the Holy of Holies or the two poles by which that ark was carried in the desert and which remained with it in the Temple.[3] They are thus a synecdoche for the site of revelation, understood as the intimate rendezvous of Israel and God. The flesh-and-blood Messiah of tradition would seem to have no place in such an encounter.

But in this poem, God and the Messiah are both separate and one, a bewildering overlapping of images, allusions, and literary personae. We can be sure that the joining of the two figures is not the result of sloppy composition or scribal errors, for the same confusion is present in a number of Ibn Gabirol's other poems on this theme. We cannot as yet say just what his purpose may have been in creating this confusion; but whatever it was, he has thereby achieved a definite literary effect. By replacing the God of the tra-

ditional allegory with the handsome, lusty, and erotically suscep-
tible David, he has intensified the erotic tone of his poems to a
level that would have been impossible had he named as Israel's
partner the transcendent God of the Jewish tradition or the abstract
God of the philosophers. When a poet refers to God as a fawn,
the reader recalls the hackneyed allegory of the Song of Songs,
perhaps overlaying it with overtones of the gazelle of secular love
poetry. But when the youthful David is called a fawn, he seems
to step right out of the secular love tradition, a handsome ado-
lescent boy like the one admired by Samuel the Nagid in his erotic
poems or like the youth whom Isaac Ibn Mar Saul compared to
Joseph for his good looks and to Absalom for his long hair.[4]

"Opening the gate" must signify Israel's redemption from exile,
but it is not immediately clear whether the speaker is standing
without, asking to be admitted (to the Temple or to the Land of
Israel), or within (the prison of exile), asking to be let out.[5] The
ultimate triumph of Israel is portrayed several times in the Bible
through the image of the ceremonial opening of the gates of Je-
rusalem or the Temple.[6] The image is even applied to Cyrus, called
God's anointed by Deutero-Isaiah, before whom no door or city
gate would be closed.[7] But the imagery of the poem presupposes
a feminine Israel awaiting her lover, the Messiah or God, rather
than a restive people awaiting the summons to march to redemp-
tion, as in poem 6. If the image of the gate is to be linked con-
sistently to the rest of the poem, we must imagine the gate as one
through which the stag has fled sometime in the past and cannot
now reenter without help. But perhaps it is best not to press for
a strictly logical clarification of the image. The opening of the gate
and the return of the stag could be parallel, though not integrated,
images of redemption.

––|◡–|–|–◡––

שַׁחַר עָלָה אֵלַי דּוֹדִי וְלֵךְ עִמִּי,
כִּי צָמְאָה נַפְשִׁי לִרְאוֹת בְּנֵי עַמִּי.
לָךְ אֶפְרְשָׂה מִטּוֹת זָהָב בְּאוּלַמִּי
אֶעֱרָךְ־לָךְ שֻׁלְחָן, אֶעֱרָךְ־לָךְ לַחְמִי.
מִזְרָק אֲמַלֵּא לָךְ מֵאֶשְׁכְּלוֹת כַּרְמִי—
וּשְׁתֵה בְּטוּב לֵבָב, יִיטַב לָךְ טַעֲמִי.
הִנֵּה בָךְ אֶשְׂמַח שִׂמְחַת נְגִיד עַמִּי
בֶּן־עַבְדְּךָ יִשַׁי, הָרֹאשׁ לְבֵית לַחְמִי!

שלמה אבן גבירול

·8·

Come to me at dawn, love,
    Carry me away;
For in my heart I'm thirsting
    To see my folk today.

For you, love, mats of gold
    Within my halls I'll spread.
I'll set my table for you,
    I'll serve you my own bread.

A drink from my own vineyards
    I'll pour to fill your cup—
Heartily you'll drink, love,
    Heartily you'll sup.

I'll take my pleasure with you
    As once I had such joy
With Jesse's son, my people's prince,
    That Bethlehem boy.

Solomon Ibn Gabirol

Ibn Gabirol's erotic vision of the redemption, imagined in the preceding poem as Israel's search for her lover, here becomes a fantasy of her ultimate reunion with him.

It might at first seem that the lover is God. In that case, the last line would mean that Israel's dream is of an ultimate union with God in place of the earlier unstable relationship with David, a final redemption by God rather than by a proxy. Reasonable as this interpretation seems, the poem's allusions to David and the evidence of Ibn Gabirol's other poems favor the Messiah rather than God as the object of Israel's fantasy.

Secular love poetry often speaks of lovers eating and drinking together, but the immediate source of this particular fantasy is the biblical picture of the intimate union of the royal lovers in Song of Songs 1:4: "The king has brought me to his chambers. Let us delight and rejoice in your love, savoring it more than wine." Most of our poem describes those chambers and expands the scene of the eating and drinking to be done there, recounting the accoutrements of the lovers' tryst in terms and phrases associated with the Temple.

Like the preceding poem, this one also makes extensive use of biblical quotations. "My heart is thirsting" appears twice in Psalms to describe the Psalmist's longing for the Temple.[1] The *ulam* in verse 2 means "hall," as translated, but can also refer specifically to the porch in the Temple that stood before the chambers in which were kept the holiest objects, including the ark with its golden cherubim. The golden bed of the poem is usually understood as referring to these cherubim. In the discussion of poem 7 we saw the erotic imagery connected with them. The "set table" also has erotic associations from the Bible. Ezekiel's allegorical harlots, representing Judah and Samaria, place a "set table" before their lovers; and the personified Lady Wisdom of Proverbs sets a table to lure foolish young men away from the seductions of Lady Folly to become her disciples.[2] But the set table also figures in the famous image of God protecting the Psalmist in the Temple.[3] Most importantly, the verb "to set" (*ʿarakh*), used twice in verse 2b as if for emphasis, has strong associations with the cult: it is used in connection with sacrifices in general, then specifically in connection with the table of the sanctuary and the shewbread, and later, for prayer.[4]

But there is another biblical passage that makes itself heard in the poem even though it is never explicitly quoted. In the opening verses of Psalm 132, David, the warrior-king, swears the following oath: "I will not enter my house, nor will I mount my bed . . . until I find a place for the Lord." The simple meaning is certainly that David took a vow of sexual abstinence until he should succeed in providing God with a home. So it was understood by tradition, in conformity with the practice in many cultures in connection with war or other important cultic rites. The narratives of his rule speak of his intention to build a Temple, though without mention of an oath.[5] It would seem that this oath provided the background for the figuring in our poem of the messianic restoration of Israel as a sexual reunion after a long period of continence. Once again, portraying David rather than God as the agent of redemption serves to heighten the level of the eroticism: since David was a human being, the reader is less inhibited about imagining him as a sexual being. And, furthermore, David's sexuality played a notable part in his life and career as recorded in the Bible.

The cherubim have already been discussed in connection with the vision of Israel's union with the Messiah in poem 7. It is important to stress that this image is not an importation from Arabic literature but is, rather, a native Hebrew development,[6] one firmly rooted in the rabbinic tradition. Although the impulse to write love poetry came from Arabic culture, and although many elements of secular love poetry entered the synagogue poetry that we are reading, it is interesting to observe that some of the most frankly sexual material in synagogue poetry seems to come from within the Jewish religious world rather than from the outside. From Arabic came only the idea of love poetry itself, and perhaps the image of the handsome young man as a theme of poetry; any further associations with Arabic literature in this poem are entirely supplementary and decorative.

—|—◡—|—|—◡—

שׁוֹכֵב עֲלֵי מִטּוֹת זָהָב בְּאַרְמוֹנִי,

מָתַי יְצוּעַי, יָהּ, תָּכִין לְאַדְמוֹנִי?

לָמָּה, צְבִי נֶחְמָד, תִּישַׁן וְהַשַּׁחַר

עָלָה כְנֵס עַל רֹאשׁ שְׂנִירִי וְחֶרְמוֹנִי?

מֵעַל פְּרָאִים סוּר, וּנְטֵה לְיַעֲלַת־חֵן

הִנְנִי לְכָמוֹךְ, וְאַתְּ טוֹב לְכָמוֹנִי.

הַבָּא בְאַרְמוֹנִי יִמְצָא בְמַטְמוֹנִי

עָסִיס וְרִמּוֹנִי, מוֹרִי וְקִנְּמוֹנִי.

שלמה אבן גבירול

·9·

O You, asleep on golden couches in my palace spread—
　　When, O Lord, will You prepare for the ruddy one my bed?

Why asleep, my handsome stag, why asleep my dear,
　　When dawn has risen like a flag on Hermon and Senir?
Turn aside from desert-asses, turn to the gazelle;
　　I am right for one like you, and your kind suits me well.
He who comes to visit me my precious stores will find:
　　My myrrh, my pomegranates, my cinnamon, my wine.

Solomon Ibn Gabirol

·9·

Perhaps the most obscure in this series of poems on redemption by Ibn Gabirol, this poem is nevertheless a fine example of the way in which the erotic depiction of redemption is treated based on materials drawn almost entirely from within the Jewish tradition.

The redeemer, who in poem 7 was invited to rest between Israel's breasts and in poem 8 to feast with her in her halls, is here urged to wake with the dawn to join his waiting beloved. The invitation to drink at dawn echoes countless Arabic and Hebrew wine poems, which usually envision the party as taking place in the morning.[1]

If we set aside verse 1 for a moment and consider the rest of the poem, it appears to be straightforwardly addressed to God, here called "the stag." Israel asks Him to abandon His temporary alliance with the unworthy nations of the world and to join Israel, His one true partner. The themes and images, especially the list of dainties at the poem's end, are already familiar from the preceding poems. They are mostly derived from the Song of Songs and are used in accordance with the rabbinic interpretation of that book.[2]

But verse 1 begins the poem by complicating this standard imagery and, as in the two preceding poems, obscuring the redeemer's identity. Whereas the sleeping addressee is *already* in the beloved's palace in verse 1, the speaker goes on to invite him to join her there in verse 4: it seems circular. Perhaps then the one sleeping in the palace is not the same as the one invited to the palace in verses 2–4. But the sleeper of verse 1 is probably God, because the golden beds must represent the golden cherubim of the Temple, as they do in the preceding poems. It makes no difference for our interpretation whether the Temple is the one in Jerusalem where God dwelt until it was destroyed, or the heavenly one where, according to a persistent rabbinic tradition, He dwells eternally.[3] And the addressee of the invitation in verses 2–4 must also be God, for what sense would it make to ask the Messiah to turn his back on the other nations, as if he presently favors them? The circle does not seem breakable.

The speaker in verse 1 asks the sleeping God to prepare a bed for the "ruddy one." This expression alludes to the biblical description of David discussed in connection with poem 7, and therefore it must again mean the Messiah. We have already seen "beds" to be Davidic language derived from Psalm 132; the allusion to the psalm is here underscored by the use of the same unusual word for bed as that used by the Psalmist. Israel seems to be asking God to act as a kind of go-between between her and her messianic lover, as in poem 7. But then in verse 2 the speaker addresses God as her lover; thus, remarkably, the Messiah-motif was raised in verse 1b only in order to be dropped. Since the bed and the banquet are complementary images of redemption, we expect the one for whom the former is prepared to be the same as the one invited to the latter.

Finally, there are just too many beds in verse 1.

All the difficulties of interpretation seem to arise because of verse 1b. It is possible that the text of this verse is not completely in order, for the manuscripts exhibit slight variants here; or these variants might represent attempts on the part of copyists to clear up an intended ambiguity. If the poem's text is correct as printed here, we must summarize the discussion by saying that here is another example of the fluidity of the characters of God and the Messiah that we have encountered before in Ibn Gabirol's poetry on redemption. Our enjoyment of the poem's erotic vision is not thereby diminished.

—ᴗ—|—ᴗ—|—|—ᴗ—

שַׁעַר פְּתַח, דּוֹדִי, קוּמָה פְּתַח שָׁעַר;
כִּי נִבְהֲלָה נַפְשִׁי גַם נִשְׂעֲרָה שַׂעַר.
לִי לָעֲגָה שִׁפְחַת אִמִּי וְרָם לִבָּהּ
יַעַן שָׁמַע אֵל קוֹל צַעֲקַת נַעַר.
מִנִּי חֲצוֹת לַיְלָה פֶּרֶא רְדָפַנִי
אַחֲרֵי אֲשֶׁר רָמַס אוֹתִי חֲזִיר־יַעַר.
הַקֵּץ אֲשֶׁר נֶחְתַּם הוֹסִיף עֲלֵי מַכְאוֹב
לִבִּי, וְאֵין מֵבִין לִי, וַאֲנִי בָעַר.

שלמה אבן גבירול

·10·

Open wide the gate, my love,
    Open wide the gate,
For terror's in my heart, my love,
    The storm does not abate.
My mother's maid is mocking me,
    Her heart is great with pride,
Because the Lord once listened
    To her little one when he cried.

Since midnight I'm chased from place to place,
    Pursued by the desert-ass;
Trampled before by the forest-boar,
    Everywhere harassed.
Keeping the end concealed, love,
    Only makes worse the pain.
In ignorance I suffer, love,
    With no one to explain.

Solomon Ibn Gabirol

·10·

The image of the opening of the gate of redemption has already occurred in poem 7, and the beginning of this messianic prayer recalls in other ways the openings of the preceding poems in this series by Ibn Gabirol. But despite the similarities, the purpose and the tone of this poem are utterly different. Its language derives neither from the Song of Songs nor from love poetry, and the confusion of God and the Messiah is completely absent. The poem is not a vision of an idyllic restoration, but a complaint about Israel's suffering in exile written in the language of rabbinic eschatology.

The mother of Israel is Sarah, and Sarah's maid is Hagar, who, through her son Ishmael, is the traditional ancestress of the Arabs. It was Ishmael's voice that the Lord heard when the boy and his mother were expelled by Abraham into the desert.[1] An angel had told Hagar on the occasion of her first expulsion[2] that Ishmael would grow up to be a "wild ass of a man." Accordingly, "wild ass" became an epithet in Hebrew poetry for the Arabs and sometimes for other nations as well.[3] In line with the decided preference of Hebrew liturgical poetry to substitute epithets for proper names, Christendom also received an animal epithet, the boar or pig. This epithet actually derives from traditional exegesis of Psalm 80, where Israel is compared to a vine transported by God from Egypt; he planted and tended it until it grew into a splendid vineyard, only to break down its fence and leave it open to passersby, human and beast: "Why did You breach its wall / so that every passerby plucks its fruit, / wild boars gnaw at it, / and creatures of the field feed on it?" The traditional epithet derived from this verse worked particularly well after the rise of Islam, to distinguish the Christian oppressor, who ate pork, from the Muslim oppressor, who did not.[4]

Animal epithets signifying the various nations and kingdoms came into use long before the rabbis began devising such interpretations of biblical verses. They probably originated in the use of such symbols in the Book of Daniel, who conceals the identity of various nations behind visions of animals, which later exegetes were at pains to interpret according to the political conditions obtaining in their own times. The bizarre visions of his book provided Hebrew apocalyptic writers and poets with much of their vocabulary.

The Book of Daniel also marks the beginning of attempts to calculate the date of redemption, partly by reinterpreting and updating the predictions of earlier prophets, partly by meditating on obscure hints revealed to the prophet by an angel or in dreams. Such calculations were much favored by Golden Age scholars, many of whose calculations have been preserved. Ibn Gabirol himself is said to have made an eschatological prediction based on astrological considerations,[5] but he may also have used exegetical techniques for the same purpose.[6]

Verse 3 of our poem, for example, is entirely in the spirit of such exegetical calculations of the redemption. Exile is often compared in rabbinic literature to night, and midnight figures both in the Bible and in the rabbinic imagination as the hour of salvation.[7] Perhaps Ibn Gabirol thought of the rise of Islam as the midpoint of the exile. If he did, this would imply the year 1175 as the date of redemption. The calculation of the Muslim era began in 622, and Jewish tradition held that the Second Temple was destroyed in 68. The first half of the night of exile thus lasted 554 years; the second half would accordingly end 554 years after the Hegira. Of course the poem may intend midnight merely as a general expression for the gloom of exile. But the last verse alludes clearly to the end of the Book of Daniel, which also hints at a specific date for the redemption. Daniel is given mysterious words that are said to contain the key to the mystery; but he is also told that the time has not yet come for their true meaning to be revealed. Thus the date remained concealed: "I heard and did not understand . . . these words are secret and sealed to the time of the end."[8]

These parallels with the Book of Daniel seem to imply that Ibn Gabirol was thinking concretely when he referred to midnight as the moment of redemption. In any case the idea was important enough to him to come back to it in another poem:

> A lion met me, a tiger arose after him
>   I fled them, abandoned my garden.
> When these had passed, there came a wild ass
>   In the middle of the night, and sat upon my place.[9]

———|⌣—|⌣—//———|⌣—|⌣—

11

נִמְתָּ וְנִרְדַּמְתָּ וְתָרֵד קַמְתָּ—/ מָה הַחֲלוֹם הַזֶּה אֲשֶׁר חָלַמְתָּ?

אוּלַי חֲלוֹמְךָ הָרָאַךְ שׂוֹנְאַךְ / כִּי דַל וְכִי שָׁפֵל וְאַתָּה רַמְתָּ?

אִמְרוּ לְבֶן־הָגָר: אֱסֹף יַד גַּאֲוָה / מִבֶּן־גְּבִרְתְּךָ אֲשֶׁר זָעַמְתָּ!

שָׁפֵל רְאִיתִיךָ וְשׂוֹמֵם בַּחֲלוֹם— / אוּלַי בְּהָקִיץ כֵּן כְּבָר שָׁמַמְתָּ,

וּשְׁנַת תח״ץ תַּתַּץ לְךָ כָּל גַּאֲוָה, / תֵּבוֹשׁ וְתַחְפֹּר מֵאֲשֶׁר זָמַמְתָּ.

הַאַתְּ אֲשֶׁר נִקְרָא שְׁמָךְ פֶּרֶא אֱנוֹשׁ / מַה כָּבְדָה יָדְךָ וּמֶה עָצַמְתָּ?

הַאַתְּ מְקָרָא פֶּם מְמַלֵּל רַבְרְבָן / וַאֲשֶׁר בְּקַדִּישִׁי זְבוּל נִלְחַמְתָּ?

הַאַתְּ חֲסַף טִינָא בְּרַגְלֵי פַּרְזְלָא / בָּאַחֲרִית בָּאתָ וְהִתְרוֹמַמְתָּ?

אוּלַי נִגַּפְךָ אֵל בְּאַבְנָא דִי מְחָת / צַלְמָא וְשִׁלַּם לְךָ אֲשֶׁר הִקְדַּמְתָּ!

יהודה הלוי

·11·

You dozed and fell asleep and rose in fear;
    What was this dream you dreamt, already unclear?
Perhaps your dream revealed to you your foe—
    You the master; he, humbled and low.

Tell Hagar's son, "Let down your haughty hand
    From Sarah's son, the rival you have scorned,
For I have seen you in my dream, a ruin;
    Perhaps in life you really are undone.
Perhaps this year, eleven-hundred thirty
    Will see your pride thrown down, your thinking thwarted.

Yes, you who now are known as "desert-ass":
    How mighty is your hand, how puissant.
Yea, thou art cleped the haughty-speaking mouth,
    Who warrest with the holy ones of heaven—
Yea, thou the clay mixed with the iron feet,
    Come at the end of days, in pride uprisen—
Haply He hath hurled the stone, smashed
    The effigy, requital for thine ancient misdeeds given."

Judah Halevi

·11·

Dreams play a prominent part in both Halevi's personal poetry and his religious poetry, which is not surprising since his general approach to religion emphasizes the direct experience of the divine through prophecy and visions. This attitude is evident throughout his great prose work on Judaism, the *Kuzari*, not only in the exposition, but in its very narrative framework, in which the motivating force is the repeated dreams of the king of the Khazars.

Our poem is divided into two unequal parts: the first two verses describe the poet's sensations on waking from a dream, and the remainder is a prophecy based on these sensations. The poet wakes with the memory of having dreamed but cannot clearly remember what he saw. His words "What was this dream you dreamt?" are the same as those of Jacob's response to Joseph's description of his prophetic dream. But the word "perhaps" in verse 2 suggests that the question is meant to resemble more the one posed by Nebuchadnezzar to his wizards when he awoke and found that not only did he not understand his dream but he could not even remember it.[1] The echo of Jacob's words is not, however, irrelevant. It quietly prefigures the poem's message, for it brings to mind a dream of the overthrow of the ruling order in which the younger (Joseph) replaces the elder (Reuben, Judah); this would parallel the desired overthrow of Ishmael (Hagar's son of verse 3) by Isaac (Sarah's son; literally "your mistress's son" in verse 3).

But the spirit of Daniel dominates the poem, for the last three verses allude to specific passages in his book. Furthermore, they are not couched in Hebrew but rather (partially) in Aramaic, a sister language of Hebrew and the language of six chapters of the Book of Daniel, including Nebuchadnezzar's dream. The shift of language, though startling, is foreshadowed: verse 6, which is in Hebrew, and verse 7, which is in Aramaic, both begin with the same syntactic pattern, in fact, with the same word, which happens to be identical in both languages. From the way the languages merge, it almost seems as if Halevi's personality has merged with that of the biblical seer. The translation here attempts to imitate the effect of the change of language in Halevi's poem by sliding into an archaic English diction.

In verse 5 the poet tries his hand at fixing the date of the redemption. Such forecasting is a feature of the Book of Daniel that gave rise to much speculation in the Middle Ages.[2] Halevi's method is a sort of number divination, by which the year of redemption is derived from the numerical value of the Hebrew letters *ttṣ* (=890). Halevi must have chosen to base his calculation on these letters because they represent the year in which the dream occurred, if it was a real biographical event, or, if it was merely a fiction, the year in which he composed the poem. Since the thousands are ordinarily dropped in citing the Hebrew dates, 890 would have meant to Halevi 4890 A.M., corresponding to A.D. 1129/1130. The three Hebrew letters in turn spell the Hebrew word *titoṣ*, "you will overturn." The root occurs in several biblical prophecies of doom, as in God's original charge to Jeremiah: "See, I appoint you this day over nations and kingdoms: To uproot and to pull down, to destroy and to overthrow, to build and to plant." The translation of Halevi's poem has to make do with alliteration to suggest this effect.[3]

The identification of the Arabs with the wild ass in verse 6 derives, as we have seen, from the rabbinic exegesis of Genesis 16:12. But the figuring of the ruling nations of the world as animals is another distinctive feature of the Book of Daniel, much of which, especially chapters 7 and 8, is devoted to visions symbolizing the nations that have subjugated Israel and that will yet do so until the redemption. Two of these visions are specifically referred to here in verses 7–9. The "haughty-speaking mouth" belongs to the small horn on the head of the terrifying fourth beast of Daniel 7, which Abraham Ibn Ezra and most other commentators who hailed from the Muslim world identified as Ishmael and the rule of Islam.[4] This horn represents the last Muslim ruler who is to wage war with the holy ones, that is, who will oppress Israel, before the final redemption.

The "clay mixed with the iron feet" ends the poem with an image taken from the dream of Nebuchadnezzar in Daniel 2, a dream alluded to obliquely at the poem's beginning. Nebuchadnezzar dreamt of a great statue made of several different materials, each part representing one of the empires of the world. The toes on the statue's iron feet were of iron and clay, materials that do not combine; a broken-off stone was thrown and struck the clay, bringing the statue down. The medieval commentators sought to identify the empires represented by the various parts of the statue and to match the prophecy to the realities of their own times. Abraham Ibn Ezra identified the iron feet and toes as the Muslim empire and the clay as that part of the Roman empire that survived the rise of Islam—the Byzantine empire in the East and Christendom in the West. Halevi may have understood the prophecy in the same way, or, like Saadia, he may have thought that the feet of the statue represented a combined Roman-Arabic empire.

The angry mood of this poem sets it noticeably apart from the others in this book. Halevi's fantasy is not simply one of release from oppression, but of revenge and of delight at the thought of the oppressor's fall. Daniel's visions, from which Halevi took his images, were composed during the persecution of the Judeans by the Seleucid Antiochus IV (167–164 B.C.); they counter Antiochus' brutal treatment of the Jews with fantasies of destruction and revenge.

It may seem odd to us that Halevi, writing during the Golden Age of Hebrew letters and under the relatively tolerant rule of Islam, should have indulged in such fantasies of destruction. It is important to realize that the tolerance enjoyed by the Andalusian Jews was only relative tolerance, not to be compared with the idea that all people are entitled to equal protection, civil rights, and respect as human beings despite cultural and religious differences. This ideal has proved difficult enough to maintain even in our time: All the more remote was it from the medieval world, where three religions held mutually exclusive views of the truth, agreeing only that sovereignty was proof of their individual claims. Muslims living under Christendom and Christians living under Islam could at least take comfort in the existence of their respective empires. But Jews could only pray for restoration of the Davidic monarchy and search Scripture and the stars for signs of an end to their subjugation. They had no expectation of what we would call tolerance. Even when there were no active persecutions, dress codes, or sumptuary restrictions, even when the way was open to wealth, power, and status, elements persisted in everyday life that never failed to remind the Jews of their dependence on the whim of the dominant society.

There is plenty of evidence, moreover, that the relative tolerance of Islam was not much comfort to the medieval Jews who enjoyed its fitful advantages. Few experienced anything like the success and esteem achieved by Maimonides, and yet even he had personally suffered from religious persecution at the hands of Islam. Forty-two years after Halevi composed our poem, Maimonides wrote:

> God has entangled us with this people, the nation of Ishmael, who treat us so prejudicially and who legislate our harm and hatred . . . . No nation has ever arisen more harmful than they, nor has anyone done more to humiliate us, degrade us, and consolidate hatred against us.

From a strictly historical point of view, Maimonides' description of the facts may be exaggerated. But the passage is certainly an accurate reflection of the feeling of Jews living under this relatively benign regime. He continues:

> We bear the inhumane burden of their humiliation, lies, and absurdities, being, as the prophet said, "like a deaf man who does not hear or a dumb man who does not open his mouth." . . . Our sages disciplined us to bear Ishmael's lies and absurdities, listening in silence, and we have trained ourselves, old and young, to endure their humiliation, as Isaiah said, "I have given my back to the smiters, and my cheek to the beard pullers."[5]

Maimonides' description of the continual necessity for discipline, self-restraint, and patient endurance provides the perfect emotional background for the angry outburst in our poem. Every Jewish child was aware that whatever the attitude of the ruling class, the anger and fanaticism of the masses and the religious leadership were never far from the surface.[6] It was not forgotten that even in tolerant Islamic Granada, once virtually ruled by the rabbi-poet Samuel the Nagid, there had been a devastating pogrom in 1066, or that Cairo had seen one in 1012. Finally, word of the fanaticism of the Almohad Berbers—who slightly more than a decade later would put an end to the Hebrew Golden Age—was already in the air.[7]

‒‒◡|‒‒◡‖‒‒◡|‒‒◡

יַעֲבֹר עָלַי רְצוֹנְךָ / כַּאֲשֶׁר עָבַר חֲרוֹנְךָ.

הַלְעוֹלָמִים עֲוֹנִי / יַעֲמֹד בֵּינִי וּבֵינֶךָּ?

וְעַד־מָתַי אֲבַקֵּשׁ / אוֹתְךָ עִמִּי—וְאֵינֶךָּ?

דָּר בְּכַנְפֵי הַכְּרוּבִים / הַפְּרוּשִׂים עַל אֲרוֹנְךָ

הֶעֱבַדְתַּנִי לְזָרִים— / וַאֲנִי כַנַּת יְמִינֶךָ.

גּוֹאֲלִי, לִגְאֹל הֲמוֹנִי / רוּם וְהַשְׁקֵף מִמְּעוֹנֶךָ!

יהודה הלוי

·12·

Pour over me your pleasure
  As once you poured your rage.
Must my sin between us
  Stand from age to age?
How long until you join me?
  Must I wait in vain?

You who dwelt on Cherubs'
  Wings, in Temple spread,
Made me slave to strangers,
  Who was your garden bed,
Savior, look from heaven,
  To save my throngs again.

Judah Halevi

The tranquil intimacy of this simple prayer may be attributed to a combination of features: its constant use of first person singular, its unadorned language, its short lines (two feet per hemistich), and the speaker's attitude, which is as passive as a petitionary prayer could possibly be. The speaker experiences God's rage passing over him and asks that it be replaced with God's pleasure. He has stood still to endure the one; he will stand still to enjoy the other. Sin has been a wall, another static image, between him and God. His hope is for God to cross that wall and join him. The speaker does not represent himself as engaged in a quest or as struggling to overcome the spiritual obstacles represented by that wall. Without loud complaints or cries of self-pity, the worshiper presents himself as one without the power or even the desire to take action—as one prepared to trust in God and accept whatever He has in store. In medieval Islamic and Jewish piety, this is a meritorious state known as *tawakkul.*[1]

Following the short opening lines suggesting intimacy and smallness of scale, the poet alters the rhythm in verses 4 and 5, lengthening the line by means of enjambment to contrast the speaker's sense of his puny self with his sense of God's tremendous power. The address to God begins with a complex epithet that fills all of verse 4 and culminates only with the verb in verse 5. In a poem of long lines and rich visual imagery, such a sentence might not stand out, but among the short, plain sentences of this poem it produces a noticeable change in rhythm and texture, highlighting the contrast between the speaker and God. It points forcefully toward the transitive verb at the beginning of verse 5 that describes God's only action mentioned in this poem: the enslavement of Israel to strangers.

The poet is not so passive as not to ask for redemption; but his petition is couched in a request for action on the smallest imaginable scale: that the tremendous God of verses 4–5 merely *look* down from heaven. That small act would be the folk's salvation.

Nor is the speaker so passive as to hide completely his feelings about the circumstances that occasioned his prayer. There is in verses 1–3 a constant alliteration of the guttural sound of the letter *'ayin*, a sound associated with sobbing.[2] The repetition of this sound, unfortunately not reflected in the translation, contributes an unobtrusive but significant acoustic commentary to the opening lines.

It has been noted that the repeated use of the first person singular lends the poem the intimacy of private conversation. This requires some clarification. Many Hebrew liturgical poems from all periods have a first person speaker. Usually, however, especially in poems about God and Israel, this speaker is the synagogue precentor acting as his people's spokesman. This convention derives from the practice of the ancient synagogue in which the precentor recited the prayers in the presence of a nearly silent congregation. This practice carried over to the liturgical poetry, to which the congregation mostly listened. Obviously the circumstances in which the poems were recited determined whether they would be understood as public, liturgical poetry, or as private and nonliturgical. But most synagogue poems also identify themselves as public, communal prayer through the use of conventional imagery and language typical of synagogue poetry. Thus Ibn Gabirol's penitential poem beginning "My joy has ended, my sorrows have multiplied, / My foe has grown great and my oppressor grown strong" sounds as if it is about the speaker's self. But in the next verse the poem says, "My end has grown long because of my sin," an unmistakable indicator that the poem is a public one, because the word "end" is a code word for the messianic age and the redemption of Israel.[3]

Our poem, by contrast, holds off until nearly the end to reveal whether it is about an individual or about the people, at which point the active verb, strongly placed at the beginning of the verse, and the epithet "garden bed" for Israel label the poem as public prayer.[4] But by verses 5–6, the personal tone is so well established that it carries over emotionally even to the last lines, making the people as a whole feel like a single worshiping individual. It may also give the momentary impression that the poet is speaking about himself despite the references to the people at the end: as if he uses the people at large as a symbol for his own personal experiences and feelings. The worshiper identifies with this self of the speaker and sees the poem as expressing inner, spiritual aspirations. A literal-minded worshiper, believing that the end contradicted this interpretation, would retroactively reinterpret the poem he had just heard. But a more versatile auditor might hold on to the other interpretive possibility and absorb the "throngs" into the individual who had been speaking so simply and affectingly until then. The tone of this poem clouds in some measure the differences between public and individual prayer, a phenomenon that will occupy our attention in the following poems.

·13·

יְעִירוּנִי / שַׂעְפֵּי לַחֲזוֹתֶךָ,

וַיַּרְאוּנִי / בְּעֵין לֵב נוֹרְאוֹתֶיךָ,

וְיוֹרוּנִי / לְהַגִּיד נִפְלְאוֹתֶיךָ —

כִּי אֶרְאֶה / שָׁמֶיךָ, מַעֲשֵׂה אֶצְבְּעוֹתֶיךָ.

מִתְהַלֵּךְ / עֲלֵי קַו חוּג שָׁמַיִם,

וּמְסַבֵּב / מְסִבָּתוֹ כָּאָבְנָיִם,

וּמְסַפֵּר / כְּבוֹדְךָ בְּלִי שְׂפָתַיִם,

וְהָאָרֶץ / עוֹמֶדֶת בְּנְתַיִם —

וְהִיא תְלוּיָה / בְּחַבְלֵי אַהֲבָתֶךָ.

שָׁם שׁוֹאֵף / הַשֶּׁמֶשׁ וְזוֹרֵחַ,

וְהוּא אוֹצֵל / מְאוֹרוֹ לְיָרֵחַ,

וְהַגַּלְגַּל / כְּמוֹ אֹהֶל מוֹתָחַ,

וְכוֹכָבִים / עָלָיו כְּגַן פּוֹרֵחַ —

לְהוֹדִיעַ / עֹמֶק מַחְשְׁבוֹתֶיךָ.

הָאֶפֶס / חֶסֶד אֵל לַעֲדֵי עַד?

וְאִם גָּבַהּ / דְּבַר נִחוּמִים וּמִסְעָד?

אִם רוֹפֵא / אוֹ הַצֳרִי אֵין בְּגִלְעָד

יְהִי מַחֲזִיק / לֵב יֶלֶד יִמְעָד —

וְהוּא דוֹפֵק / שַׁעֲרֵי חֶמְלָתֶךָ?

משה אבן עזרא

·13·

My thoughts awaken me to see You;
They show me in my hearts's eye Your deeds;
They teach me to tell Your wonders,
   "When I behold Your heavens,
   The work Your fingers made."

Around its course the disk of heaven walks,
A potter's wheel enwhirling the world;
It has no lips, and yet it tells Your glory
To earth, unmoved within its orbit,
   Suspended in the void,
   By cords of Your love stayed.

Thither the sun yearns, and there burns,
And of his light some to the moon he lends.
While heaven's sphere is spread out like a tent,
With stars blooming on it, a garden,
   Proclaiming how profound
   The plans that You have laid.

Can God's compassion be exhausted?
Can comfort and support be far off?
Can Gilead's balm afford no healing
Or help to hold upright a stumbling child,
   Who knocks upon Your gates,
   Who pleads to You for aid?

Moses Ibn Ezra

·13·

The poet's starting point is Psalm 8:4: "When I look at Your heavens, the work of Your fingers . . . what is man that You have been mindful of him . . . ." On it he constructed a monorhymed leading-stanza that links the three strophes by rhyming with the last line of each. This leading-stanza lends its overtones to the three strophes, so that all the statements made in them seem to emerge from the poet's intellectual contemplation of the cosmos.

The poem appears to culminate in a plea for the redemption of Israel, using the words of Jeremiah: "Is there no balm in Gilead? Can no physician be found? Why has healing not yet come to my people?"[1] "Comfort" recalls the rabbinic expression for the fulfillment of the messianic prophecies of the Bible.[2] The "child" recalls Jeremiah's famous words of comfort for Ephraim, God's delight.[3] And the gate upon which the child knocks, the gate of mercy, may remind us of the gate that Ibn Gabirol several times begs God to open as the first act of redemption, as we have seen. The whole stanza pulses with a warmth and tenderness that is in line with the religious love poetry in general, though it is not at all erotic.

But the context in which this plea is set is not traditional at all. The whole complex of ideas connecting God's love of Israel with Israel's exile, subjugation, and national humiliation is absent from the leading-stanza and the first two strophes. The poem is an individual's hymn to the creator of the universe.

Within Psalm 8, the verse quoted at the beginning of our poem expresses awe and wonder, a heightened—but static— spiritual state: if the Psalmist is led by his observations and feelings to reflect, it is to reflect upon himself. But the leading-strophe built around this verse adjusts its meaning to suit a more outward-looking and a more dynamic spiritual state.

This leading-stanza adumbrates the themes governing the following stanzas. Its first three lines are dominated by three verbs that are syntactically parallel and morphologically similar: $y^{e\varsigma}iruni$ (they awaken me), $yar^{\jmath}uni$ (they show me), and $yoruni$ (they teach me). All three have at least some connection with light and vision and all share the sound of the letter *r*, which seems to derive from the verb *er'e* (I look) in the verse from Psalm 8. But this "seeing" is not the sight of the eyes; it is a seeing of the intellect, stimulated by thinking and performed with "the heart's eye"; it is the application of reason to the phenomena of the universe, which leads to knowledge of God.[4] This is exactly the conception of the true religious life embraced by philosophical-minded religious thinkers of the age. The Psalmist's attitude of passive wonder has been translated into a dynamic, intellectual mode, and the ideal act of worship presupposed is therefore of a character quite different from that of the Psalmist. This theme is connected with Psalm 19:2, "The heavens tell the glory of God," alluded to in verse 7 of the poem. According to Abraham Ibn Ezra, it means that the heavens provide man with clues as to the workings of the universe and information on the basis of which to draw conclusions about God and creation. Abraham Ibn Ezra regards this act of intellectual seeing as the highest religious duty: "Whoever knows the way of the spheres has knowledge of the divine."

The first three lines of the leading-strophe are subdivided by meter and rhyme into two uneven parts, the first ending in *nī* (= me) and the second rhyming in *t*ᵉ*kha* (= you).[5] These pronoun-rhymes balance the speaker and the addressee, establishing a kind of equilibrium between the human and the divine that a poet might use either to emphasize the distance or to reduce it by creating an intimate dialogue. The poet has set himself the task of building a bridge from the worshiper to God out of the scientific data yielded by human observation of the universe and speculation as to its origins and nature.

The first and second strophes sketch some elements of medieval cosmology, not as an awe-inspiring catalog of transcendent wonders but as objects that the poet can color with feeling. The motion of the heavens is described as "walking," a form of the verb associated with the righteous Abraham, Noah, and Enoch, but more importantly with God Himself in the Garden of Eden.[6] The garden reappears as the culmination of the cosmology in the second strophe, where the stars are compared to a garden, a common image in secular poetry of the period. In the context of this comparison, a medieval reader would have associated the tent in the preceding line with a pavilion erected in a garden for a drinking party. The overtones of such a comparison are not of riotous carousing, but of tranquil pleasure in nature and in the reunion of friends.[7]

The theme of the garden is not far removed from the theme of love, which is also present in the poem. The celestial bodies are all in constant motion around the earth, yearning to repeat their cycles, as is hinted in line 10.[8] The image of the heavens turning like a potter's wheel is more than a description of their circular motion: it also suggests the creative power that emanates from them as they impart their motion to the lower spheres. The word for potter's wheel also has biblical associations with fecundity, in particular, in connection with childbirth.[9] Both descriptions of motion thus employ words and images that invest the list of natural phenomena with human feeling and point to their creative power.

The power of love is named explicitly in the poem, not in connection with motion but with stasis, for in the center of the rotating spheres stands the earth, suspended by nothing but love.[10] This is a love that has nothing to do with God's love for Israel; it is not even God's love for the world. Rather, it is the world's passionate desire to return to its source.[11] Having as its theme the universe as a whole and man as a species, the poem in some ways resembles the secular poetry of love more than it does the traditional poetry of the synagogue. Even the individual worshiper and the sufferings and joys of his personal life are not the concern of this poem. As we descend from the One through the spheres of the stars and the luminaries and the world of man, the next natural station is man's soul, which, like the rest of the noncelestial beings, yearns for upward motion so that it may return to its original place.

After all this, how are we to interpret the plea of the third stanza? It could very well be on behalf of the people Israel, on the basis of the hints and allusions to biblical passages that were mentioned earlier in this discussion. But considered in the context of the leading-strophe and the first two stanzas, a national reading of the poem seems forced. The most natural reading is to see the soul of man as the stumbling child, lost and comfortless in the world of matter, knocking on the gate of redemption so that it can return to the upper world where it originated. But the meaning is not clearly stated, and the reader is left to choose. Thus, the language of national redemption and God's love has been quietly transferred from the nation to mankind.

14

אֲיֻמָּתִי, עֵדֶן שָׁמֵמְתְּ! / קוּמִי עָלַי כִּי רֵחַמְתְּ;
מַה יָּפִית וּמַה נָּעֵמְתְּ!

בַּת חֵיקִי, בְּפָנַיִךְ, / חַיִּים וְצוּף בְּשָׁנַיִךְ.
יָפְיִי וְחֵן אָזְנַיִךְ, / עֲגִילַיִךְ בְּאָזְנַיִךְ,
וְעֵינַיִךְ / כְּפוּךְ שָׂמְתְּ.

רְעִיתִי בֵּין יְעֵלוֹת, / קוּמִי עָלַי בַּלֵּילוֹת,
וְהֵן תֵּצְאִי בִמְחוֹלוֹת / וְשָׁדַיִךְ כְּאֶשְׁכֹּלוֹת;
אִם אֲשַׁמְתְּ—/ בְּאוֹב קָסַמְתְּ.

הֵיךְ הָיִית לִקְצָפָה, / בַּנָּשִׁים הַיָּפָה,
כַּשַּׁחַר נִשְׁקָפָה; / וְכִי שָׁמוּךְ לַגְדוּפָה
אִם נָפַלְתְּ—/ הוּקַמְתְּ קָמְתְּ!

מַה תִּתְאוֹנֵנִי, בִּתִּי, / קוּמִי לָךְ צְאִי אִתִּי!
אֲבִיאֵךְ לְבֵית תִּפְאַרְתִּי, / אֲנִי אִישֵׁךְ וְאַתְּ אִשְׁתִּי.
עֲדִי עֶדְיֵךְ / וְהִתְגַּחַמְתְּ!

אברהם אבן עזרא

·14·

Awesome one, in rags are you?
Rise, for I have pitied you.
How lovely, ah, how sweet are you!

Dearest child with honey mouth,
You who grant life with your face,
You with rings upon your ears,
You with stores of charm and grace,
Eyes made up in blackest hue—

In this night of exile rise,
Among gazelles my only girl,
You with breasts like clustered grapes:
Go and join the dancers' whirl—
Your beauty may your sins undo.

Ah, to think you had such grief,
Lovely lady, fairest fawn!
That you had to bear such shame,
You whose face gleams like the dawn,
No more fallen, raised anew.

Weep no longer, dearest child.
Rise and come away with me.
To my palace I will bring you,
Man and wife for aye to be.
Put on your gems; away with rue!

Abraham Ibn Ezra

·14·

This strophic poem closely resembles secular love poems of the *muwashshaḥ* type.[1] Like many other sacred poems of the period, it is built on the conjunction of the Song of Songs with elements of secular love poetry. Nearly every line contains a reminiscence of the Song of Songs or of some other part of the Bible in which God's love for Israel is represented as love between man and woman. The penultimate line in the Hebrew text thus echoes and reverses the meaning of Hosea 2:4: "For she is not my wife and I am not her husband."[2]

At the same time the poem also lacks some of the typical elements of the love poetry of national redemption; against the background of the other poems of this type, it may almost seem like an outsider. Its vision of redemption is colorless, making no mention of the familiar eschatological signs such as the dawn, the Messiah, or the vision of the Jews streaming homeward from the ends of the earth. The picture of the oppressors, too, is relatively bland and unspecific. There is no explicit mention of their subjugation of Israel or of their rivalry for God's affection; and there is none of Israel's dream of vindication and revenge. In fact the only reference to the nations of the world is in the word "gazelles" in verse 10.[3] This very usage seems contrary to convention, for though liturgical poetry commonly refers to the nations of the world as wild animals, the word "gazelle" and others deriving from the secular love tradition are normally reserved for Israel. Finally, the Temple, which plays a prominent role in so many poems of national redemption, is alluded to only in the vague expression here rendered "my palace," literally "my house of splendor." True, this is a recognizable and appropriate designation for the Temple;[4] and the sentence in which it occurs can be traced to Song of Songs 3:4 or 8:2, both of which have been interpreted as referring to the return of God and Israel to the Temple. But compared with the golden cherubim and other concrete references to the restored Temple to which other poems have accustomed us, "the house of my splendor" is flat, having little evocative power. The phrase passes, leaving no image behind.

The vagueness of the national elements in this poem leaves it open to a spiritual reading. By avoiding very concrete allusions to the national destiny, the poet allows the philosophical-minded worshiper to apply the poem to the exile of the soul as well as to the exile of the nation. A sophisticated worshiper of Abraham Ibn Ezra's time must surely have identified the woman of the poem with the soul of man, imagined as an exiled beauty, awaiting the voice of her lover to call her home to himself. Such pictures would soon emerge in allegorical stories of a philosophical type, in the writings of Jacob b. Eleazar and Ibn ʿAqnin.[5] When Ibn Ezra's poem was recited in the synagogue, the average worshiper could hear in it the traditional national allegory, but the philosophical-minded could think of it in more general terms as addressing an inner-directed intellectual life.

·15·

—–◡—–◡—–◡∥—◡—–◡—–◡

בְּכָל לִבִּי, אֱמֶת, וּבְכָל מְאֹדִי / אֲהַבְתִּיךָ, וּבְגָלוּיִי וְסוֹדִי.

שְׁמָךְ נֶגְדִּי—וְאֵיךְ אֵלֵךְ לְבַדִּי? / וְהוּא דוֹדִי—וְאֵיךְ אֵשֵׁב יְחִידִי?

וְהוּא נֵרִי—וְאֵיךְ יִדְעַךְ מְאוֹרִי? / וְאֵיךְ אֶצְעַן?—וְהוּא מִשְׁעָן בְּיָדִי!

הֱקִלוּנִי מְתִים לֹא יָדְעוּ כִּי / קְלוֹנִי עַל כְּבוֹד שְׁמָךְ כְּבוֹדִי.

מְקוֹר חַיַּי—אֲבָרֶכְךָ בְחַיַּי, / וְזִמְרָתִי—אֲזַמֶּרְךָ בְעוֹדִי!

יהודה הלוי

·15·

With all my heart—O Truth—and all my might
  I love You, with my limbs and with my mind.
Your name is with me: Can I walk alone?
  With it for lover, how can I be lorn?
    With it for lamp, how can my light go dim?
    How can I slip with it the stick
      By which I stand?

They mock who do not understand: The shame
  I bear because I bear Your name is pride to me.

Source of my life, I bless You while I live;
  My Song, I sing to You while yet I breathe.

Judah Halevi

15

There is no difficulty in seeing this poem as another in the series of declarations of Israel's love for God set against a background of suffering in exile and longing for redemption. The precentor speaks in the first person singular on behalf of the people; the mockers are the nations of the world whose insults Israel bears with pride. But the "I" is extraordinarily prominent. It recurs as part of the rhyme syllable.[1] The pronoun or its characteristic vowel occurs at the end of every hemistich; it is suffixed to no fewer than five of the eight words of the opening line; and it appears at least twice in every hemistich. There is just too much "I" in this poem for it to be felt merely as a public poem. It cries out for an inner, personal application.

The rhetorical structure of verse 1 also points in this direction. The poem begins as a meditation on part of the *Sh^ema^c*, one of the central prayers of Israel's worship.[2] The poet is not concerned with the solemn public declaration of the opening of the *Sh^ema^c* but, rather, with what follows, the fundamental rule of personal piety in Judaism: "You shall love the Lord your God with all your heart, with all your soul, and with all your might." In the first verse the biblical "heart" and "might" are paired chiastically with words meaning literally "my public self . . . my inner self." These words reflect such terms of Islamic pietistic literature as *ẓāhir* and *bāṭin*, to which they are roughly equivalent in meaning. They also recall the complementary pair "duties of the limbs" and "duties of the hearts," characteristic of that literature, the source of both theme and title of Baḥya Ibn Paquda's Jewish classic.[3] As a commentary on "all your heart . . . and all your might," they point away from the nation and toward the individual.

Comparing verse 2 with its biblical source leads us to a more exact idea of the poem's spiritual message. The corresponding verse of the *Sh^ema^c* is a commandment bidding the individual to keep God on his mind when he sits at home and walks by the way; but the speaker declares it a given that God is with him on these occasions and speaks about the comfort he derives from the assurance of God's continual presence. The speaker is not smugly calling attention to his own obedience in keeping God in mind, but is rather expressing confidence in God's providence. The words "Your name is with me" seem to confirm this idea, for they recall the verse of Psalms so beloved of Jewish pietists, "I have set the Lord before me always";[4] the poet does not say "I set God's name before me," but "God's name *is* before me." The verbal allusion to the verse underscores the difference between the *Sh*ᵉ*ma*ᶜ, which demands that man take the spiritual initiative, and the poem, with its satisfaction in God's having already taken it.

Yet comparison with the poem's source, the *Sh*ᵉ*ma*ᶜ, shows that the speaker has also replaced the authoritarian voice of Deuteronomy with a vulnerable one that expresses itself in rhetorical questions. "How can I walk alone" are words one might say to oneself precisely when one *feels* alone. This sense of whistling in the dark is only intensified by the use of pronouns referring not to God Himself but to God's name. The effect is one of distancing: for a moment God is not "You" but "he" or "it."

This "name of God" represents not merely the thought of God but also something divine that the poet feels to be an integral part of himself. The impression is confirmed by the words "He is my lamp," which immediately recall Proverbs 20:27: "The soul of man is the lamp of God." On this verse, Abraham Ibn Ezra says: "For the (rational) soul of man is emanated from His light . . . ; Thence it gives light to the animal and vegetative souls with its intelligence so that they see by its light." It is the rational soul, a part of God in man, that guides the poet on his spiritual way.

Who then are the mockers of verse 4? We know them well from the love poetry, and we have seen the terms used here applied to Israel's national enemies. But the soul, isolated in the material world and yearning to return to her source, is also beset, for the body and the senses are to the soul what Edom and Ishmael are to the Jewish people. Ibn Gabirol also expressed the hostile relationship of body and soul in national terms, most notably toward the end of his great poem on the soul, where he prays on the soul's behalf:

> Heal her wound, be her hope and her help;
> Call for her salvation, erase her sin, as she comes near . . .

> Behold her misery, hear her weeping to you, Lord . . .
> Shaddai, mock the enemies who have mocked her,
> Avenge her shame and humiliation.
> Be a rock, a fortress against her enemy in her plight;
> Do not deliver up the Only One, the one you raised.[5]

The intimate tone of this poem, the vulnerability of its speaker, and the weakness of its national references all remind us of poem 12. With its allusions to the soul and to its status as a divine captive in a hostile material world, the poem also points in the direction of the many poems in which the soul speaks directly rather than through the voice of the people Israel. It is to such poems that we turn our attention in Chapter II.

2

God and the Soul

THE SOUL IN PHILOSOPHY AND POETRY

In Chapter I we observed the turning inward of the theme of love, as the focus of the poems shifted from the national to the individual sphere. In the poems that follow, it is the soul, whether of the individual worshiper or of worshiping mankind, that stands at the center of the religious experience. The specifically Jewish element of the liturgy is either completely suppressed or drastically reduced, and the theme of love all but disappears.

Yet the poems we are about to read are related to those of Chapter I in that their form derives from secular Arabic and Hebrew poems on love and wine drinking. Like them, they are short monorhymed poems in Arabic meters; like them, their language, though heavily influenced by Arabic, is very close to that of the Bible. Like them, their form is an innovation of the Golden Age, instantly distinguishable from the liturgical poetry of earlier periods and even from the Golden Age liturgical poetry that carried on in the old vein. Not only the form but also the warmth, the intimacy, and the quiet intensity associated with secular and religious love poetry are carried over into these poems. But they are not religious *ghazals*; their theme sets them apart as an independent genre.

In the introduction to Chapter I we saw how the medieval poets' concern with the soul brought about the possibility of a reinterpretation of the idea of redemption. Further exploration of the poets' idea of the soul reveals how they reinterpreted the idea of prayer as well.

It is important to bear in mind that the courtier-rabbis were also philosopher-rabbis, whose intellectual life was formed not only by the Bible and Talmud but also by Arabic humanism and philosophy. Their serious thoughts were of the nature of man and of the human mind, of the nature of the universe, of metaphysics, of the nature of God and His relationship to the individual soul. They pursued these studies not merely out of the need to defend Jewish doctrine against competing ideas and religions but for the sake of truth. For all the loyalty to the community that the poets displayed in their public lives and in their other literary activities, for all the yearning that they expressed on behalf of their subjugated people, as we have seen in Chapter I, they also were conscious of belonging to a category larger than the Jewish people alone—to the whole race endowed with reason and, within that race, to the class devoted to the fullest cultivation of this endowment, namely, the philosophers.

It was axiomatic for these thinkers that the chief guide to truth is reason, and that reason's chief tool is logic. Saadia had asserted that reason was the basis of true knowledge and that God had given the Torah out of kindness, to spare mortals the difficulty and uncertainty of working out its truths on their own. Even a pietist like Baḥya cited first the logical arguments for each point in his book on religious conduct, and only afterward, the supporting statements from Scripture and rabbinic lore. For such thinkers, reason and revelation were complementary.

From this position it was but a short step to seeing revealed religion not as complementary but as secondary to reason. Not all took this step; nor did all those who took it express themselves openly. We can observe Levi Ibn al-Tabban hovering at the brink of it in the first two stanzas of a strophic poem written to introduce the benediction over the luminaries in the Morning Service:

Reason and religion are two luminaries,
Restoring man's soul, enlightening his eyes.

Philosophers, the wise, have taught
That reason sheds its light over the soul,
Ever revealing to it whatever is hidden,
Wandering around it, teaching it
To go in God's straight paths.

So too those who keep the Torah's law,
Dearer than all things, in truth;
It brings out to light all who walk in darkness;
An adornment of grace, a diadem for your head,
For God's words are words of truth . . . [1]

The stanzas are so ordered as to imply that reason and reve-
lation are complementary and equal in status. But the metaphor
in the leading-line is ambiguous. The word "luminaries" recalls
the creation of the sun, moon, and stars in the opening chapter
of Genesis. According to rabbinic tradition, the sun and the moon
were created equal; but the interesting thing about them is that
they have decidedly not been equal since the fourth day of creation.
Without raising the problem directly, the poet permits the reader
to entertain the question: Which of the two is the source of truth
and which is merely its reflected image?[2]

If there is any doubt as to whether this was an acceptable at-
titude in the liturgies of the Golden Age, Abraham Ibn Ezra ad-
dressed the issue quite openly:

I have seen You with my heart's eye,
And *afterward* in Your Torah.[3]

But the poets were not consciously trying to break with tra-
dition. Medieval Jews that they were, they assumed that the truth
self-evident to them was already present in the classic religious
texts, including the prayer book. They probably did not believe
that they were innovating or changing anything by introducing
philosophical notions into their liturgy. They intended only to use
their poetry to call attention to the parts of the liturgy that best
fitted their understanding of religion and to bring out the message
that their spirit discovered there.

Already Saadia Gaon, in one of the two prose prayers he composed for individual worship, was thinking along these lines:

> Everything comes from You, everything belongs to You, everything is Your witness. All who seek You grasp You intellectually in their hearts, and all who look for You find You in their thoughts. You are near to them in their innermost spirit. For our souls are Your trustworthy witnesses to us, and our bodies testify to us truly, teaching us that we are clay and You our potter, that You are the creator and that we are all the works of Your hands.[4]

And as Bahya expressed it so strikingly in his meditation:

> Even if someone tried to deny You . . . , his very soul would cry out like a stone from the wall, or his spirit would answer as a rafter answers from the woodwork.[5]

Further, Abraham Ibn Ezra concludes a short poem about the soul by interpreting a biblical verse in a way diametrically opposed to its original meaning:

> One generation tells God's praise to another,
> And a people created new praises God.[6]

The "people created new" in Psalm 102:19 is redeemed Israel, according to Abraham Ibn Ezra the commentator. But Abraham Ibn Ezra the poet is writing about the soul, not about Israel: the phrase in the poem more likely means all people who benefit from being created, that is, mankind at large.

Finally, we recall that earlier in this book we twice had occasion to note how Ibn Gabirol stretches the limits of medieval—and even modern—tolerance to recognize all seekers of God as members of a single brotherhood of rational beings.[7]

As the locus of man's rational powers, the soul became one of the chief themes of Golden Age liturgy. Saadia, in what may be the very first reference to philosophical themes in liturgical poetry, composed a cycle of poems for the Day of Atonement based on Psalm 104:1ff., "Bless the Lord, O my soul." The first of these poems is a meditation on the similarities and differences between the soul of man and God.[8] The Neoplatonic myth of the descent of the soul into the body and of its yearning for restoration came to be seen as underlying the very impulse to pray. Prayer came to be understood not merely as a requirement of religious law or as the peculiar institution of a particular religion but as a universal impulse stemming from the nature of the human soul itself. The following selection from a strophic poem by Joseph Ibn Ṣadiq shows how these thoughts cohere. The "charming girl" is, of course, the soul of man:

> Lovely is the charming girl hidden from every eye.
> Consider, men of wisdom, her "where," her "how," her "why."

> Descended to live in clay when matter and form were joined,
> Hidden unwilling there, imprisoned perforce in flesh,
> Enslaved, but by no man's hand; sold, but not with coin,
> To till the body's earth, to make man splendid and dread
> As his due, to set him apart from the beasts with his mind.

> . . . .
> The soul, the Only One, sought release from her toils,
> A day of rest, a day when her labors would lightly lie.
> For eternal matter is hers; she does not perish at death.
> Before the body existed, she existed of old;
> But she is rewarded or punished according to her deeds.

> O God, Your word is manna; to praise You, Lord, is sweet;
> Your works display Your greatness and testify to Your might;
> Have mercy on Your folk joined in Your house of prayer!
> The souls of the world's throngs depend on You like slaves;
> Their voice never ceases: "Praise Him who created every soul."[9]

The last stanza is particularly important. Its third line refers to the congregation and the liturgical occasion, but otherwise all four stanzas are about the soul. In Chapter I we saw how the idea that the soul of man is in captivity in this world, yearning continually for redemption, gave rise to a new, spiritual interpretation of the idea of redemption. Here we see how the essential similarity of the soul and God give rise to a new idea of the praise of God, of the hymn. It is essentially the soul's celebration of her own origins, and the expression of her yearning to return, a spontaneous impulse that is shared by all creatures in whom she resides. This is the point of the last two lines: the soul's yearning is connected to the words of praise, in a sweeping statement that embraces all of humanity: "The souls of the *world's throngs* depend on You like slaves, / Their voice never ceases: Praise Him who created *every soul.*"

This consciousness of a mysterious kinship that joins all rational beings to each other and to God informs a good deal of the poetry in this chapter.

A NEW GENRE

The poems of Chapter I were for the most part attached to points in the liturgy that had been nodes for poetic embellishment since the very origins of liturgical poetry; though innovative in their themes, form, and imagery, they were still traditional in their liturgical function. By contrast, for the new poetry on the soul— the poems to be taken up in this chapter—a new liturgical function was devised. They were designed for parts of the service that had never before attracted poetic embellishment. The poets sought a new liturgical context because they had a completely new theme to contribute to the liturgical repertoire. The new poems may thus be considered the most distinctive liturgical innovation of the Golden Age.

The standard public liturgy for the Morning Service, as described in the Introduction, consisted of the *Sh^{e}ma^c* with its framing benedictions, the *'Amida*, and the silent Supplication. The service opened with a ritual summons to prayer, called *Bar^{e}khu*, in which the precentor said, "Bless the Lord, the blessed," and to which the congregation responded, "Blessed forever is the blessed Lord." This summons to the public service was preceded by benedictions and psalms, which, though originally intended as private preparatory devotions, by the tenth century had already evolved into a kind of preliminary service. On Sabbaths and festivals this preliminary service was concluded by a hymnic piece known as *Nishmat* (The Breath), from its opening word. This was followed by *Kaddish* (Sanctification) to mark the end of the preliminary service, then by the summons to the service proper, as described above.

The Andalusians introduced the practice of prefacing short poems to each of the three prayers—*Nishmat, Kaddish,* and *Barᵉkhu* —that form the transition between the preliminary service and the Morning Service proper. Such poems were called *rᵉshut* (plural *rᵉshuyot*). The name probably derives from the older practice of the precentor offering a private prayer before introducing a complex series of *piyyuṭim*. This practice has left traces in the Ashkenazic rite.[10] It may be the only liturgical genre in which the "I" of the precentor actually represents the precentor as an individual, for ordinarily when the precentor uses the first person pronoun, he speaks in the name of the congregation. In the ancient *rᵉshut*, the precentor petitions God to accept the prayer that he is about to recite on behalf of the congregation. He protests his unworthiness to speak for the congregation, excusing himself on the grounds that the deterioration of the age has left it without a truly worthy spokesman. He asks for fluency and eloquence (a reminder that the liturgical poetry was not fixed like the statutory prayers) and prays that his fear will not impede his mission. Furthermore, he pleads that his prayer be heard so that the congregation not be disappointed in their trust in him.

These themes are all quite uniform from poem to poem. Like the rest of the classical *piyyuṭim*, they are not an individual statement of the precentor's own religious personality. Even in his private prayer, then, the precentor merges with the congregation. He separates himself from the congregation only to the extent that he highlights his function as their spokesman, sometimes even as their intermediary. Yet this degree of distancing was sufficient to permit the emergence of a truly individual voice. And the Golden Age poets exploited the opportunity by transferring the occasion for a personal statement by the precentor to the transitional prayers between the preliminary service and the service proper.

Rᵉshuyot were thus prefaced to prayers occurring at the end of the part of the service that was originally private, more flexible, and less rigidly regulated. It was natural for the new themes to seek a new place in a part of the service not already encumbered by tradition. Moreover, this part of the service was an intrinsically logical site for the new subject matter, for in it national themes like the covenant and the Torah play no role whatsoever and the vicissitudes of Jewish history, though not completely absent, are far from central. This is especially true of *Nishmat*, the substance of which is the praise of God, a praise not qualified as the activity of any particular group of humanity or as an expression of gratitude for any particular benefaction. The praise of *Nishmat* is that which arises spontaneously from all creation to the mighty and bountiful force that exists unseen in the world.[11] It is complemented by similarly universal ideas of the praise of God in the two prayers that follow it. The sequence is:

> *The breath* of every living thing blesses Your name, Lord, our God; the spirit of all flesh ever glorifies and extols You . . .

> *Magnified* and sanctified be His great name in the world He created . . . .

> *Bless the Lord* who is blessed!

The *rᵉshut* usually alludes in its last line to one of the three fixed prayers to which it was to be prefaced. Here are examples of the linkage between poems and the three prayers, taken from poems to be discussed in the body of this chapter. The last line of each poem is translated literally here to demonstrate its connection with the prayer that it introduces:

> Poem 20:
> . . . therefore I
> Will praise You while God's *breath* stays with me.[12]

> Poem 21:
> And so the soul *is magnified* to sing Your praise.[13]

> Poem 23:
> At all times, "O my soul, *bless the Lord*."[14]

Most of the *rᵉshuyot* in this chapter are monorhymed poems in quantitative meters and biblical diction. They almost always have the acrostic of the poet's given name at the beginning of the lines and usually have only as many lines as the poet's given name or at most one additional line. Hardly ever does the acrostic of a monorhymed *rᵉshut* include the poet's patronymic as well. Besides these short *reshuyot* of three to five lines, there are also longer, strophic *reshuyot*. As meditations preparatory to the recitation of the standard prayers, the *reshuyot* provide the poet, acting as precentor, with the opportunity to formulate his own interpretation of the fixed liturgy, a liturgy created centuries earlier in a very different intellectual climate.

Many of the new poems take as their point of departure the precentor's traditional theme: the expression of humility in stepping forward to offer prayer. Often this theme expanded into a meditation on the nature of prayer itself and on the relationship between God and man. Here the poets' different philosophical positions and religious personalities imbue their poems with a distinctive character that is unprecedented in the earlier liturgy. And only rarely in the new poems does the speaker refer to his function as precentor; more often he speaks as though no one but he and God were present. The use of the first person singular is not in itself the innovation it is sometimes made out to be, however. What is new is the virtual absence of the congregation from the background of the poems. The first person singular pronoun is not only used, but it is used insistently; often the rhyme is a suffix meaning "I" or "me." Sentences are often framed in such a way that pronouns designating the speaker alternate with pronouns designating the addressee—the "I" of the speaker with the "You" of God. This back and forth lends the poem a personal flavor quite different from and considerably more intense than that of the traditional *reshut*.

We must however be careful as to how we think of this poetry as individual and personal. It is not ordinarily individualistic in the sense of depicting or being inspired by strongly idiosyncratic views or experiences, like the poetry of a John Donne, a Christopher Smart, or a Gerard Manley Hopkins. Though intimate, it is not the kind of poetry from which a specific person's spiritual biography can be inferred. The *reshuyot* are less individualistic than they are inward. They are celebrated for the warmth that they derive from their characteristic search for God in the worshiper's heart and mind. They put into actual religious practice the philosophical commonplace of the day that man is a microcosm, that whoever wants to find God should therefore examine himself. At their best, they are not routine mouthings of conventional pieties, but are paradoxical delvings into the soul of man in order to mine a transcendent God. Informed as they are by a sincerely religious spirit, their spiritual nuances vary from poet to poet.

But like its ancestor, the traditional r⁵shut, the Andalusian r⁵shut is public religious poetry intended to express the values of the worshipers who delegated the poet-precentor to serve as their spokesman. Beneath the surface of the conventional language and themes we are often able to discern the distinctive spiritual fingerprints of the great creative religious personalities like Ibn Gabirol and Judah Halevi. But despite all its innovations vis-à-vis traditional rabbinic prayer, the Andalusian r⁵shut ordinarily remains conventional, within the framework of the conventions of Golden Age Jewry.

The relationship of the individual to the community in the r⁵shut is analogous to the relationship between the individual and the community that obtains in the secular love poem. There, too, biographical events are excluded or are so abstracted that they no longer allow the possibility of discerning the historical realities behind the texts. There, too, the poet is the spokesman of a communal ideal: the service of beauty. Though formally he addresses the object of his love, his real audience is his circle of fellow courtiers and poets. The "self" that loves is not an individual, though it speaks through an individual; it is the values and aspirations of the group speaking through the mouth of an individual lover. The lover portrays himself as a man apart, severed from society by the uniqueness of his feelings and the uniqueness of the gazelle whom he loves; but in stressing his uniqueness he is actually a force for cohesiveness.[15] Likewise in the r⁵shut, the individual soul speaks to God, but for all his insistence on the "I" he is still spokesman for his community of fellow worshipers. The poet hopes that the congregation that empowered him to express its collective convictions listens and identifies with his words.[16]

·16·

—ᴗ—|—|—|———|—‿|—//—ᴗ—ᴗ—|—|———|——ᴗ

לְבָבִי יְעִירֵנִי כְּשׁוֹאֵל לְשַׁחֲרָה / וְעֵינִי לְעַפְעַפֵּי שְׁחָרִים מְשַׁמְּרָה.

וְאָקוּם לְעֹפֶר חֵן וּפָנָיו אֲכַפְּרָה / בְּפִי מַעֲנֶה לָשׁוֹן כְּבוֹדוֹ אֲסַפְּרָה.

יְקָרוּ בְקָהָל רָב וְצִדְקוּ אֲבַשְׂרָה / וְרוּחִי בְּעוֹד תִּהְיֶה בְּקִרְבִּי אֲזַמְּרָה.

לוי אבן אלתבאן

·16·

To rise with the dawning
    My heart awakens me.
I watch for the eyelids
    Of sunrise impatiently.
I rise to my Fair Gazelle,
    And beg Him to pardon me.
With words He imparted
    I speak of His sovereignty.
His splendor, His righteousness
    I hymn to His community,
And praise Him as long as
    His spirit remains with me.

Levi Ibn al-Tabban

·16·

The sunny poem with which we open Chapter II is quite explicit about its public function, for the speaker calls attention in the third verse to his role as spokesman for the community. The references to morning at the beginning and to the prayer *Nishmat* at the end also point to the Morning Service as the specific liturgical occasion for which the poem was designed. The present translation into short lines is an attempt to imitate the characteristic movement of the original, a limping variant of an otherwise ordinary meter, the limp being emphasized by hemistich-rhyme.

The "Fair Gazelle" of verse 2 is, of course, God; but the expression is not developed or extended in any way; the secular love poetry tradition explored in Chapter I has contributed nothing to our poem but the word "gazelle" itself. The image of God as a lover has been reduced to an inert epithet of the type characteristic of the classic *piyyuṭ*.

The last verse contains an important ambiguity that I have not been able to convey in English. Literally translated, the words mean "and my spirit, as long as it is in me, I sing." The translation reflects the more obvious interpretation, according to which "and my spirit" is understood as the anticipated subject of the temporal clause. But there is neither a grammatical objection nor (since the word order is in any case unusual) a stylistic objection to interpreting "my spirit" as the object of the main clause. This would result in the translation "I will sing *of my spirit* as long as it is in me" or, simply, "I sing my spirit as long as . . . " This reading would view the spirit of the poet as the object of his praise.[1] Another interesting, paradoxical possibility is to understand the spirit not as the theme but as the contents of the poet's praise, to identify the poet's spirit with his song.

Both of these less obvious interpretations suit the intellectual climate of the Golden Age and provide a convenient introduction to our new subject. For all the philosopher-poets, the soul of man was in one way or another divine; thus, to sing of one's soul could very well be an—admittedly daring—way of praising God. But to think of the soul as the song itself is perhaps not all that daring;

we shall soon see Ibn Gabirol making this idea explicit. Either way, the divine character of the *soul* lends divine character to the *song*: the song itself is in some mysterious way a part of God.

This theme is prepared by the words *ma'ane lashon* in verse 2b, which mean literally "utterance of the tongue." The phrase is here translated "words He imparted" because I believe that the poet has in mind Proverbs 16:1: "The plans of the mind belong to man, but the utterance of the tongue is from the Lord." This verse was often cited by synagogue poets, both in the Golden Age and in the earlier liturgical tradition, in prefatory prayers of the type described in the introduction to this chapter as the possible precursor of the Golden Age *r'shut*.[2] The meaning is that the words are not merely the poet's craft, decorative dressing to adorn his own pious thoughts, but, rather, they are words of divine efficacy, put in his mouth by God, as God put into Moses' mouth the words that would eternally guarantee His people's atonement.[3] This is more than a metaphorical way of saying that God bestows eloquence upon man. It means that the words are conceived as being a part of God that is returned to Him through the act of prayer, and in this case, through poetry. The prayer is thus analogous to man's soul, which has descended from God and by its nature returns to Him. We are quite far from the notion of poetry as mere decorated speech, so characteristic of the Golden Age.[4]

Rereading the poem, we cannot help noticing how little its public liturgical function has to do with its contents. The community may have provided the formal occasion for prayer, but the prayer itself seems to be almost a private meditation on the interaction between God and the soul. The worshiping body, a religious corporation led by a spokesman, is present only in the background. In the foreground is the individual heart of man, gifted with the power of reason and the ability to see beyond the particular.

‒‒ᴗ|‒‒ᴗ|‒‒ᴗ//‒‒ᴗ|‒‒ᴗ|‒‒ᴗ

יְחִידָה, שַׁחֲרִי הָאֵל וְסִפְיו, / וְכִקְטֹרֶת תְּנִי שִׁירֵךְ בְּאַפָּיו:
הֲלֹא אִם תִּרְדְּפִי הַבְלֵי זְמַנֵּךְ, / וְתֹאמְרִי כִּי אֱמֶת הֵם כָּל כְּשָׁפָיו,
וְתִזְלִי אַחֲרָיו לֵילֵךְ וְיוֹמֵךְ / וְהֶעֱרַב לָךְ תְּנוּמָה מִנְּשָׁפָיו
דְּעִי כִּי אֵין בְּיָדַיִךְ מְאוּמָה / אֲבָל עֵץ יֵיבְשׁוּ מָהֵר עֲנָפָיו.
הֲיִי לִפְנֵי אֱלֹהַיִךְ וּמַלְכֵּךְ / אֲשֶׁר בָּאת לַחֲסוֹת תַּחַת כְּנָפָיו.
שְׁמוֹ יִגְדַּל וְיִתְקַדַּשׁ בְּפִי כֹל / אֲשֶׁר נִשְׁמַת אֱלוֹהַּ חַי בְּאַפָּיו!

יהודה הלוי

·17·

My soul, seek God at dawn, attend His house,
  And set your song like incense before Him.
For if you run to try to trap Time's vapors,
  Mistaking his illusions for the truth,
And wander wayward, night and day behind him,
  Loving lazy mornings after nights of pleasure—
Know that nothing really is your own
  Except a tree whose boughs will one day wither.

Then be before your Lord, your God and King,
  From whom you seek protection underneath His wing.
His name be ever magnified and sanctified:
  Let every mouth that breathes His greatness sing.

Judah Halevi

This is another poem that alludes at its beginning to morning as the time of day for which it was intended, and at its end to the statutory prayers that it was designed to precede, *Nishmat* and *Kaddish*.[1] But unlike the preceding poem, which explicitly refers to its public function, this one seems to be directed inward from its very first word, "My soul."[2] This inward-looking quality is especially striking when one considers the poem against the background of the genre with which its theme is normally associated. Poems preaching asceticism and the rejection of the ephemeral goods of the world, known in Arabic as *zuhdiyāt*, probably derive ultimately from the wisdom literature of the ancient Near East. They are ordinarily directed outward, as if representing a father instructing his son, or a preacher, his listeners. This Arabic literary tradition was amalgamated in the synagogue with a genre of liturgical poetry known as the *tokheḥa*, or poem of admonition, which derived from the ancient practice of preaching repentance on fast days.[3] In these poems the precentor, whose prayers and poems are normally addressed to God, turns (figuratively) toward the congregation. In our poem, the kind of admonition that would ordinarily be directed outward is directed instead to the poet's own self.[4]

Morning is a time for pursuing; but what goals are worthy of pursuit? This poem presupposes that most people naturally spend their lives pursuing "Time" and its vanities.[5] Time appears under two broad aspects in Arabic literature and in the Hebrew literature influenced by it. Especially in pre-Islamic poetry, but also later, it personifies the black fate that predestines all creatures to disaster. Similarly, it is used to represent the circumstances that stand between a person and the object of his ambition or desire. In the gnomic tradition, by contrast, Time stands for all mundane things, disparaging them by calling attention to their transience. One term thus represents both the objects of worldly desires and the obstacles to their attainment. The two meanings seem to converge in a third usage in which Time personifies the vicissitudes of life and the mutability of human circumstances, a kind of demigod that bestows pleasure, power, and wealth, only to withdraw them without warning. Time in this sense may also be depicted as a magician who charms people with sleight of hand into believing in his illusions, for no other purpose than the malign pleasure of watching man's eventual disappointment. Here is the source of the expression "Time's illusions" (literally "his wizardry") in the poem. The image of the conjurer who gleefully disguises the temporal world with superficial decorations in order to lure man into complacency and then destroy him is actually found in the Quran, where it is attached to Satan.[6] Moses Ibn Ezra gave epigrammatic expression to this thought in a secular poem:

> Beware of Time: the gifts that he bestows
> Are venom mixed with honey to taste sweet.[7]

In the intellectual life of the philosopher-poets, time and change are associated with motion. It was axiomatic to them that motion resulted from a deficiency in the moving object and was a cause of its dissolution, or at least evidence of its perishability. In their view, motion affected only the created, composite, and therefore impermanent world. The progress of time and the motion of the world were bound together in their minds. God, by contrast, was outside both and unaffected by them—everlasting, unchanging, and still.

Pursuit in verse 2 is thus identified with the transient. It is complemented in the following verse by another verb of motion, the rather rare word vᵉtezli. I have translated it as "wander wayward," to capture the overtones of two different possible etymologies.[8] In the same verse, even the expression "night and day" is incorporated into the theme of motion, for lelekh (your night) is a homonym of the rabbinic Hebrew form of the verb "to go." Man's constant motion in pursuit of temporal pleasure and success is a motion that does not go anywhere, like the desiccation in the tree in verse 4, like the endlessly wearisome motion of the sun, winds, and waters in Ecclesiastes.

Stasis, the opposite of motion, is what the poet finally recommends in verse 5, after all his negative observations. The verb that signifies the shift from negative to positive, from motion to stasis, is *h*^a*yi* (be), complemented not with an adjective or noun, but awkwardly with a prepositional phrase. Not "be pious" or "be trustworthy" or "be good," but "be before the Lord." Several important religious ideals are encapsulated in this recommendation: first, the plain meaning, to be in the synagogue, where the poem is being recited; second, to trust in God by not pursuing the things of this world; and, finally, by imitating His unmoved serenity, to be as much like Him as is possible for imperfect, material, composite man.

‒◡‒|‒◡|‒‒◡|‒‒◡

18

יְשֵׁנָה בְחֵיק יַלְדוּת, לְמָתַי תִּשְׁכְּבִי?

דְּעִי כִּי נְעוּרִים כַּנְּעֹרֶת נִנְעָרוּ!

הֲלָעַד יְמֵי הַשַּׁחֲרוּת? קוּמִי צְאִי —

רְאִי מַלְאֲכֵי שֵׂיבָה בְּמוּסָר שִׁחֲרוּ;

וְהִתְנַעֲרִי מִן הַזְּמָן, כַּצִּפֳּרִים

אֲשֶׁר מֵרְסִיסֵי לַיְלָה יִתְנָעָרוּ.

דְּאִי כַדְּרוֹר לִמְצֹא דְרוֹר מִמַּעֲלֵךְ

וּמִתּוֹלְדוֹת יָמִים כְּיַמִּים יִסְעָרוּ.

הֱיִי אַחֲרֵי מַלְכֵּךְ מְרֻדֶּפֶת, בְּסוֹד

נְשָׁמוֹת אֲשֶׁר אֶל טוּב יְיָ נָהָרוּ!

יהודה הלוי

·18·

O you who sleep in childish folly's lap—
  Childhood is chaff to be thrown off:
      Awake!

Do black-haired days endure?
  Go out and see the gray-clad messengers
      Who greet you with their lessons every dawn,

And shake off Time
  As birds shake drops
      Of night-dew when they wake.

Like swallows, soar o'er sin,
  And free yourself from Time,
      That seething sea.

But be pursuing God, in the river of those souls
  That toward His bliss with radiant faces flow.

                                        Judah Halevi

·18·

The image of sleeping and waking in a moral or spiritual context is common enough in both Arabic and Jewish writing. This poem, in fact, has no specifically Jewish content at all: its imagery, worked out against a richly textured background of wordplays and plays on sound, conveys a message that would be acceptable to any monotheist.

Like the preceding poem, the present one is a morning exhortation to the worshiper to devote his day to God. But "day" here is more explicitly a metaphor for "life." And, reversing the imagery of poem 17, our poem takes pursuit and motion as positive images of the religious life rather than as emblems of vanity; stasis here would represent turpitude. Indeed, the poet echoes the age-old call of the moralist to the young man to rise with the dawn and use the day for accomplishment, a call that can be heard from the Book of Proverbs (6:9–10) through the morning call of the muezzin ("Verily prayer is better than sleep") to Poor Richard and beyond. The addressee is urged to go out, to shake off, to soar, and, in wording that seems almost an intentional counterpart to the penultimate verse of poem 17, to "be pursuing" (instead of the static "be before"). The ultimate reward of this true and pious motion is conveyed in the poem's last word, which describes the river of righteous souls flowing to their Lord at the end of time.

This last word, however, can also mean "to shine," an image certainly relevant to a poem intended to awaken the addressee both literally and spiritually. The words here translated "childhood is chaff to be thrown off" (literally "youth is shaken off like tow") make use three times of the root letters ʿr, which are associated with waking.[1] By referring to youth as "black-haired days," the poet paradoxically links youth with nighttime and therefore with ignorance and folly; while the "gray-clad messengers" are associated with dawn, since every morning we find ourselves closer to old age—and, therefore, to enlightenment.[2]

If all these references to light were not sufficient to stir us in our warm beds, the poet also alarms us with sound effects. This short poem is crammed with them, beginning with the triple play in verse 1b on ʿr, a sound that continues to echo through verse 3, where verbs derived from the root nʿr begin and end the verse. Verse 3 also imitates the birds' tossing off the beads of night-dew by connecting the ṣr of the Hebrew word for bird with the rs of the word for dewdrops. All these sounds, especially r, anticipate the swallows. These appear in verse 4, where the word deror occurs twice, first with the meaning "swallow," then with the meaning "freedom."[3] It is almost as if the sleeper hears the birds' sound at first only in his half-conscious state, then picks out the sound as that of birds, finally identifies the birds as swallows in verse 4, when he is fully awake.

We have already met personified Time in poem 17; here we encounter the "seed of Time" (literally "the generations, or descendants, of Time"). The figure reflects a common Arabic idiom in which any abstract idea may be said to have children, which are the specific occurrences of the idea. Thus, if Time represents disaster, the children of Time would be individual disasters; if Time represents the mundane, to pursue the children of Time means to cultivate individual this-worldly concerns, to look away from man's ultimate end.

The instability and transience of the mundane world is often compared to the ebb and flow of water. Halevi draws on this tradition, turning the lovely drops of night-dew that sparkle in the morning sun as the swallows shake them free, into raging oceans of worldliness. These cannot be so lightly tossed off; they threaten to drown anyone who cannot escape by soaring over them. But those who succeed in doing so are able to join a more gentle kind of flow: the river of the righteous streaming toward the Lord.[4]

—⌣—|—⌣—|—⌣//—⌣—|—⌣—|—⌣—⌣

יְעִירוּנִי בְשִׁמְךָ רַעְיוֹנַי / וְיָשִׂימוּ חֲסָדֶיךָ לְפָנַי.

הֲבִינוּנִי דְבַר נֶפֶשׁ יְצַרְתָּה / קְשׁוּרָה בִי—וְהִיא נִפְלָאת בְּעֵינַי.

וְלִבִּי רָאָה וַיַּאֲמֶן בָּךְ / כְּאִלּוּ מֶעֱמָד הָיָה בְסִינַי.

דְּרַשְׁתִּיךָ בְחֶזְיוֹנַי וְעָבַר / כְּבוֹדְךָ בִּי וְיָרַד בַּעֲנָנַי.

הֲקִימוּנִי שְׂעִפַּי מִיְצוּעַי / לְבָרֵךְ שֵׁם כְּבוֹדֶךָ אֲדֹנַי.

יהודה הלוי

·19·

My meditations on Your name aroused me,
They set before my face Your acts of love,
Revealed to me the soul that You created—
Bound to me, yet past my understanding.

My heart beheld You and was sure of You,
As if I stood myself at Sinai mountain.
I sought You in my dreams; Your glory passed
Before my face, on clouds descending, landing.

My thoughts awakened me to rise from bed,
To bless Your glorious name, O Lord, commanding.

Judah Halevi

·19·

Neither the morning sun nor birdsong awakens the poet here. Rather, he is awakened by his thoughts, which lead first to understanding, then to a vision. We have already had occasion to note the importance for Halevi's religious mentality of such direct spiritual experiences. We also saw a hint in poem 16 of the idea that religious behavior is set in motion by "thought," and we will see it again in poems to come. Here revelation through a dream and the activity of the intellect together shape the poet's experience.

The starting point is the poet's meditation on the soul of man, the wonder that this spiritual substance should be attached to his body. "Wonder"—the mood of man contemplating his origins— is the theme of Psalm 139:14, from which the words of verse 2 are borrowed:

> I praise You
> For I am awesomely, wondrously made;
> Your work is wonderful;
> I know it very well.[1]

This psalm was regarded in the Middle Ages as a particularly profound spiritual statement.[2] For many it was a model for the idea that man can know God by looking at himself, that by studying the miraculous skill with which God crafted man he can come to see God with the eye of the intellect. The passage from Psalms is quoted by Baḥya as the preamble to a long and beautiful passage describing the wonderful nature of man's body and intellect. It was axiomatic for Baḥya and some of his contemporaries that, although we cannot grasp God directly, we can see traces of Him in His works, and especially in the way that man, the microcosm, is made. To seek these traces of God is the first step (after intellectual conviction of God's existence and unity) on the way to true worship.[3] Halevi follows Baḥya's spiritual plan. Like him, he goes beyond the psalm in seeing the union of man's body with his intellect as the greatest wonder of man's composition. Halevi progresses from thinking (verse 1) to understanding (2a) to wonder

(2b). But, characteristically, Halevi surpasses Baḥya's practical breed of pietism, to achieve an actual vision òf revelation (3–4).

This vision is specifically of the revelation of the Torah at Mount Sinai, which is referred to in verse 3. The image of God descending upon the poet like a cloud recalls the story of the giving of the Torah, as well as Moses' second ascent to the mountain after breaking the tablets.[4] Following this private theophany, the poet's thoughts rouse him from bed. Since this awakening is the physical one that brings the dreamer-poet to the synagogue to sing God's praise by reciting our poem, it becomes apparent in retrospect that the "waking" of verse 1 referred not to the physical waking from sleep but to a spiritual awakening into the dream. The poem thus embodies the quasi-mystical paradox that true awakening occurs in the world of prophetic dreams.

We are to understand that intellectual meditation on the soul by day led the poet to a nighttime vision in which he saw himself present at Mount Sinai, when God descended to join His people. This spiritual awakening is followed by physical awakening and regular morning worship. This pattern is exactly in accord with Psalm 139:17–18:

> How weighty Your thoughts seem to me, O God,
> How great their number!
> I count them—they exceed the grains of sand;
> I awake—but am still with You.

To this, Abraham Ibn Ezra says:

> "Your thoughts" means that when I think with my heart to know Your thoughts it is like a vision of God: the body is recumbent and the soul of man clings to the highest soul.[5] There it sees marvelous forms. Therefore, "I awaken and am still with You," for this is not like all [ordinary] dreams."

This last remark seems to mean that those sensitive souls who are granted spiritual visions of God in dreams receive them also during the day.[6]

For the religious thinkers of the Golden Age, the revelation on Mount Sinai represented the highest level of spiritual development attainable by mortals, and Moses, the man who had come closest to fulfilling this human spiritual potential. Halevi's dream is thus in keeping in a general way with the religious sensibilities of his age. But his dream may also have been related to the specific subject of the meditation that induced it. Halevi tells us that he had been contemplating the miraculous junction of the soul and the body. God's descent on Mount Sinai was likewise a miraculous joining of the divine and mundane worlds on the plane of Jewish history. Perhaps in his dream, Halevi—obsessed as he was with the national history and seeing revelation rather than creation as the central fact of religious life—translated the theme of his meditation into the language of this particular biblical episode and woke believing for a moment that he had experienced a "vision of God" comparable to the one beheld by the ancient Israelites. It would not be farfetched to assume that a medieval poet and philosopher would interpret the biblical episode as an allegorical representation of a philosophical truth.[7]

The poem thus embodies several transformations. (1) The moralist's awakening from sloth to activity (poem 17) is transformed into a spiritual awakening from the waking to the sleeping state, where there exists a spiritual life of an intensity not accessible to the merely active. (2) The historical experience of Israel is transformed into an inner experience of the union of God and man; the national experience of Israel is completely revalued and acquires metaphysical significance.[8] (3) The public ritual of prayer is converted into a symbol of individual spiritual life that derives ultimately not from the community of Israel but from the nature of man as such.

·20·

‏——|‿—|—|‿—//—|‿—|—|‿—‎

‏שַׁחַר אֲבַקֶּשְׁךָ, צוּרִי וּמִשְׂגַּבִּי; / אֶעֱרֹךְ לְפָנֶיךָ שַׁחְרִי וְגַם עַרְבִּי.‎
‏לִפְנֵי גְדֻלָּתְךָ אֶעֱמֹד וְאֶבָּהֵל / כִּי עֵינְךָ תִרְאֶה כָל מַחְשְׁבוֹת לִבִּי.‎
‏מַה זֶּה אֲשֶׁר יוּכַל הַלֵּב וְהַלָּשׁוֹן / לַעֲשׂוֹת, וּמַה כֹּחַ רוּחִי בְּתוֹךְ קִרְבִּי?‎
‏הִנֵּה לְךָ תִּיטַב זִמְרַת אֱנוֹשׁ, עַל כֵּן / אוֹדְךָ בְּעוֹד תִּהְיֶה נִשְׁמַת אֱלוֹהַּ בִּי.‎

‏שלמה אבן גבירול‎

·20·

At dawn I come to You, my Rock, my Strength;
      I offer You my dawn and evening prayers.
Before Your majesty I stand in fear,
      Because Your eye discerns my secret thoughts.

What is there that man's mind and mouth
      Can make? What power is there in my body's breath?

And yet the songs of man delight You; therefore I
      Will praise You while I still have breath from God.

Solomon Ibn Gabirol

·20·

Probably the most famous poem in this book, one familiar even to English readers through its inclusion in many prayer books,[1] this apparently simple, straightforward prayer begins with ideas and images that are themselves long familiar from the Psalms and earlier prayers. The first two verses might even seem to be routine rephrasings of old ideas if the meter did not lend some novelty to the old thoughts, especially through its power to thrust the thought forward.[2] But in the course of the poem the poet seems to move from comfortable old pieties to new, unsettling realizations and finally to resolution.

Routinely approaching God with his daily prayers in verse 1, the poet is awed by God's majesty in verse 2a. Realizing that God sees directly into man's heart, the poet suddenly understands that there is nothing appropriate for man to say at all. This sensation of being transparent before God's eye brings the poet in verse 3, the poem's core, to a state of paralysis.

Taken by themselves, the words of verse 3 seem merely to state the familiar religious idea that human means are inadequate to express God's majesty. This idea is of course standard in rabbinic literature and is actually one of the themes of *Nishmat*, the prayer that our poem was written to introduce.[3] But in *Nishmat* this idea is merely a rhetorical device, praising God by saying that He is beyond praise. Our poem goes beyond *Nishmat* both formally and conceptually in treating this theme.

Meter and sound effects combine to focus attention on the religious paradox that follows from the overwhelming sense of God's majesty expressed in verse 2a. The rhythm of the line reflects the poet's resulting sensation of breakdown; and alliteration in the verse's center points an arrow at the problem:

> *ma ze asher yukh*al hal*ev veha la*shon
> la ʿsot . . .

Rhythmic manipulation supports or, better, expresses the idea, through the enjambment of the word *la ʿsot* in 3b (can make). The forward thrust of the syntax forces the reader to land hard on this word; and what remains of verse 3 is too short to feel metrically complete. The first hemistich is thus made to seem too short to contain the complete syntactic unit that expresses the poet's thought, and the short second hemistich comes out feeling limp. Just so the mind of man is unable to contain within its compass the complete thought of God, and thus it is unable to praise Him. It would be hard to imagine a verse better designed to demonstrate the importance of reading these poems in accordance with the original meters, for here the metrical shortfall is the whole point of the line. The translation makes a pale attempt at imitating these effects by means of alliteration, a long row of unstressed syllables, and a metrically short line.

That God's omniscience renders the worshiper's prayer banal is a traditional idea, and that this consciousness should inhibit him from speaking is also not unprecedented. But that it should inhibit his intellectual activity is new. That the mind of man, his divine spirit, should be caught up in the paralysis of the body seems an almost irresponsible hyperbole, for medieval thinkers like Ibn Gabirol assert again and again that it is through the mind that man apprehends God, insofar as he is able. But this last reservation—insofar as he is able—is exactly what troubles Ibn Gabirol. Even the soul falls short, because while we live it is inextricably tied to the body, as is suggested by the alliteration at the verse's center, *lev* and *lashon* (heart/mind and tongue/mouth).

It has already been pointed out that the phrase derives from a rhyming Arabic maxim, "The heart and tongue are the whole of man."[4] It was Ibn Gabirol's good fortune that the Hebrew words for "heart" and "tongue" alliterate. (They do not in Arabic.) It was his genius that seized on the alliteration for the purpose of building his paradox.

Just as the problem was given its full expressive force by the organization of the rhythm in verse 3, so it finds resolution in the rhythmic organization of verse 4. The gap that logic and argument fail to bridge between the desire to praise God and the incapacity of mind and tongue is here bridged by the verse form. The two sentences of verse 4 are distributed between the two hemistichs in exactly reverse proportion to the distribution of the two sentences of verse 3. Thus, the assertion that man's song delights God ends two syllables before the hemistich break, just as the statement of man's frailty in verse 3 ended two syllables beyond it—and the rhythmic imbalance of verse 3 has been redressed. One concludes with the impression, following the speaker's meandering, seemingly uncontrolled expression of doubt, that his conviction of human worth is firm and authoritative.

The rhythmic solution is supported by the words. The temporary spiritual imbalance is overcome by the belief in an intrinsic commonality between man and God: man has a divine soul, which entitles him to address God. One meaning of the verse is that the poet will praise God as long as that divine spirit is in him. The other meaning—the one that answers the doubt of verse 3—is that it is the presence of the divine soul in man that makes the praise of God at all possible in the first place.

Ibn Gabirol returns to this question of what it means for man to praise God in the next poems. He also deals with the broader philosophical question: How could imperfect man proceed at all from God? We know from this poem not to expect philosophical answers founded on strict logic. Ibn Gabirol speaks in this book as an artist, not as a philosopher. He addresses himself to the reader's feelings about philosophical problems, not to the problems themselves, which he took up with all due rigor in his philosophical work.

—⌣—|—⌣—|—⌣—/⌣—|—⌣—|—⌣—|—⌣—|—⌣

שְׁפַל־רוּחַ, שְׁפַל־בֶּרֶךְ וְקוֹמָה,/אֲקַדֶּמְךָ בְּרֹב פַּחַד וְאֵימָה.

לְפָנֶיךָ אֲנִי נֶחְשָׁב בְּעֵינַי/כְּתוֹלַעַת קְטַנָּה בָּאֲדָמָה.

מְלֹא עוֹלָם, אֲשֶׁר אֵין קֵץ לְגָדְלוֹ—/הֲכָמוֹנִי יְהַלֶּלְךָ, וּבַמֶּה?

הֲדָרְךָ לֹא יְכִילוּן מַלְאֲכֵי־רוֹם—/וְעַל אַחַת אֲנִי כַּמָּה וְכַמָּה!

הֱטִיבוֹתָ וְהִגְדַּלְתָּ חֲסָדִים/וְלָךְ תַּגְדִּיל לְהוֹדוֹת הַנְּשָׁמָה

שלמה אבן גבירול

With lowly spirit, lowered knee and head
   In fear I come; I offer Thee my dread.
But once with Thee I seem to have no worth
   More than a little worm upon the earth.

O Fullness of the World, Infinity—
   What praise can come, if any can, from me?
Thy splendor is not contained by the hosts on high,
   And how much less capacity have I!
Infinite Thou, and infinite Thy ways;
   Therefore the soul expands to sing Thy praise.

Solomon Ibn Gabirol

The religious feeling that gave rise to poem 20 was the poet's sense of being transparent before God; in the present poem it is his feeling of smallness and insignificance.

The rabbis of the Talmud already recognized the inadequacy of man's praise of God. This poem may remind us of the Talmudic anecdote of the rabbinic master who rebuked his disciple for praising God at too great length. But the master's ironic "Have you finished saying all of God's praise?"[1] is founded on an essentially logical problem: since God's infinitude must by definition outstrip human vocabulary, any praise that pretends to completeness actually diminishes Him. The religious attitude of our poem arises not out of this logical problem, which led some rabbis to limit the free composition of hymnic prayers, but out of awe, like the prayer of Solomon to which it alludes: "Even the heavens to their innermost reaches cannot contain You; how much less this house that I have built."[2]

We might even say that it is the sense of man's smallness, more than that of God's greatness, that gives the poem its particular flavor. And if by the poem's end the problem has been resolved, this only confirms that the focus of the poem is on man more than it is on God, for it is our impression of man alone that will change in the course of the poem. The rhyme syllable *mā* makes every verse seem to end with the question "what?"[3] It is hard to believe that Ibn Gabirol was not thinking of Isaiah 2:22 when he composed the poem around this syllable: "Oh cease to glorify man, who has only a breath in his nostrils! For by what [*bame*] does he merit esteem?"

If we dwell upon the meaning of this verse as it appears in Isaiah, we can clearly see how Ibn Gabirol has turned it around. The verse concludes a stern oration on God's terrifying appearance at the end of time, when He will judge man and his idols. Since man exists only thanks to a vapor, the breath (*nᵉshama*) in his nostrils, and perishes the instant this breath is gone, he is as nothing compared to this tremendous God of judgment.

But to a medieval thinker, man owes his essential character

not to the physical breath in his nostrils but to his divine soul, which is also called *n*^e*shama*. The purpose of the poem is to take us from Isaiah's deprecation of man for having merely *n*^e*shama* (breath) to a new sense that thanks to the *n*^e*shama* (soul) man is in fact commensurable with God and has the power and the right to praise Him.

The repeated "what" of the poem's rhyme-syllable thus raises a question that is fully resolved only by the poem's last word, *n*^e*shama*. Since the soul of man is of divine origin, man does in some sense contain God. For all man's smallness and insignificance as a creature of the material world, he is entitled by virtue of his soul to speak of Him. We shall now see how the poem uses the rhythmic potential of Hebrew verse to resolve this paradox.

True to the rules of quantitative metrics, this poem contains exactly the same number of syllables in each hemistich—eleven— and all hemistichs have theoretically the same duration in time. Metrical uniformity does not, however, mean rhythmical uniformity: it merely provides a background beat against which the poet can create a rhythm by varying the number and placement of words (hence stresses) in each hemistich.

The somewhat routine statement of pious humility in verse 1a is couched in a rapid measure of five words to the hemistich. Verses 1b and 2a slow the pace to four stresses per hemistich. By the time we reach the point, in verse 2b, where the poet stands completely outside himself and sees himself from God's perspective as a little worm on the ground, the measure has slowed to a ponderous three words to the hemistich. Motion seems to have come to a halt. Now reversing the point of view and taking the measure of God, the poet utters a rapid burst of six words in hemistich 3a. Though this hemistich is equal in duration to 2b, its sheer fullness of words makes it seem to last forever. At the same time, the words themselves seem to move by quickly, since they are forced into a fairly rigid time frame. In verse 3b the perspective again shifts back to the speaker, and again his view of himself is compressed into three words, and rather bland ones at that. This line contains the widest rhythmical contrast; it is the middle line of the poem; and it makes the poem's most radical statement of the gap between God and man. Here is where the problem of the poem is most formally stated.

Verse 4 seems to restate the problem of verse 3. But the fact that its hemistichs are evenly balanced, with the word count in a ratio of 5:5 (as opposed to 6:3 in verse 3), alerts us to a shift in tone; and, indeed, this verse also contains, in verse 4b, the poem's first statement about man that is not one of complete humility. It is as if the poet's will to deny man's divine status is running out. He now expresses himself not in imagery as in verse 2, nor in clear negation as in verse 3, but in an ambiguous logical calculation, deflating the lofty tone with a cliché of rabbinic Hebrew. The words call attention to themselves partly because the use of nonbiblical diction is contrary to the poetics of the Golden Age and most unusual. The idiom used here ordinarily denotes the inference that an attribute admittedly belonging to one subject must apply even more certainly to another. Ibn Gabirol's point is coldly logical: since even the angels cannot contain God's splendor, certainly man cannot. But something in the wording of the idiom implies "more" rather than "less," an undertone that in this context seems to reverse the logic and imply that man can do *more* than what the angels can do—the opposite of the denotation of the words.

The final answer does not come in the abstract language of philosophy. Rather, it comes in a loose rhetorical equation that reflects on the relationship between God and man. The verb *higdil* (to be great) is applied to God's acts of grace in 5a and to man's praise of Him in 5b, as if the two can be brought into balance, reason notwithstanding. God's grace in 5a is His act of creating man with a soul that derives from Himself. This soul is a kind of overflow onto the human clay of God's abundance, which cannot be contained by the heavens. This overflow fills man with soul; and man is able to praise Him by a matching overflow. Within Ibn Gabirol's oeuvre, this train of thought is not unique. We shall see it more explicitly developed in the very next example. Nor is it unique to Ibn Gabirol, for we find it also in a poem by George Herbert:

> Prayer . . .
>> God's breath in man returning to his birth,
>> The soul in paraphrase . . . [4]

—ーᴗᴧ—ᴧ—ᴧ—ᴗᴧᴧ—ᴧ——ᴧ—ᴧ——ᴗ

שִׁחַרְתִּיךָ בְּכָל שַׁחְרִי וְנִשְׁפִּי / וּפָרַשְׂתִּי לְךָ כַּפַּי וְאַפִּי.

לְךָ אֶהְמֶה בְּלֵב צָמֵא, וְאֶדְמֶה / לְדַל שׁוֹאֵל עֲלֵי פִתְחִי וְסִפִּי.

מְרוֹמוֹת לֹא יְכִילוּךָ לְשִׁבְתָּךָ—— וְאוּלָם יֵשׁ מְקוֹמְךָ תּוֹךְ סְעִפִּי!

הֲלֹא אֶצְפֹּן בְּלִבִּי שֵׁם כְּבוֹדְךָ / וְגָבַר חִשְׁקְךָ עַד יַעֲבָר־פִּי.

אֲנִי עַל כֵּן אֲהוֹדֶה שֵׁם אֲדֹנָי / בְּעוֹד נִשְׁמַת אֱלֹהִים חַי בְּאַפִּי.

שלמה אבן גבירול

·22·

At morning and at evening I seek You;
　　I offer You my face and outspread palms.
For You I yearn, to You I turn, Your grace to earn,
　　Like someone at my door who asks for alms.

The heavens do not have room for You to dwell,
　　And yet You have a palace in my mind.
For in my heart I hide Your holy name;
　　Your love spills over, it cannot be confined.

And so I praise God with my poetry,
　　While yet He breathes the living soul in me.

Solomon Ibn Gabirol

This poem, like the one preceding, is a meditation on the paradox of God's infinitude and man's seemingly irrational urge to praise Him. But here the relationship of man to God in worship is not presented as a problem to be solved. Its paradoxical nature is given. The formulation of the paradox in verse 3 provides the foundation of a poetic explanation of the nature of prayer in verse 4.

Let us start by examining verse 3 more closely. As in the preceding poem, there is an allusion to Solomon's prayer at the dedication of the Temple, with its paradox of dedicating a mere building to house an omnipresent God. Perhaps in the background lies the familiar rabbinic adage, "The world is not His place, but rather He is the place of the world."[1] But the idea that the heart of man is God's true place resonated even closer to Ibn Gabirol's world. The Sufis attributed to Muhammad a tradition according to which God said, "My earth and My heaven contain me not, but the heart of My faithful servant containeth Me." And for Ibn Gabirol, the emanationist, man's soul is God's natural place, perhaps even more so than the corporeal heavens themselves.[2]

Ibn Gabirol's language in this line reflects the rabbinic tradition that God has a temple in heaven, an exact analogue of the Temple in Jerusalem.[3] The conjunction chosen by Ibn Gabirol to join the two halves of verse 3, *ve'ulam*, alludes to the Temple, for it happens to be a homonym of a word used in Kings in connection with Solomon's Temple.[4] By means of this latent pun, Ibn Gabirol hints that the Temple reputedly in heaven is actually located in man's heart. It is, incidentally, interesting to observe how much more powerful is Ibn Gabirol's playful hint that the heart is a Temple than is Abraham Ibn Ezra's explicit resolution to make his heart a Temple:

> I give thanks to the Lord, I call upon His name
> I make my heart a Temple where He can dwell.[5]

or his plea, to be discussed below in connection with poem 29, that God make His temple in the poet's heart.

Once we understand that Ibn Gabirol assumes God's presence within man's heart, we are in a position to recognize the hint in verse 2 that had prepared the way for this idea. The image of the beggar at the door that ends the verse is surprising on two counts: it is hackneyed; and its pronominal suffixes (e.g., *my* door) have no apparent meaning. Now it is true that even Ibn Gabirol is capable of using a tired image on occasion; and it was routine for the synagogue poets to tack pronominal suffixes onto words merely for the sake of the rhyme. Perhaps the pronouns are justifiable as indicating that the poet feels as humble as the beggars who have come to beg at his own door. But the internal rhyme at the beginning of the verse signals something noteworthy, and with a little reflection on Ibn Gabirol's theme we can see what he is really hinting at. For man to approach God he has not to look outward at a remote being that even the heavens cannot contain, but inward, at a God compressed within the compass of a man's soul. The supplicant thus must stand like a beggar at his own door and at his own threshold in order to speak to God.

This interpretation, which might seem forced to a reader not steeped in Ibn Gabirol's kind of piety, is confirmed by a line from another poem, a line, incidentally, that bears a notable rhythmic similarity to the one under discussion. The poem is Ibn Gabirol's great meditation on the soul, and it is to the soul that the "she" refers:

> To You she bows, her heart bound; she watches,
> Sounding her sorrowful prayer at *her* gate, at *her* portal.[6]

The paradox that the transcendent God, who overflows the heavens, can be contained in man's soul is the poem's pith. This image, to which we have alluded in the discussion of the preceding poem, explains and justifies the act of worship. The same divine abundance that overflows the heavens cannot help but overflow the heart of man as well. It is *in* man, but it cannot be contained in him. Ibn Gabirol rejoices that the pressure of the divine presence bursts the confines of the body and pours from his mouth in the form of prayer. Prayer is thus God returning to Himself, an anticipation of the soul's ultimate return to its source.

The sensation of the pressure of the divine within man bursting forth in verbal form is found already in Jeremiah, where, in the context of the poet's anguish, the imagery is of fire. Here the emotional context is ecstasy, and the image is of water.[7] In both instances, God's presence inside the poet is understood as words that cannot be contained. But in the poem, prayer, like prophecy, is seen as the very substance of God.[8] Although Ibn Gabirol's language in this line does not derive from love poetry, the theme of the difficulty of keeping love secret was a commonplace of love poetry and theory, and it might have contributed to the emotional response of a medieval audience on hearing these lines.[9]

Though Ibn Gabirol's idea derives from Neoplatonic speculation on the nature of the soul, it is tempting to see in it also an extension of one of the unspoken assumptions of the Jewish liturgy. This is the tendency of Jewish prayer in all ages to stay close to the words of Scripture, as if man can come close to God by returning His words to Him.[10] Perhaps this idea underlies Ibn Gabirol's thinking and is here given a Neoplatonic interpretation.

·23·

ـ‌ـ‌‌ـ‌ﺍ‌ـ‌ـ‌ﺍ‌ـ‌ـ‌ﺍ‌ـ‌ـ‌‌//‌ـ‌ـ‌ﺍ‌ـ‌ـ‌ﺍ‌ـ‌ـ‌ﺍ‌ـ‌ـ‌ﺍ‌ـ‌ـ‌ﺍ‌ـ‌ـ‌ﺍ‌ـ‌ـ‌ﺍ‌ـ‌ـ‌‌∪

שְׁלֹשָׁה נוֹסְדוּ יַחַד לְעֵינַי, / יְשִׂימוּן זִכְרְךָ תָּמִיד לְפָנָי:

לְשָׁמֶיךָ—אֲנִי אַזְכִּיר שְׁמֶךָ, / וְהֵם עֵדַי לְעֵדַי נֶאֱמָנִי.

מְקוֹם שִׁבְתִּי—יְעוֹרֵר מַחֲשַׁבְתִּי, / בְּרָקְעוֹ אֶזְכְּרָה רֹקַע אֲדָנִי.

הֲגִיג לִבִּי—בְּהַבִּיטִי בְּקִרְבִּי: / בְּכָל עֵת בָּרֲכִי, נַפְשִׁי, אֲדֹנָי:

שלמה אבן גבירול

·23·

Three things there are, together in my eye
    That keep the thought of You forever nigh.
I think about Your great and holy name
    Whenever I look up and see the sky.
My thoughts are roused to know how I was made,
    Seeing the earth's expanse, where I abide.
The musings of my mind, when I look inside—
    At all times, "O my soul, bless Adonai."

Solomon Ibn Gabirol

·23·

Of all of Ibn Gabirol's poems, this miniature masterpiece most clearly, succinctly, and beautifully evokes the inward-looking character of his religious thought and experience.

The contemplation of a series of God's manifestations—the sky, the earth, and the mental life of man—brings the poet to praise Him. The author of the Psalms might very well have been inspired by sky and earth to praise God; but that the mind of man should also be a source of inspiration is a distinctively medieval contribution to religious thought.[1]

The expression "in my eye" in the poem's opening is concrete. Calling attention to the organ as it does, it suits the observation of heaven and earth. But it does not prepare the reader for such an abstraction as the promised third item. Having discovered that the climax of the series is the mind of man, we realize that "eye" had not been meant literally but was intended as the equivalent of "the heart's eye," the ability of man's intellect to know God by observing and reflecting on His creations.[2] The poet, we see, is thinking in verses 2 and 3 not merely of passive emotional ecstasy at beholding the grandeur of nature but also of the way in which his mind is engaged by the material cosmos and how this engagement leads him toward God. The philosopher-poets held this notion to be man's highest religious duty.

Ibn Gabirol gives his idea a distinctive twist by having the "eye" roam from the distant, literally visible sky to the nearer, more plainly visible earth and from there to the inner, invisible mind. The progression is from sky to self; from remote to proximate; from that which is least subject to man's control to that which is most so; and from that which is least graspable to that which is most so. The logic is that the more abstract kind of seeing is the clearest and that the clearest view of God is gained through the soul. This is because man's soul is itself part of God, as we have seen in poem 22.

The poem's sound patterns are carefully orchestrated to support these ideas. The dominant sounds derive from the personal pronominal suffixes. As the suffixes are repeated, the meaning comes to be so firmly associated with the sounds that it is sustained even when the sounds appear independent of the suffixes.

The poet starts by speaking of "Your thought," "Your heaven," and "Your name." That is the last time he addresses God. He then speaks of "my dwelling place" and "my thoughts." At the poem's climax in verse 4 we have "my mind" (literally "my heart"), "when I look" (literally "in my looking"), and "inside" (literally "into my inside"); in each of these phrases the pronoun consists simply of the vowel *ī* suffixed to a noun. But besides these three occurrences of the first person pronoun, there are no fewer than four other occurrences in the verse of its characteristic vowel or its short equivalent, *i*. The result is a salvo of *ī*'s:

hagīg libī bᵉhabītī bᵉqirbī

so that the poem climaxes acoustically on the "I" of the poet rather than on the "You" of God.

There is another form of the first person pronoun that helps to determine the poem's structure and meaning. This is the vowel of the rhyme syllable *ai*, a pronominal suffix meaning "my" used with nouns in the plural. In conformity with the rules of prosody, this rhyme-syllable occurs at the end of the first hemistich and at the end of each of the poem's four verses. At the end of verse 3 the poet prepares us for the climax when he rhymes with the relatively uncommon word *adanai* (my foundations), a word distinguished from the name of God by only a single vowel. The actual climax comes at the end of the final verse: the same consonants form the rhyme word, but the vowel is changed so that the poem actually does end (as an alert listener might almost have anticipated) with God's name. The sacred word closes the poem on a ringing note, in part because its arrival seems inevitable, having been hinted at at the end of the preceding verse. Further, we have noted the sense of finality lent by biblical verses to the last line of a poem. In this case the concluding words are part of a very familiar quotation, "Bless the Lord, O my soul," from Psalm 104:1.[3]

But precisely because the name of God forms the climax of a poem that turns so decisively on the various forms and sounds of the first person singular pronoun, the semantic content of its own suffix is stressed. Since *adonai* has become a fixed term meaning God, an equivalent of His name, its literal meaning is not ordinarily given any special weight. But here we cannot escape the reminder that the name of God itself contains the first person pronoun, since literally it means "my lord." In this final verse, then, both of the sounds associated with "I"—*i* and *ai*—come together in God. The vivid sound effects create the illusion that the poem's meaning could almost be derived from them alone, without recourse to the imagery of verses 1–3.

The biblical verse at the poem's end draws attention to itself also through a breakdown in symmetry between verse 4 and the two preceding verses. In verses 2 and 3 observed objects, the heavens and the earth, are matched with the thought of God's creative activity. The third object is not matched with an idea but with an action.[4] Taken by itself, and literally, this verse might appear to mean nothing more original than that man's reason, after contemplating the phenomena mentioned in verses 2 and 3, tells him to praise God.[5] This would be standard theology; but it bespeaks too indirect a link with God for the Ibn Gabirol who wrote poems 21 and 22. Rather, the breakdown of the parallelism tells us that here again we have a leap from observation and reason to automatic action. When man's mind progresses from contemplation of God in externals to the contemplation of God within, his thinking itself becomes an act of worship, and the act of contemplation, an act of praise.

——╴┤——╴┤——╴╷╷//—╴┤——╴┤——╴╻

יְדַעְתִּיךָ בְּשֵׁם נִשָּׂא וְגֵאֶה / וְשֵׁרַתִּיךָ בְּמִפְעָל לֹא בְנִרְאֶה.

צְפוּנְי דַעְתְּךָ הֶלְאוּ חֲכָמִים / וְדַעַת נִשְׂגָּבָה נִפְלֵאת וְתִלְאֶה.

חֲקַרְתִּיךָ—וְהִנֵּה בֵין זְמַמַי / בְּעֵין לֵב אֶמְצָאֶה אוֹתְךָ וְאֶרְאֶה.

קְשׁוּרַת כְּסֵאֲךָ נֶפֶשׁ נְפָחְתָּהּ—/ וְאִם שָׁכְנָה בְּגוּף נִדְכֶּה וְנִכְאֶה.

אֱנוֹשׁ נִרְאֶה וְלֹא רוֹאֶה הֲיַשִּׂיג / כְּבוֹד נוֹרָא בְּלִי נִרְאֶה וְרוֹאֶה?

יצחק אבן גיאת

·24·

By name I know You, High and Lofty One;
    Your deeds reveal You to me, not my eye.
The secrets of Your mind weary the wise—
    Too wonderful, too lofty, too profound.

I sought You out and found You in my thoughts:
    My heart has eyes within that let me see.
The soul You breathed in me clings to Your throne,
    Though it resides in a battered, aching clod.

Can seen, unseeing mortals hope to grasp
    The awful, glorious, unseen, seeing God?

Isaac Ibn Ghiyath

·24·

This poem by Isaac Ibn Ghiyath follows a pattern of thought already familiar to us from Ibn Gabirol. God can be seen only indirectly, by the application of the mind (the "heart's eye") to the mystery of creation. The nearest object of such study, and the most direct route to God, is therefore the soul of man, implanted by God in the perishable body. The theme is fortified by allusions to Psalm 139, which, as we have seen, was a key biblical text for medieval Jewish religious thinkers.[1] But our poem alters the language of the psalm and reverses the roles of knower and known.

The psalm begins with the feeling of transparency described by Ibn Gabirol in poem 20: as the creator, God knows man's thoughts better than man does himself. In the words of the Psalmist: "O Lord, You have searched me, and You know." In our poem this becomes "I searched You out and found You in my thoughts." Whereas in the psalm God searches out man's inner thoughts and thereby knows the man, in the poem man searches out *his own* inner thoughts and thereby comes to know God. The idea is formulated clearly enough in verse 3 of the poem, but it gains even more certainty when the verse is contrasted with the source of its wording.[2]

An even more daring reversal of biblical material occurs in the opening sentence,"By name I know you" alludes to Exodus 33:12, where God is said to have known Moses by name, a key passage for philosophical-minded exegetes. It occurs in the course of the confrontation between God and Moses after the incident of the Golden Calf. Moses needs to be reassured that God will not withdraw His protection from the people during their trek through the desert. In stirring language, he evokes the intimacy of his relationship with God until that point: "You have said, *'I know you by name* and you have found favor in my eyes.'"[3] In the Exodus story the expression means that God knew Moses with great familiarity, brought him close to Himself, and showed him favor. But to our philosopher-poets Moses represented the highest possible level of human spiritual development, and this passage is one of the descriptions of that state. By using a phrase associated with Moses' relationship to God, the poet implies that his internal examination has brought him to Moses' level of spiritual insight. He goes even a step further by reversing the Bible's pronouns: it is not that God knows him but that he knows God. This daring reversal confirms the reversal of Psalm 139, which also uses the words "You know," as we have already noted.

The last verse ends the poem with wonderful riddle-like rhetorical density, balancing man and God and contrasting their powers in such a way as to emphasize their similarity. The rhetoric plays on the theme of seeing, and once again the poet reverses the meaning of a traditional phrase. The midrash says that God is "seeing, yet unseen."[4] But the poet has already told us that he sees God with his "heart's eye," and he compares himself in this respect to Moses. God is, in this sense, visible, and man can see Him. This recalls the other half of the midrash, which says that the soul resembles God in that it too is "seeing, yet unseen." Thus man is more like God than he is used to imagining.

The formulation of the last line uses rhetorical means to undermine its own logical content. The words mean that man cannot see God, but the sounds stress the essential identity of man and God: if man and God are separated, it is not by much, for only the placement of the letter *nun*, the mark of the passive voice, tells us which one is visible and which one invisible. Teasing us with sound effects, the poet shows us that man and God share even that *nun*, for he calls them, respectively, *enosh* (literally "the weak one") and *nora* (literally "the awesome one"). Thus acknowledging the doctrinally correct idea that man cannot really know God, the poet manages to confirm at the poem's end the audacious immanence expressed in the poem's opening.

———|◡—|◡—◡—//———|◡—|◡—

לִקְרַאת מְקוֹר חַיֵּי אֱמֶת אָרוּצָה—/עַל כֵּן בְּחַיֵּי שָׁוְא וָרִיק אָקוּצָה.
לִרְאוֹת פְּנֵי מַלְכִּי מְגַמָּתִי לְבַד—/לֹא אֶרֶץ בִּלְתּוֹ וְלֹא אַעֲרִיצָה.
מִי יִתְּנֵנִי לַחֲזוֹתוֹ בַחֲלוֹם—/אִישַׁן שְׁנַת עוֹלָם וְלֹא אָקִיצָה.
לוּ אֶחֱזֶה פָנָיו בְּלִבִּי בֵּיתָה—/לֹא שָׁאֲלוּ עֵינַי לְהַבִּיט חוּצָה.

יהודה הלוי

Toward the source of life, of truth, I run,
   Impatient with a life of vanity,
To see my Master's face is all I want,
   None other do I fear, none else revere.

If only I could see Him in a dream,
   I'd sleep at ease, not caring if I died.
If I could see His face within my heart,
   My eyes would never turn their gaze outside.

Judah Halevi

This is probably not a liturgical poem, but it belongs here by virtue of its close thematic relationship with the preceding poems.

The "source of life" is, of course, God, from whom the soul indirectly emanates. The term is part of the Neoplatonic legacy to medieval Jewish thought, and it figures prominently in the poetry of the Golden Age as well as in philosophical texts.

Halevi longed for divine visions, for personal contact with God. His language is similar to that of the Muslim mystic Dhū 'l-Nūn al-Miṣrī: "My wish is that once before I die I might know Him for an instant."[1] Next to such aspirations, everything else in life would seem insipid. In contrasting the "life of vanity" with the "source of life," Halevi is not, like the moralists, merely contrasting a life of bad values and materialism with the life of virtue and piety. Rather, he is condemning all of life in the mundane world—everything that is not God—and advocating total absorption in the eternal.

The mystic's longing to see God in a dream is related to a theme of secular love poetry, where the separated lovers are said to visit each other in night-visions. To see the beloved in a dream is one of the chief desires of the frustrated lover in Arabic and Hebrew love poetry. The echo of this erotic visitation, audible to readers familiar with the traditions of love poetry, lends verse 3 a degree of tenderness.

The longing for visions of God, though common to the religious poets of the Golden Age—poem 24 was a good example—is a typically Halevian theme. We have already seen in Chapter I how Halevi tends to seek the more concrete and unmediated manifestations of religious experience; he does not stress the quest for God through the workings of the rational faculty, so central for Ibn Gabirol. Likewise, the aspiration for a passive reception of God's presence, expressed so beautifully in verses 3–4, is pure Halevi and closer to the religious world of some of the Muslim mystics than to the world of the Neoplatonists. Rābiʿa, for example, preferred not to look at flowers in spring; instead, she closed the windows and contemplated the creator of flowers and springtime.[2] Compare this with the last verse of our poem. Halevi shares with her a preference for the internal experience, for being alone with God, for direct experience of Him. It is thus probable that Halevi would have judged as frivolous Ibn Ghiyath's cheerful, confident acceptance of man's limitations, as expressed in poem 24.

——◡|——◡|——◡||——◡|——◡|——◡

שְׁחִי לָאֵל, יְחִידָה הַחֲכָמָה, / וְרוּצִי לַעֲבֹד אוֹתוֹ בְּאֵימָה.

לְעוֹלָמֵךְ פְּנִי לֵילֵךְ וְיוֹמֵךְ, / וְלָמָּה תִרְדְּפִי הֶבֶל וְלָמָּה؟

מְשׁוּלָה אַתְּ בְּחַיּוּתֵךְ לְאֵל חַי, / אֲשֶׁר גֶעְלָם כְּמוֹ אַתְּ נַעֲלָמָה.

הֲלֹא אִם יוֹצְרֵךְ טָהוֹר וְנָקִי— / דְּעִי כִּי כֵן טְהוֹרָה אַתְּ וְתַמָּה.

חֲסִין יִשָּׂא שְׁחָקִים עַל זְרוֹעוֹ— / כְּמוֹ תִשְׂאִי גְוִיָּה גֶאֱלָמָה.

זְמִירוֹת קַדְּמִי,   נַפְשִׁי, לְצוּרֵךְ / אֲשֶׁר לֹא שָׂם דְּמוּתֵךְ בָּאֲדָמָה.

קְרָבִי, בָּרְכוּ תָמִיד לְצוּרְכֶם / אֲשֶׁר לִשְׁמוֹ תְּהַלֵּל כָּל נְשָׁמָה.

שלמה אבן גבירול

·26·

Submit to God, my cerebrating soul,
    And run to worship Him in holy dread.
To your true world devote your nights and days—
    Why, why so bent on chasing empty breath?

For you, like God, have everlasting life,
    And He is hidden just as you are hid;
And is your God immaculate and pure?
    You too are pure, you too are innocent.
The Mighty One bears the heavens in His arm,
    Just as you bear the mortal, speechless clay.

My soul, greet God, your Rock, with gifts of praise,
    For nothing has He put on earth like you.
My body, bless your Rock for evermore,
    To whom the soul of All sings ever praise.

Solomon Ibn Gabirol

This poem builds on a series of comparisons between God and the soul of man, a theme that had its origins in the ancient Stoic philosophers and that left traces in the Talmud and midrash. The resemblance between God and man, that is, the conception of man as microcosm, was also taken up by Muslim and Jewish philosophers and mystics.[1]

In the Middle Ages the animating part of man was understood to consist of three souls: living, sensing, and thinking, the last of which is of divine origin. Ibn Gabirol refers to it here as "wise soul," literally "wise Only One," which I have taken the liberty of translating "cerebrating soul." We have seen that the biblical term "only one" suited the purposes of the philosopher-poets particularly well. It could be understood to allude to their conception of the soul of the individual as part of the universal soul, separated from it temporarily in order to animate a particular person, but destined eventually to return to its source.[2] It also suggested loneliness, implying a personified soul that feels out of place in the mundane world, where it is isolated from its divine source.

In verse 2 the poet exhorts his soul to seek its own world, the divine world where it rightly belongs, as opposed to the world of vanity. Two words for vanity are employed. The first is *hevel*, literally "a breath of air," commonly used to denote something of no substance. The second, *lamma*, is rather more complicated. Its ordinary meaning is "why," and this is the meaning used at the beginning of the hemistich. On a first impression, the hemistich is most naturally interpreted as "Why pursue vanity, why?" The translation follows this, the simplest interpretation, as best conveying the sense of cajoling produced in the Hebrew by having the line begin and end with the same word of interrogation. But in several early sources, *lamma* is used as a synonym for vanity.[3] According to this usage the hemistich should probably be understood as meaning "Why pursue vanity and nullity?" But even more interesting is yet a third usage, which derives from the vocabulary of philosophy. "Why" is one of the four questions that may be asked about anything: Does it exist? What is it? How does

it exist? Why does it exist? The first of these questions applies to
God; the others apply only to lower beings. The question asked
in verse 2 is really "Why concern yourself with things of which
one may ask, Why?" that is, with anything other than God.[4]

Thus the "world" to which the soul is urged to devote all its
attention is not the mundane world (which is the ordinary mean-
ing of 'olam in Golden Age poetry) but the upper world, where
the soul is truly at home. For that reason it is called "*your* world."[5]
As if to demonstrate the kinship between the soul and this divine
world, the poem then enumerates the points of comparison be-
tween it and God.

The versions of the list of comparisons, as they appear in the
poem and in the various rabbinic sources, are not identical, though
the poem is closest to the Midrash on Psalms. These differences
are of less concern to us, however, than is one significant formal
difference: in some versions, God is compared to the soul; in oth-
ers, the soul is compared to God. Because the direction of the com-
parison is consistent within each version, it is not particularly strik-
ing. Our poem differs from the rabbinic sources in having no
consistent formulaic pattern for the comparison and no consis-
tent direction of comparison. The compared objects keep shifting
position: you are eternal, like God; God is invisible, like you. He
is pure—so are you; he carries the heavens just as you carry the
body. The poet seems to be playing with the hierarchical relation-
ship of the two items of comparison, mixing them up so that now
God, now the soul serves as the pivot around which the other
turns. Logically, of course, God is the dominant figure in the com-
parison, but the formulation teases us with the notion that the
soul and God are a reversible equation, an idea often hinted at by
Ibn Gabirol, as we have seen.

One attribute shared by God and the soul in most of the rab-
binic versions of this tradition is that each is unique in its own
sphere. Ibn Gabirol does not put this item in terms of a comparison
but simply asserts in verse 6 that God made the soul unique in its
sphere, the lower world. The reader can be counted on to infer
that this, too, is a point of comparison with God, who is unique
in the universe. By ending the series of comparisons with an ab-
solute statement of the soul's uniqueness, the poet provides an

explanation of the epithet "Only One" at the poem's beginning. The poet may have understood the wording of the passage in the midrash as an explanation of that term. Thus, the passage in the Midrash on Psalms reads, "Just as the soul is unique [y*ḥida*] in the body, so God is unique in the world."

But more importantly, ending the list with this assertion of the soul's uniqueness allays any doubts that may have been raised by the shifting wording of the poem's middle section as to whether it is the soul or God that dominates the poet's religious imagination. As we have seen before with Ibn Gabirol, however attentive he is to God's tremendous majesty, it is nevertheless the soul of man that is always at the center of his religious consciousness.

The last explicit comparison between God and the soul occasions a reference to the body, which is called literally "the mute corpse." "Mute" is a very suitable adjective for use in contrasting body and soul, because the Arabic word *nāṭiq* and its medieval Hebrew equivalent *m*e*daber* mean both "speaking" and "rational." Among the three animating forces within the body it is the rational faculty, identified with speech, that sets man apart from other beings, animate and inanimate.

Since the body is mute, it is the soul that is exhorted in the first instance to sing God's praise. But the body is not neglected; it, too, must do its part in the service of the soul. The object exhorted to praise God in verse 7 is called, literally, "my insides." It is tempting to understand this word as referring to the soul, like "my soul" of verse 6. This seems especially reasonable in view of the passage in Psalms to which the poet here alludes. These two words are used there in parallel clauses, apparently as synonyms:

> Bless the Lord, O my soul
> And all my insides, [bless] His holy name.[6]

But that would not advance the theme at all. Besides, *qerev* is often used in the Bible to mean the flesh-and-blood inside of the body, specifically, the entrails. It sounds as if a contrast with verse 6 is intended. This impression is confirmed by Abraham Ibn Ezra's comment on the passage from Psalms:

["My soul":] this is the upper soul [*n^eshama ^celyona*]; "and all my insides" is said of the body, which is the flesh . . . . It is [to be understood] thus: "Bless the Lord, O my soul, and all my insides bless His holy name." . . . He mentions the ineffable name explicitly together with the soul and the name of God with the body; . . . he does not mention the ineffable name together with the insides explicitly, but only by allusion.

This is exactly the kind of distinction that Ibn Gabirol had in mind. He was surely thinking of Psalm 103:1, which figures prominently in the liturgy, when he wrote the poem.

———|–◡–|–◡–//———|–◡–|–◡–

טֶרֶם הֱיוֹתִי חַסְדְּךָ בָאַנִי, / הַשֵּׁם לְיֵשׁ אַיִן וְהִמְצִיאַנִי.

מִי הוּא אֲשֶׁר רָקַם תְּמוּנָתִי? וּמִי / עַצְמִי בְכוּר יָצַק וְהִקְפִּיאַנִי?

מִי הוּא אֲשֶׁר נָפַח נְשָׁמָה בִי? וּמִי / בֶּטֶן שְׁאוֹל פָּתַח וְהוֹצִיאַנִי?

מִי נִהֲגַנִי מִנְּעוּרַי עַד הֲלֹם? / מִי לִמְּדַנִי בִין וְהִפְלִיאַנִי?

אָמְנָם אֲנִי חֹמֶר בְּקֶרֶב יָדְךָ; / אַתָּה עֲשִׂיתַנִי, אֱמֶת, לֹא אָנִי.

אוֹדֶה עֲלֵי פִשְׁעִי וְלֹא אֹמַר לְךָ / כִּי הֶעָרִים נָחָשׁ וְהִשִּׁיאַנִי.

אֵיכָה אֲכַחֵד מִמְּךָ חֲטָאַי? הֲלֹא / טֶרֶם הֱיוֹתִי חַסְדְּךָ בָאַנִי!

שלמה אבן גבירול

·27·

Before I was, Your kindness came to me,
        When You made nothing be, when You created me.

Who was it wove my form? Who poured
        And fired my matter in the kiln?
Who was it breathed in me the soul? Who opened
        Sheol's womb and let me go forth free?
Who guided me till now from infancy?
        Who gave me thought, my gift distinctively?
True, to you I never can be more than clay.
        True, You made me; never I made me.

I own my guilt; I do not say I strayed
        Because some snake beguiled me craftily.
How could I hide my sin from You? For see:
        Before I was, Your kindness came to me.

                                    Solomon Ibn Gabirol

With its identical beginning and end,[1] its anaphoras, and its evocation of the contrary emotions of wonder and horror at the vision of the foundry where life was created, this poem cannot help but remind the English reader of *The Tyger* by William Blake. Like Blake's poem, it is a song of experience; to read it as a song of innocence is to miss the point.[2]

The poem begins on a positive note with an allusion to the election motif of Jeremiah 1:5, where God says: "Before I created you in the womb, I selected you; before you were born, I consecrated you." But already in verse 1b we are caught in a web of ambiguity. The Hebrew words with which God is addressed, *"hasam l*e*yesh* c*ayin,"* can legitimately be translated "O You who made nonbeing into being"; but it would not naturally occur to one hearing the poem for the first time to understand it so. The meaning that comes to mind on a first hearing is precisely the opposite: "O you who made being into nonbeing."[3] The auditor comes around to the doctrinally correct interpretation as an afterthought. I have done my best to reproduce this ambiguity, because it is essential for interpreting the poem correctly. In expressing apparent gratitude to God for creating man, the poet has chosen words implying that this loving act of physical creation was actually an act of destruction.

This bitterness has to do not so much with the creation of any individual person (though much of Ibn Gabirol's personal poetry is gloomy to the point of utter despair) as with the human species. True, the expressions for the creation of man in verse 2 derive from biblical passages in which individuals speak of their own prenatal formation and birth.[4] And true, the pronominal suffix meaning "I" at the end of each verse of the poem lends it a characteristically personal tone. But the end of the first line already frames the discussion in broader terms by using the philosophical terminology of "being" and "nonbeing." Further, the rephrasing of the biblical passages in verse 2 brings together the words "form" and "matter" in balanced hemistichs. Taken alone, neither word calls attention to itself, but once juxtaposed they bring the reader into the realm of philosophical discourse and raise the subject matter to the level of the species. The reference to God's breathing the soul into man alludes to the quickening of Adam, and therefore keeps the discourse on this level.[5]

Even when the words of the poem seem to point more to the individual, as in verse 4, the poet's eye is always on the species. "I am clay" in verse 5 means "I am Your creature for You to mold," as in the famous parable in Jeremiah 18. But the word translated "clay" also has the technical meaning "matter" in the language of philosophers, that is, the substratum of all things, that which receives forms. The personal tone of the line is at odds with its theoretical content. The speaker adopts such personal diction in speaking of the species of man because his reflections arise from introspection, from the habit of studying himself, the microcosm, as a key to understanding the macrocosm, from the habit of seeing the individual as a reduced version of the whole. We have seen this poet filled with wonder when contemplating the meaning of the soul. Here we see him filled with despair as he contemplates the meaning of flesh.

The workshop in which this flesh of man was made is not Eden but Sheol. To disregard the connotations of such a striking phrase, to explain it merely as a metaphor for the mother's womb, citing biblical proof texts and medieval commentators, is to miss the poem's complexities and to betray the poet.

The expression "the belly of Sheol" occurs once in the Bible: Jonah uses it in his psalm of thanksgiving to describe the trouble from which God saved him, a situation unrelated to our poem.[6] More important is the fact that it corresponds in meaning to the expression "the underneath of the world," where the Psalmist in Psalm 139:15 locates his own origins.[7] This passage was undoubtedly on Ibn Gabirol's mind, as it is alluded to by the word *ruqamti* ("formed," here translated "wove") in verse 2.[8] Although the Aramaic translation of the psalm understood the "underneath" of the world as the womb, it seems on the literal level more suitable to the origin of the species than of the individual. At least one philosophical-minded medieval commentator understood it so.[9]

When Ibn Gabirol says that God opened the belly of Sheol to release the newly made man, he is expressing philosophical anguish over man's very nature. To say that the body and the soul were united in the place where the Bible locates the shades of the dead, in a world whose name is synonymous with the grave, is to say indirectly that the life of man is spiritual death. This idea comes as no surprise to readers of Ibn Gabirol's secular poetry, where he more than once adopts this notion of extreme Islamic asceticism. Compare, for example, his famous line "The day of my joy is the day of my death; / and the day of my death, my joy."[10]

Verse 5 sums up the series of God's actions on behalf of man in two sentences that affirm God's total responsibility for man's creation. Each sentence contains a word of affirmation, here translated "truly." These words would be poetically weak unless they were intended to call attention to something that might otherwise be overlooked. Their purpose is probably to alert us to the double meaning of the statements they affirm: "I am clay in Your hands" means that man is completely in God's control and owes Him gratitude; it also means that man can be no better than God made him. This is "the cry from the house of the potter, 'Why hast thou made me thus?'"[11] It lays the groundwork for the two verses that conclude the poem with the acknowledgment of sin, which is the point of the poem.

Verses 6 and 7 alone, or in some other poem, might express humble contrition, as if to say, "I admit my sin, I do not seek extenuation on the grounds of having been led astray by cunning seducers." But after the hints in the preceding verses, they cannot mean anything of the kind. On the contrary, they seek extenuation; they deny responsibility on the part of the speaker and refer the sin to the One who made man what he is.

Verse 6 returns to the Garden of Eden. If we insist on reading the poem from the perspective of the individual worshiper, we might interpret it as follows: I admit my sin; I do not try to blame it on seducers outside myself. But if we keep our eye on that serpent, we are reminded that we are speaking of the origin of mankind, not of individual man. In Ibn Gabirol's allegorical interpretation of the Garden of Eden, the serpent represents the vegetative and the animal souls.[12] God knows that man is made partly of base elements; there is no need to remind Him that man must inevitably sin. How could man think to hide his sin from God, when God's favor—the joining of form to matter, of soul to body—preceded the individual man and is the very foundation of the species? The verbatim repetition of the opening hemistich is now a bitter reflection on the destructiveness of God's act of creating man: the sullying of the soul, the turning of being into nonbeing. "How could I hide my sin from You" is not the humble expression of that feeling of being transparent before God that we have seen before. Rather, it is a taunt. Thus, when the words of the opening hemistich return at the poem's end, they are laden with bitterness, a stunning reversal of their emotional content.

It is even possible that the word *ḥesed* has literally changed meaning in the repetition, that it is not an ironic use of the word meaning kindness but a homonym with a different meaning altogether. In Leviticus 20:17 the word is used in connection with the sins of the flesh to mean "something disgusting." Could Ibn Gabirol have wanted us to think of this meaning of *ḥesed* at the poem's end? Whether we go this far or not, it certainly is no exaggeration to see irony in the use of a form—the repetition of the opening hemistich at the end—otherwise associated with poems of humble contrition.

—‒◡|—‒◡|—‒◡//—‒◡|—‒◡|—‒◡

יְדַעְתַּנִי בְּטֶרֶם תְּצָרֵנִי, / וְכָל עוֹד רוּחֲךָ בִי—תִּצְּרֵנִי.

הֲיֵשׁ לִי מַעֲמָד אִם תֶּהְדְּפֵנִי, / וְאִם לִי מַהֲלָךְ אִם תַּעְצְרֵנִי?

וּמָה אֹמַר?—וּמַחְשָׁבִי בְּיָדְךָ! / וּמָה אוּכַל עֲשֹׂה עַד תַּעְזְרֵנִי?

דְּרַשְׁתִּיךָ בְּעֵת רָצוֹן—עֲנֵנִי, / וְכַצֹּנָּה רְצוֹנְךָ תַּעְטְרֵנִי.

הֲקִימֵנִי לְשַׁחֵר אֶת דְּבִירֶךָ, / וְאֶת שִׁמְךָ לְבָרֵךְ עוֹרְרֵנִי.

יהודה הלוי

Before I came to be, You did select me,
 And while Your breath is in me You protect me.
Where can I stand steady if You shake me?
 How can I find my way if You deflect me?
What can I say?—My very thoughts are Yours.
 Whatever can I do if You neglect me?
I come to You in time of favor—hear me!
 Shield me with Your grace, do not reject me.
Rouse me at dawn to come into Your temple,
 To bless Your great and holy name direct me.

Judah Halevi

The verb *yada‘* with which this poem opens means "to know," with that verb's overtones of intimate, even sexual, knowledge. But beyond that, the nearly verbatim allusion in the first hemistich to Jeremiah's inaugural vision justifies seeing it as an expression of the poet's personal feeling that he stands in a special protected relationship with God. At the same time, the allusion and the common opening that this poem shares with the preceding poem invite comparison.

We have on more than one occasion noted the tone of intimacy in these short poems, the sense of mutuality between God and the speaker evoked by the constant balancing of the speaker's "I" with God's "You." We have also seen how this claim to intimacy is related to the notion of the divine origin of the soul, the poet's consciousness of an essential kinship between God and himself, the notion that in some mysterious way God exists within man.

This poem maintains the same tone of intimacy but reverses diametrically the relative positions of man and God. Every phrase of this poem places God *outside* man. The speaker feels himself wholly subject to a transcendent, omnipotent will, to which he submits in love and trust. His religious stance is not the complex, bitter piety of poem 27 but the accepting, tranquil mood of *tawakkul*.

Yet considered in abstract theological terms, this poem does not differ from the preceding ones in seeing the soul as a piece of the divine implanted in man. The theological assumptions are the same; the difference resides in the poet's different orientation toward that assumption. His response to the realization that he embodies a divine soul is not to feel a surge of divine power that seeks to burst the bounds of his body, or that raises him to the level of the angels, or that embitters him because it is hemmed in by flesh. It is, rather, a consciousness of God's controlling, sustaining, protecting efforts on his behalf.

The effect is won partly through the poem's syntactic organization. Ten verbs have God as subject and the speaker as object; the speaker is the subject of only three verbs, and of these, two occur in parallel clauses that assert the speaker's lack of power to act independently. The speaker's only direct action is to pray (verse 4, "I seek You"), and that, he stresses, only at a time acceptable to God: God controls even the poet's turning to Him. And what is the content of the speaker's prayer on that occasion? Nothing more ambitious than to be shielded and to be granted the ability to continue to rise and pray.

The studied passivity of this poem is most palpable in the last verse, where the poet cannot even rouse himself to pray unless God wakes him and grants him the words. It is a devotion of gentle submission that contrasts starkly with the stormy outbursts of Ibn Gabirol that we have read.

אַחֲלַי יִכּוֹנוּ דְרָכַי / לִשְׁמֹר חֻקֶּיךָ,
כִּי מְנוּחָה לֹא מָצָאתִי / כִּי אִם בְּחִשְׁקֶךָ.
עַבְדְּךָ אֲנִי—הַדְרִיכֵנִי / בְּדֶרֶךְ צִדְקֶךָ.
הֵן שְׁאֵלָתִי אַחַת הִיא— / לְהָפִיק רְצוֹנֶךָ.
לֹא אֲבַקֵּשׁ מִלְּפָנֶיךָ / כִּי אִם פָּנֶיךָ.

בֶּאֱמֶת אֵין עֲרֹךְ אֵלֶיךָ— / וְאֵיךְ אֲמַשִּׁילֶךָּ?
אוֹ לְמִי אֲדַמֶּה פְּעָלֶיךָ? / וְהַכֹּל פָּעֳלֶךָ!
אַתָּ בְּרָאתַנִי—וּמָה אוֹסִיף / לְדַבֵּר אֵלֶיךָ?
מַחְשְׁבוֹת רוּחִי וְקִנְיָנִי / הֵם קִנְיָנֶךָ.
לֹא לְמַעֲנִי אַתָּה עוֹשֶׂה / כִּי אִם לְמַעֲנֶךָ.

רֹאשׁ וְסוֹף אֵין לַחֲסָדֶיךָ— / וּמִי לֹא יוֹדֶךָּ?
וֶאֱמֶת אֵין בִּלְעָדֶיךָ / וּמַעֲשֵׂה יָדֶיךָ;
וַאֲשֶׁר בְּשִׁמְךָ כְּחָשׁוּ— / הֵם הֵם עֵדֶיךָ.
יַחֲשֹׁב לִבִּי כֹּה וָכֹה— / הִנֵּה הִנֶּךָּ!
אֶפְגָּעֲךָ בָךְ, כִּי אֵין מַבְדִּיל / בֵּינִי וּבֵינֶךָ.

מִלְּפָנֶיךָ אֲנִי יוֹצֵא / וְרוּצִי אַחֲרֶיךָ.
מַחֲזֵה בַּל חָזוּ עֵינַי / לְבַד מֵהֲדָרֶךָ;
מַאֲמָר לֹא שָׁמְעוּ אָזְנַי— / רַק מַאֲמָרֶיךָ.
אוֹת חָתְמוּ לִבִּי—הִנֶּךָ / רוֹאֶה בְעֶגְנֶיךָ,
וַאֲשֶׁר סֵפֶר פִּי—הִנֶּה— / עוֹלֶה בְּאָזְנֶיךָ!

עַל אֲסִיר יֵצֶר רַע צַוֵּה / יְשׁוּעוֹת פָּנֶיךָ.
זָכְרֵךְ בְּפִיו שִׂים, וּבְלִבּוֹ / בְּנֵה בֵּית מְכוֹנֶךָ.
רַחֲמֵהוּ בְּשֵׂאתוֹ עֵינָיו / לְכִסֵּא מְעוֹנֶךָ.
הֵט זְרוֹעֲךָ וּתְהִי יָדְךָ / עַל אִישׁ יְמִינֶךָ,
וּבְמַחֲשַׁכִּים עָלֵינוּ / נְסָה אוֹר פָּנֶיךָ.

אברהם אבן עזרא

O for a clear way to keeping Your commands!
For only in Your love do I find rest.
I am Your servant; guide me in Your ways.
    I have no care but to deserve Your grace;
    I only ask that I may see Your face.

Nothing is like You; what trope can I use
For You or for Your works, when they are everything?
You made me: what else should I say to You?
    To You belong my thoughts and all my wealth.
    You made them not for me, but for Yourself.

Your grace is infinite; who would not praise?
For nothing else is; only Your works and You,
As those who deny Your name themselves attest.
    Whichever way I seek You, You are there,
    No bar between us—You are everywhere.

I turn from You, and, turning, to You I turn.
No vision can I see except Your light;
No speech is in my ear except Your word.
    The secret sealed in me Your eye sees clear;
    Before I speak, my speech is in Your ear.

Send grace to save Your creature, evil's slave.
Put Your name in his mouth, in his heart Your home.
Pity him as he lifts his eyes toward Your throne.
    Stretch forth Your hand, and let it on Your folk alight.
    We live in darkness—lift Your face to give us light.

                         Abraham Ibn Ezra

This poem has the peculiarity, very noticeable when it is read aloud, that each of its lines ends with the suffix meaning "you." At the same time, it fulfills all the rules of the complicated strophic poems described in the Introduction, in that it employs two different rhyme schemes: a fixed rhyme at the end of each strophe contrasting with varying rhymes peculiar to the individual strophes. The constant repetition of the suffix almost overshadows the strophic rhyme pattern and lends the poem a somewhat obsessive note. It also echoes the idea of God's constant presence in the mind's eye of the poet.

The poem begins, most unusually, with a verbatim biblical quotation, Psalm 119:5: "Would that my ways were firm in keeping Your laws"—as if the opening quotation were meant to announce that the poem is to be an exposition of the psalm as a whole. Indeed, the psalm and the poem seem to share a peculiar combination of gentle tone and passionate desire for intimacy with God. This effect is achieved in both works by the frequent recurrence of the pronouns "I" and "You," by the use of brief sentences consisting of a few ideas and key phrases that repeat over and over again, and by the avoidance of complex imagery and rhetorical fireworks. Yet the theme of God's laws is not further developed in the course of the poem. For despite the similarities, our poem is not a biblical devotion, but a medieval one, and its actual contents reflect quite a different view of what intimacy with God might actually mean.

For Psalm 119, the key to religious life is the Torah, God's laws, and God's ways. As the Masora points out, every verse but one refers to one of the following terms: God's way, Torah, testimony, precepts, speech, law, commandment, judgment, or word. In other words, the Psalmist is concerned mainly with the way one leads one's external life. In all doubts, trials, and vicissitudes, he clings to pious conduct and obedience to God's command for protection, comfort, and guidance. He keeps the rules of conduct out of love for God—and out of love for the rules themselves.

The opening of our poem is remarkably similar to Psalm 119, and not only because of the quotation in verse 1. Verses 2 and 3 are so similar in rhythm and content to many of the psalm's verses that a reader may be excused the impulse to consult the concordance to see if they too are not also quoted from it.[1] But there is a difference. Though in form and mood, a sentence like "I find rest only in Your law" would fit perfectly in Psalm 119, in the poem we read instead, "I find rest only in Your love."

The final couplet of the first stanza gives a clearer intimation of the direction the poet will take. But however the sentence is translated, it can yield its meaning only in the original, for the English words with the same meaning as the Hebrew idioms do not permit constructing a sentence with the same rhetorical balance. Literally the words mean "I seek nothing from Your face but Your face." It is possible to say in Hebrew that one seeks a thing from someone's face because "from your face" is a slightly indirect, and therefore a respectful, way of saying "from you"; it is the appropriate way to address God. It is possible to say "I seek Your face" because "face" is sometimes used in figurative expressions for "favor."[2] The advantage of using the two idiomatic faces in the same verse is that it makes the poet's desire sound mysteriously circular. The Hebrew formulation suggests the tone, if not the meaning, of paradox, as if the thing desired moves from God's face and back again.

It would be possible to render the line as "All I ask of You is You." That would convey the lexical content of the sentence, but it would mean abandoning the image of God's face, presumably the last thing to which the poet would have consented. The two faces of this line are doubtless intended to call to mind Moses, who saw God face-to-face. In his commentary on Exodus, Abraham Ibn Ezra describes Moses as the paragon of human spiritual development, having achieved in his lifetime that knowledge of God which is denied to others, even prophets and philosophers, until after death.[3] Verse 5 makes us think of this event in Moses' life, because its theme of seeking God's face reminds us of his speech to God in Exodus 33:13ff.: " . . . Pray let me know Your ways, that I may know You," of God's reply, "My face will go and I will lighten your burden," and Moses' rejoinder, "Unless Your face goes, do not make us leave this place." On rereading the stanza, the object of the speaker's yearning in verse 1, God's "way," is seen to have shifted meaning. At first it represents the Psalmist's desire to know God's laws and rules of conduct, but now it represents the philosopher's desire to know God Himself.

Stanza 2 also begins with language familiar from other poems, even from the standard liturgy. That God is incomparable is said repeatedly in the Bible, reiterated in the prayers, and given hard philosophical definition by theologians like Saadia and his followers. But the seemingly innocent parallel in the second line of the stanza gives the overly familiar idea a startling twist. That God is incomparable is a given. But are His creations, the contents of the cosmos, likewise incomparable, as the poet says? What is the meaning of this transference of one of God's attributes to His creations? We are, after all, used to comparing God's creations to one another. More than a linguistic convenience, such comparisons are the very essence of figurative language, of poetry. Yet the poet asks, apparently in all seriousness, what is the logic in such comparisons, seeing that everything in the universe is God's work? He seems to take as his axiom that all God's creations are identical by virtue of having been created by God. This reasoning leads to the additional paradox that God and His creatures are in fact comparable in their very incomparability, each in his own sphere. It is a dazzling revision of the traditional cliché that God is beyond comparison; the very idea that comparison is possible becomes empty when we give free rein to the idea, implicit in the emanationist principle, that the world is continuous with God.

The idea is personalized in the second part of the second strophe. We are familiar with the topos that human speech is inadequate to express divine truths. We have even seen in Ibn Gabirol the idea that human speech is logically unnecessary because God knows man's thoughts. Abraham Ibn Ezra takes this a step further when he says in line 9 that God Himself is the author of man's thoughts. There seems to be no reason for the poet to stop here. We prepare ourselves to hear him say that not only is God the author of man's thoughts, but that man's thoughts and God's thoughts are the same.

And indeed the third stanza takes us to the very brink of pantheism. Once again, the words are traditional, for "there is none but You and the works of Your hands" is a truism and would be unexceptionable in a traditional liturgical context. But as with the "faces" of line 5, the meaning is determined by the rhetorical formulation, not by the strict logic of the words. The internal rhyme joins the two clauses—which individually are orthodox—into a new, rhetorically dangerous whole. Line 12 now seems to give a pantheistic twist to the familiar phrase from the liturgy, "There is no God but You," as if the esoteric meaning were "There is nothing, God, but You."

The boundary of pantheism seems to be crossed in the following verses, where the poet says that whatever direction he contemplates there is nothing but God,[4] that he actually comes into contact with God because there is no boundary between them, that there is nothing to see but God's splendor, nothing to hear except God's speech. Even those who refuse to acknowledge God are testament to Him by their very existence. All that saves these verses from pantheism is that the poet still speaks as if there is an "I," an individual consciousness apart from God. His selfness is not yet identified with God, but that is the direction in which his thinking moves. The tension in the poem derives from his passionate longing to have this last barrier fall.

The first verse of stanza 4 expresses this idea by using a famous paradoxical expression, probably adopted from Arabic. The sentence, which, literally translated, reads, "When I leave Your presence I am running after You," has its origin in a tradition of Muhammad, who is said to have prayed, "I take refuge in God from God." Muhammad is supposed to have meant by this that he seeks protection in God's mercy from His anger. This is the usual meaning of the phrase, whether in Arabic or Hebrew.[5] Abraham Ibn Ezra has given it a characteristic twist, diverting it from its original context of repentance, forgiveness, and divine mercy into the realm of the existential, as if it meant "When I flee from God I find that I am fleeing to God, for there is nothing but God."

In the final stanza the language is less intense and more traditional, as the vocabulary shifts to that of the prayers for national redemption. The poet has come down to earth. He has withdrawn from his flirtation with the identification of the cosmos with God and has come to recognize that man's soul is after all bounded by the body, at least in life. At this point we are no longer surprised to find phrases taken from the traditional eschatological prayers being revalued. The traditional plea "Rebuild your Temple" is explicitly reworded here so as to ask for a temple in the worshiper's heart; and the "man at your right hand"[6] means neither Israel nor the Messiah but those who are spiritually and intellectually developed enough to achieve the knowledge of God to which philosophical-minded thinkers like Abraham Ibn Ezra aspired. Redemption here is purely a metaphor for man's realization of the divine potential in him.

———|—◡—|—◡———//———|—◡—|—◡—

כָּל כּוֹכְבֵי בֹקֶר לְךָ יָשִׁירוּ, / כִּי זָהֳרֵיהֶם מִמְּךָ יַזְהִירוּ,

וּבְנֵי אֱלֹהִים עוֹמְדִים עַל מִשְׁמָרוֹת / לַיְל וְיוֹם שָׁם גֶּאֱדָר יַאְדִּירוּ,

וּקְהַל קְדוֹשִׁים קִבְּלוּ מֵהֶם, וְכָל / שַׁחַר לְשַׁחֵר בֵּיתְךָ יָעִירוּ!

יהודה הלוי

·30·

To You the stars of morning sing,
 Because their lights from Your lights spring.
Like them the angels on their watches
 Night and day extol their King.
Your holy people follows them:
 Each dawn their songs from Your house ring.

Judah Halevi

They were medieval people, in the end. Their intellectual ideals may have taught them to value universals above particulars; their philosophical training may have stressed mankind's common heritage of a rational faculty, uniting men with each other and with God; and some even quietly taught that the specific doctrines and practices of particular religious communities could not represent absolute truth. Yet for all that, the mundane world that they inhabited was structured by monotheistic religions, each laying exclusive claim to the truth. Especially for the Jews, consciousness of their peoplehood and loyalty to their particular tradition were living issues. They constantly had to protect themselves from the common wisdom of the age: that they had been abandoned by history and were out of the running in the contest for divine favor. Halevi, who ends our anthology, in a way marks the end of the entire Golden Age. It was he who, late in life, voluntarily threw over its values and abandoned Spain to turn pilgrim just when the Almohad invasion was about to end it for his contemporaries perforce. It was also he who, in his *Kuzari*, put Israel and its revelation back at the center of religious thought in an attempt to break the hold of philosophy on his contemporaries.

This little poem harks back to a theme of the ancient liturgy. The angels in heaven praise God; Israel on earth praises God. The choirs of angels respond antiphonally to each other; Israel responds antiphonally to them. The theme occurs in the statutory prayers every day, and it was poetically elaborated by hundreds of poets throughout the Middle Ages. It was a theme that answered the desperate need of the Jews, hounded and isolated as they were, to feel themselves alone with God as the earthly members of His circle of courtiers, shutting out the nations of the world that had shut them out of the circle of historical events. It represents a supremely national view of the theme of the praise of God.

Here the universe is divided not into two but into a three-part scheme: the stars of dawn, the angels, and the holy ones. This division of the cosmos, though not usual, is also not unique. Abraham Ibn Ezra speaks of it in his Biblical commentaries.[1]

The phrase "the holy ones" of course refers to the people Israel, who share this epithet with the angels in the old liturgy. But even here, where the national theme could have been most forcefully expressed, it is muted. The three parts of the poet's universe are each assigned one line of the poem. By giving two thirds to the upper world, the poet keeps the reader's attention directed upward; and by not naming Israel explicitly, he keeps the weight off the theme of her special status. Halevi does not deny this special status; that is simply not his focus in this poem, which is, rather, the experience of praying in tandem with the heavenly spheres and the angels.

This lovely miniature encapsulates in its small scale and lofty vision the medieval Jewish dialectic of universal and particular. It thus seems a fitting conclusion to our picture of the religious poetry of the Hebrew Golden Age.

Afterword

The Golden Age of Hebrew poetry that had begun in the tenth century under the caliphate of Cordoba lasted through the successive periods of the Party Kingdoms and the Almoravids. The departure from Spain of Judah Halevi and Abraham Ibn Ezra in 1140 heralded the eclipse of Andalusian Jewry, for the following decade saw the conquest of the country by the Almohads, a fanatical Islamic revival movement that suppressed Jewish activities and forced many prominent Jewish families to flee the country. Among the refugees were the young Maimonides; the Ibn Tibbons, who were to achieve fame as translators into Hebrew from Arabic; and the Kimḥis, grammarians and Bible commentators.

The refugees carried the fruits of the intellectual tradition of the Golden Age to their new lands. But Spanish Jewish scholarship and literature were already known and esteemed throughout the Mediterranean world. Secular poetry in forms developed by the Spanish Hebrew poets was already being composed in Egypt and Iraq; poets in other parts of the Arabic-speaking world would soon be composing liturgical poetry in the new style as well; and even the synagogue poets of Christian Europe, who knew no Arabic, began to experiment with forms that had originated in the Bedouin ode. In Spain itself, though new poetry continued to be composed, some of the works of the Golden Age poets came to be adopted permanently by the various communities for their liturgies. After the expulsion in 1492 the new wave of refugees carried these works, including many of the poems in this book, to their new homes in Italy, the Ottoman Empire, and Northern Europe.

In Spain about a generation passed before the Jewish community recovered from the Almohad persecutions. By the end of the twelfth century literary activity had resumed, now relocated in the new centers of Jewish culture in the north of Spain. With the gradual decline of the prestige and influence of Arabic culture and the rise of the vernacular literatures in the various Romance languages of the peninsula, the character of Hebrew literature also changed. The second half of the literary history of Spanish Jewry, dating from about 1200 to the expulsion in 1492, is no longer considered merely epigonic. It is different from the Golden Age and deserves separate treatment.

The question has been raised as to whether the term Golden Age is still appropriate for the period covered by this book, the period of Arabic dominance in Spain. Some historians point out, quite rightly, that its high culture touched only a tiny fraction of the Jewish community; that the tolerance which the Jews enjoyed among the Muslims did not amount to equality with them; and that much of the Jews' intellectual activity did not involve the new areas of philosophy and secular poetry but merely continued their ancestral preoccupation with religious law (and, it may be added, liturgical poetry of the traditional type).[1] The historians point to the ideological considerations that motivated the German Jewish historians of the nineteenth century to attach the label Golden Age to the period.[2]

Yet, if we judge strictly by literary criteria, the Hebrew literary work written in Andalusia from the mid-tenth to the mid-twelfth century is worthy of a name that highlights its special place in the history of Hebrew letters. The Hebrew poetry of tenth-century Spain is completely revolutionary, whether we consider the innovations in poetic functions, forms, or themes, as is amply demonstrated in *Wine, Women, and Death* and in the present book. In these respects, the special character of the period was just as clear at the time as it is today.

The term Golden Age is particularly justified when we consider two criteria that are even broader than the functions, forms, and themes of poetry.

In tenth-century Spain, after six hundred years in which it produced little else but virtually anonymous communal poetry, the Hebrew language suddenly became a vehicle for the voice of the individual poet. With all the reservations with which this phrase must be qualified, there is simply no mistaking the difference between the many voices that speak in this book and the single voice of the hundreds of poets of the preceding centuries. The Golden Age produced much more than a number of prolific poets writing in new forms for new functions; it produced a number of such poets who knew how to make use of these tools to express distinctive personalities, powerful minds, sensitive souls. The only premodern Jewish community that can compete with Spain in this regard is Italy. If we value the individual voice over the monolithic voice of the community, as we twentieth-century people generally do, we owe the age that first gave these individual voices the means of self-expression an epithet that expresses our admiration and sense of kinship.

Further: In tenth-century Spain, after six hundred years in which the intellectual content of Hebrew poetry was all but restricted to themes that can ultimately be traced to the exegesis of Scripture, the Hebrew poets began to address themselves to the intellectual life they shared with serious thinkers of the rest of the world. Though they continued to make use of Scripture and scriptural exegesis as vehicles for expressing this intellectual life, and though they were loyal adherents of the covenant and active members of the Jewish community, their minds were receptive to the best thought of their age, whatever its source. This openness to the world was not a permanent legacy to Jewish history; it was too dependent on the peculiar nature of Jewish society in Muslim Spain. Again, a similar development may be observed in the Hebrew poetry of Renaissance Italy. But Spain was the pioneer, and Muslim Spain produced great figures in far greater concentration. If the Judaism we value is one that fearlessly unlocks the door to the larger world rather than the self-protective Judaism that shuts itself in, we need feel no inhibition about crowning the Hebrew poetry of Muslim Spain with a title that expresses our esteem.

It is precisely at this point that a disturbing note has recently entered the literature evaluating the achievement of the Golden Age poets. Was the discovery of the individual voice in liturgical poetry in fact desirable? It has been argued that this voice represented a centrifugal tendency within the medieval Andalusian community. Was the incorporation of science and philosophy into the outlook and writings of the poets a positive achievement? It is argued that this tendency represents a dilution of the native spirit of the religion and therefore of communal cohesiveness. By failing to suppress both tendencies, it is argued, the community prepared the way for its own disintegration when it came under pressure from Christianity in the following centuries. The behavior of the Spanish Jews in preferring conversion, Marranism, or flight to martyrdom is, by implication, compared unfavorably with that of the Jews of the medieval Rhineland.[3]

It would seem reasonable to question whether a literary movement of the tenth to twelfth centuries can be used to explain a social movement of the fourteenth and fifteenth. By the time of the mass conversions of 1391, many other historical and intellectual currents had contributed to shaping the character of Hispanic Jewry, so that the discussion of what predisposed this community to its particular reaction to oppression must take into account many other factors than the intellectual life that prevailed two or three centuries before. Furthermore, as pointed out in the Introduction to this book, much of that community's intellectual activity, including liturgical poetry, carried on the forms and themes of the Jewish tradition, modified only by evolution and unaffected by the peculiar and revolutionary traits of Golden Age literature.

But more is at stake here than such historical arguments. The critique appears to reflect a defensive reaction to the whole Andalusian experiment, as if Jewish survival necessarily depends on limiting the scope of individual expression and restricting outside influence. A dreary prescription for Jewish survival!

It seems absurd to fault the medieval Andalusian Jewish aristocracy for holding an outlook on life that so resembles our own, even allowing for all the differences between their world and ours. The mentality of Andalusian Jewry at its best seems like an ideal program for a high culture of diaspora Jewry today: individualism and worldliness in creative combination with authentic, concrete textual knowledge of the Jewish literary tradition. To fault it for its supposed outcome—even granting that the historical analysis is correct—would be to reject a positive cultural success out of fear of an unknown, unpredictable future. This is not the way of a living culture. To withhold our approbation out of a wish that the medieval Andalusian Jews had been something other than what they were is to wish that we were something other than what we ourselves are, something far less abundant with possibilities for the future.

Notes

Abbreviated Titles of Editions and Anthologies Frequently Cited in the Notes

Abraham Ibn Ezra, *Shire haqodesh*   Yisra'el Levin, ed. *Shire haqodesh shel avraham ibn ezra.* 2 vols. Jerusalem: Israel Academy of Sciences and Humanities, 1975–1982.

Carmi, *Penguin Book*   T. Carmi, ed. and trans. *The Penguin Book of Hebrew Verse.* New York: Penguin Books, 1981.

Goldstein, *Hebrew Poems*   David Goldstein, *Hebrew Poems from Spain.* New York: Schocken Books, 1966.

Ibn al-Tabban   Dan Pagis, ed. *Shire levi ibn altaban.* Jerusalem: Israel Academy of Sciences and Humanities, 1967.

Ibn Gabirol, *Selected Religious Poems*   Israel Zangwill, trans., and Israel Davidson, ed. *Selected Religious Poems of Solomon Ibn Gabirol.* Philadelphia: Jewish Publication Society of America, 1923.

Ibn Gabirol, *Shire haqodesh*   Dov Jarden, ed. *Shire haqodesh lᵉrabi shᵉlomo ibn gabirol.* 2 vols. Jerusalem: Dov Jarden and the American Academy for Jewish Research, 1971–1972.

Ibn Gabirol, *Shire shᵉlomo ibn gabirol*   Ḥayim N. Bialik and J. C. Ravnitzky. *Shire shᵉlomo ben yᵉhuda ibn gabirol.* 3 vols. Tel Aviv: Dvir, 1924–1932.

Ibn Ghiyath, *Shire ibn giyat*

Yonah David, ed. *Shire r. yiṣḥaq ibn giyat 1038–89.* Jerusalem: Akhshav, 1987–1988.

Judah Halevi, *Dīwān*

H. Brody, ed. *Dīwān des abū-l-Ḥasan Jehuda ha-Levi.* 4 vols. Berlin: Schriften des Vereins Mekize Nirdamim, 1894–1930.

Judah Halevi, *Selected Poems*

Nina Salaman, trans., and H. Brody, ed. *Selected Poems of Jehudah Halevi.* Philadelphia: Jewish Publication Society of America, 1928.

Judah Halevi, *Shire haqodesh*

Dov Jarden, ed. *Shire haqodesh lᵉrabi yᵉhuda halevi.* 4 vols. Jerusalem, 1978–1985.

Moses Ibn Ezra, *Selected Poems*

Solomon Solis-Cohen, trans., and H. Brody, ed. *Selected Poems of Moses Ibn Ezra.* Philadelphia: Jewish Publication Society of America, 1945.

Moses Ibn Ezra, *Shire haḥol*

H. Brody, ed. *Moshe ibn ezra: shire haḥol.* Vols. 1 and 2. Berlin and Jerusalem: Schocken, 1934–1942; Dan Pagis, ed., Vol. 3. Jerusalem: Schocken, 1977.

Moses Ibn Ezra, *Shire qodesh*

Shimeon Bernstein, ed. *Moshe ibn ezra: shire qodesh.* Tel Aviv: Masada, 1956–1957.

Petuchowski, *Theology and Poetry*

Jakob Petuchowski. *Theology and Poetry: Studies in the Medieval Piyyuṭ.* London: Routledge and Kegan Paul, 1978.

Schirmann, *Hashira haʿivrit*

Ḥ. Schirmann. *Hashira haʿivrit bisᵉfarad uvᵉprovans.* 2 vols. Jerusalem and Tel Aviv: Mosad Bialik and Dvir, 1954–1956.

Schirmann, *Shirim*

Ḥ. Schirmann. *Shirim ḥadashim min hagᵉniza.* Jerusalem: Israel Academy of Sciences and Humanities, 1965.

Wine, Women, and Death

Raymond P. Scheindlin. *Wine, Women, and Death: Medieval Hebrew Poems on the Good Life.* Philadelphia: Jewish Publication Society, 1986.

INTRODUCTION

1. Moses Ibn Ezra, *Shire qodesh*, pp. 62–63 (poem 57, lines 15–24). Bernstein correctly notes that the background to these lines is the life of pleasure pursued by the Andalusian Jewish aristocracy, but he misses the point that this group was Moses Ibn Ezra's own social circle.

2. For example, folly appears as a seductive woman in Prov. 7:5, 9:13–18.

3. *Wine, Women, and Death*, p. 91. For the garden as a symbol of the good life in Golden Age secular poetry, see pp. 3–8.

4. The Christian reconquest of Spain actually began in the eleventh century with the capture of Toledo in 1085, but for Jewish culture the watershed was c. 1145, when the capture of the Muslim territories by the fanatical Muslim Almohads drove the Jewish intelligentsia into the Christian territories and many of its members

out of Spain altogether. For a sketch of the history of Muslim Spain, see W. Montgomery Watt, *A History of Islamic Spain* (Edinburgh: University Press, 1965), and David Wasserstein, *The Rise and Fall of the Party Kings: Politics and Society in Islamic Spain 1002–1086* (Princeton: Princeton University Press, 1985).

5. For the sociopolitical status of the Jews under medieval Islam, see Bernard Lewis, *The Jews of Islam* (Princeton: Princeton University Press, 1984); for the history of the Iberian Jewry under Islam, see Eliyahu Ashtor, *The Jews of Moslem Spain*, 3 vols., trans. Aaron Klein and Jenny Machlowitz (Philadelphia: Jewish Publication Society, 1973–1984); and Wasserstein, *Rise and Fall*, pp. 190–223.

6. *Wine, Women, and Death*, pp. 30–31; Raymond P. Scheindlin, "Rabbi Moshe Ibn Ezra on the Legitimacy of Poetry," *Medievalia et Humanistica*, n.s., 7 (1976): 101–115; Ross Brann, *The Compunctious Poet: Cultural Ambiguity and Hebrew Poetry in Muslim Spain* (Baltimore: Johns Hopkins University Press, 1991).

7. Quran 26:224–226, cited from Mohammad M. Pickthall, *The Meaning of the Glorious Koran* (New York: New American Library, n.d.). The classic treatment of the antithesis of the tribal values of the Age of Ignorance and the religious values of the Age of Islam is Ignaz Goldziher, *Muslim Studies*, ed. S. M. Stern and trans. C. R. Berber and S. M. Stern (London: George Allen and Unwin, 1967), 1:16–44 (first published in 1888). See also Annemarie Schimmel, *As through a Veil: Mystical Poetry in Islam* (New York: Columbia University Press, 1982), pp. 11–14.

8. Thor Andrae, *Islamische Mystik*, 2d ed. (Stuttgart: Verlag W. Kohlhammer, 1980), pp. 13ff.

9. Abū 'l-ʿAtāhīya, *Dīwān* ed. L. Cheikho (Beirut: Jesuit Press, 1887). I wish to thank Professor Julie Scott Meisami of Wolfson College, Oxford, for providing me with this example.

10. For further discussion of *zuhd* as a secular theme, see *Wine, Women, and Death*, Chapter III, and below, pp. 21–22.

11. The formulation is that of Annemarie Schimmel, *Mystical Dimensions of Islam*, (Chapel Hill: University of North Carolina Press, 1975), pp. 98–99. The whole chapter "The Path" is relevant, pp. 98–186. For the cosmopolitanism of Sufism, see, for example, Reynold A. Nicholson, *The Mystics of Islam* (London: G. Bell and Sons, 1914), pp. 68–101; Marshall Hodgson, *The Venture of Islam*, 3 vols. (Chicago: University of Chicago Press, 1974), 1:401.

12. Georges Vajda, *La théologie ascétique de Baḥya Ibn Paquda* (Paris: Imprimerie Nationale, 1947), pp. 6–13; Ḥava Lazarus-Yafeh, *Some Religious Aspects of Islam* (Leiden: E. J. Brill, 1981), pp. 76–77.

13. The text was *On Medical Substances* by Dioscorides; see Ashtor, *Jews of Moslem Spain* 1:166–168.

14. Abraham Ibn Ezra composed a Hebrew adaptation of Avicenna's philosophical allegory *Ḥayy ibn yaqẓān*; see his *Ḥai ben meqiṣ*, ed. Yisrael Levin (Tel Aviv: The Katz Research Institute for Hebrew Literature, Tel Aviv University, 1983).

15. The relative indifference of Muslim philosophers to specific religious traditions has often been noted. For the Brethren of Purity, see T. J. De Boer, *The History of Philosophy in Islam* (London: Luzac and Co., 1903; New York: Dover Publications, 1967), pp. 93–94; for Avicenna, see pp. 144–145; for Ibn Tufail, see p. 185; for Averroës, see p. 199.

16. Gideon Libson, "*Pᵉraqim misefer hameṣranut lᶜrav shᶜmuʾel ben ḥofni gaʾon,*" *Tarbiz* 56 (1986–1987): 61–107; Naphtali Wieder, *Islamic Influences on Jewish Worship* (Hebrew) (Oxford: East and West Library, 1947).

17. Ps. 106:35. See *Wine, Women, and Death*, p. 31 and n. 27.

18. Section 8 of the poem in Schirmann, *Hashira ha'ivrit* 1:261; Ibn Gabirol, *Shire haqodesh* 1:42; Ibn Gabirol, *Selected Religious Poems*, p. 86; Solomon Ibn Gabirol, *The Kingly Crown*, trans. Bernard Lewis (London: Vallentine and Mitchell, 1961), p. 31. For further discussion of this passage, see below, introduction to Chapter I and n. 23.

19. The standard description and history of the liturgy is Ismar Elbogen, *Hat'fila b'yisra'el b'hitpathutah hahistorit*, rev. Joseph Heinemann et al. (Tel Aviv: Dvir, 1972); an English translation by Raymond P. Scheindlin is forthcoming (Philadelphia: Jewish Publication Society). For the fullest exploration of the fluidity of liturgical texts in the Talmudic period, see Joseph Heinemann, *Prayer in the Talmud: Forms and Patterns*, trans. Richard Sarason (New York: de Gruyter, 1977). On the extent to which we may actually speak of a "canonization" of the liturgy, see Lawrence A. Hoffman, *The Canonization of the Synagogue Service* (Notre Dame, Ind.: University of Notre Dame Press, 1979). For an overview of the various approaches to the problems of the history of Jewish liturgy, see Richard S. Sarason, "On the Use of Method in the Modern Study of Jewish Liturgy," in *Approaches to Ancient Judaism*, ed. William Scott Green (Missoula, Mont.: Scholar's Press for Brown University, 1978), 1:97–172, reprinted in Jacob Neusner, ed., *The Study of Ancient Judaism* (New York: Ktav, 1981), pp. 107–179.

20. Deut. 6:4–9, 11:13–21; Num. 15:37–41.

21. Most familiar are "Blessed God," inserted on weekdays, and "God, the Lord," inserted on the Sabbath; but see Ezra Fleischer's monumental study *Hayos'rot b'hithavutam uv'hitpathutam* (Jerusalem: Magnes Press, 1983–1984) for an idea of the enormous quantity of such poems.

22. For a discussion of the medieval and modern critique of the language of the early *piyyut*, see Yosef Yahalom, *S'fat hashir shel hapiyut ha'eres yisr'²eli haqadum* (Jerusalem: Magnes Press, 1985), pp. 11–19, 183–196. Much energy has been expended over the past nine centuries in vilifying Kallir and the style associated with his name. This is because most of the judges have been either medieval or modern worshipers who had definite, divergent ideas of what they wanted in prayer. Other critics approached him from the point of view of Romantic European poetry, and they too were inevitably disappointed. Yet his work was immensely popular for centuries, and his style was imitated and even taken to further extremes by some of his followers. The time has come to reformulate the question of *piyyut*: Just what was the nature of the religious experience that he and his followers were trying to achieve? A sympathetic examination of *piyyut* from this point of view would yield a valuable contribution to the study of Jewish religiosity.

23. The continuity between Spanish liturgical poetry and that of geonic Iraq has been stressed by Ezra Fleischer. See the summary in his *Shirat haqodesh ha'ivrit bime habenayim* (Jerusalem: Keter, 1975), p. 333; his *Hayos'rot*, pp. 475ff.; and his earlier articles cited there.

24. See, for example, Ibn Gabirol, *Shire haqodesh* 1:122–135 (poems 32, 33, 34) and 1:243ff. (poem 76).

25. For more information, see *Wine, Women, and Death*, p. 16; for secular examples, see pp. 90–109.

26. For the cultural conditions underlying this development, see Dan Pagis, *Hidush umasoret b'shirat hahol ha'ivrit bis'farad uv'²italya* (Jerusalem: Keter, 1976), p. 56.

27. Aharon Mirsky, *"Haziqa sheben shirat s*farad lid*erashot hazal,"* Sinai 64 (1968–1969): 247ff.; idem, *"Shte dugma'ot midrash mishirat s*farad."* in *Mehq*re sifrut mugashim l*shim 'on halqin,* ed. Ezra Fleischer (Jerusalem: Magnes Press, 1973), pp. 115ff.; Jonathan Wittenberg, "A Reshut to *Nishmat,"* Prooftexts 8 (1988:340–345).

28. Yosef Tobi, "The Liturgical Poems of Rav Sa'adia Gaon: Critical Edition (of the Yoseroth) with a General Introduction to his Poetic Work" (Hebrew) (Ph.D. diss., Hebrew University, 1982), pp. 292–293.

29. Even more spectacular is the monumental cycle of poems for the Day of Atonement by Isaac Ibn Ghiyath *(Shire ibn giyat,* pp. 7–114).

30. Moses Ibn Ezra, *Kitāb al-muḥāḍara wa 'l-mudhākara.* ed. and trans. A. S. Halkin (Jerusalem: Meqize Nirdamim, 1975), p. 60.

31. I have also benefited from consulting the translations and notes to Halevi's religious verse by Franz Rosenzweig in his *Jehuda Halevi: Zweiandneunzia Hymnen und Gedichte Deutsch* (Berlin: Verlag Lambert Schneider, 1926), though it is not ordinarily cited in the notes. I was not able to make use of the translations by Raphael Loewe in his book *Ibn Gabirol* (London: Peter Halban Publishers Ltd., 1989), which reached me only after *The Gazelle* was set in type.

1 · GOD AND ISRAEL

Introduction

1. Judah Halevi, *Shire haqodesh* 1:212 (poem 94).

2. See Fleischer, *Hayoṣ*rot,* pp. 475–604, for a detailed treatment of the development of the cycle in Spain.

3. See Georges Vajda, *L 'Amour de dieu dans la théologie juive du moyen age* (Paris: Cahiers de la Société Asiatique, 1957), p. 91; Karl Dreyer, *Die religiöse Gedankenwelt des Salomo Ibn Gabirol* (Leipzig: E. Pfeiffer, 1930), pp. 36–37.

4. Ephraim E. Urbach, "The Homiletical Interpretations of the Sages and the Expositions of Origen on Canticles, and the Jewish-Christian Disputation," *Scripta Hierosolymitana* 22 (1971): 249. G. D. Cohen has suggested that the allegorical exegesis of the Song of Songs is considerably older, that in fact the book was always understood by the rabbis as an allegory; see his "The Song of Songs and the Jewish Religious Mentality," in the *Samuel Friedland Lectures, 1960–1966* (New York: The Jewish Theological Seminary of America, 1966), pp. 1–21. Daniel Boyarin *("Sh*ne m*vo'ot l*midrash shir hashirim,"* Tarbiz 56 {1986–1987]: 479–500) argues that rabbinic exegesis was not truly allegorical and that it functioned rather differently from the way described here; but he would not deny that exegesis in this period tended to connect key events in Israel's sacred history with the Song of Songs. Although there are several indications that the allegorical interpretation of the Song of Songs was especially cultivated during the period between the destruction of the Second Temple (70) and the Bar Kokhba revolt (132–135), the chronology is very uncertain. Two passages in tannaitic literature connect the allegorization of the Song of Songs with R. Akiba, who died c. 135.: his statement in Mishna Yadaim 3:5 defending the book's sanctity, and his exegesis of Songs 5:9–10, 1:3, 2:16 quoted in the *Mekhilta (M*khilta d*rabi shim 'on bar yohai,* ed. J. N. Epstein and E. Z. Melamed

[Jerusalem: Sumptibus Mekize Nirdamim, 1955], p. 79; *Mᵉkhilta dᵉrabi yishimaᶜel*, ed. H. S. Horovitz and I. A. Rabin, 2d ed. lJerusalem: Bamberger & Wahrman. 1960], p. 127). The apocryphal book II Esdras (IV Ezra), which dates from roughly the same period, uses, at 5:24 and 26, certain figures of speech that seem to derive from the allegorical exegesis of the Song of Songs.

5. Schirmann, *Hashira ha ᶜivrit* 1:182.

6. Hebrew *ayala is* associated with beautiful women not through the Song of Songs but through Prov. 5:19. Hebrew *ᶜofer/ᶜofra* may be intended as a substitute for Arabic *ᶜafrāᵓ* (dust-colored antelope), occasionally used as a generic name for the beloved in poetry. Cf. Ibn Rashīq, *ᶜUmda* (Beirut: Dār al-Jīl, 1907), 2:121–122.

7. Ibn Gabirol, *Shire qodesh* 2:519 (poem 180).

8. Trans. Willis Barnstone (New York: New Directions Publishing Company, 1972), p. 57.

9. Zvi Krol, *"Ha ᵓahava bᵉshire r. shᵉlomo ibn gabirol."* *Mizrah uma ᵓarav* 2 (1928–1929): 276–279. Krol does not explain why the use of secular themes in a sacred context is unthinkable for Ibn Gabirol but thinkable for whoever assigned the poem to the liturgy.

10. Schimmel, As *through* a *Veil*, pp. 37–41.

11. There is a magisterial study of al-Ḥallāj by L. Massignon, *The Passion of al-Ḥallāj: Mystic and Martyr of Islam*, 4 vols., trans. Herbert Mason (Princeton: Princeton University Press, 1983); more briefly, one may consult Massignon's article in the *Encyclopaedia of Islam*, new ed. (Leiden: E. J. Brill, 1960–1986), 3:99; on Ḥallāj's poetry, cf. also Schimmel, As *through a Veil*, pp. 30–36.

12. See above, pp. 23–25.

13. The influence of Sufi poetry on Golden Age religious verse has been suggested by Y. Levin, *"Habᵉriha min ha ᶜolam el ha ᵓelohim,"* in Zvi Malachi, ed., *ᶜAl shira vᵉsiporet* (Tel Aviv: Tel Aviv University, 1977), p. 156; *"Biqashti et she ᵓahava nafshi."* *Hasifrut* 3 (1970–1971): 123. But no systematic research has yet been done on this topic, probably because, with the exception of the poems of al-Ḥallāj, the Arabic texts themselves have never been collected. I plan to devote myself to a thorough investigation of both the Arabic and the Hebrew side of this question in the near future.

14. The Arabic original is lost. It was translated into Latin by Johannes Hispalensis and Dominicus Gundissalinus in the twelfth century; this version was translated into Hebrew by Jacob Bluwstein, *Sefer mᵉqor hayim lᵉrabi shᵉlomo ibn gabirol*, ed. Abraham Zifroni (Jerusalem: Mahbarot lᵉsifrut, 1925–1926); Part 3 is available in English translation in *The Fountain of Life (Fons Vitae) by Solomon Ibn Gabirol*, abridged and trans. H. E. Wedeck (London: P. Owen, 1963).

15. *Meqor hayim*, trans. Bluwstein, 5:43, p. 221.

16. *Ibid.* 3:56, p. 137; translation quoted from Wedeck, *Fountain*, pp. 127–128.

17. Vajda, *La théologie ascétique*, pp. 27–29; idem, *L amour*, p. 88. For this theme in Bahya Ibn Paquda, Moses Ibn Ezra, Judah Halevi, and Abraham Ibn Ezra, see Vajda, *L'amour*, pp. 99–115.

18. Yisra ᵓel Levin and Reuven Zur have glimpsed Ibn Gabirol's train of thought; Georges Vajda has seen it clearly. See Levin, "Neoplatonic Mystical Trends in the Poetry of Solomon Ibn Gabirol" (Hebrew), in Zvi Malachi, ed. *Aharon Mirsky Jubilee Volume: Essays on Jewish Culture* (Lydda: Habermann Institute for Literary Research 1986), p. 311 n. 52, reprinted in Levin's *Hasod vᵉhayᵉsod: Mᵉgamot shel mistorin*

b^eshirato shel ibn gabirol [*Mystical trends in the poetry of Solomon Ibn Gabirol*] (Lydda: Habermann Institute for Literary Research 1986), p. 163 n. 52; Zur, *'Iyunim bashira ha'ivrit bime habenaim* [*Studies in medieval Hebrew poetry*] (Tel Aviv: Daga Books, n.d.), p. 23n; but above all, Vajda's trenchant statement, *L'amour*, p. 91, which however, stops just short of recognizing the bivalent nature of many of these poems. See also Vajda, *L'amour*, p. 109 on Halevi.

On the shift in Jewish eschatology from the national to the individual, with very interesting examples from various prose writers, including Abraham bar Ḥiyya, another eleventh-century Iberian author, see Moshe Idel, "Types of Redemptive Activity in the Middle Ages" (Hebrew), in *M^eshiḥiyut v^e'esthatologia: qoveṣ ma'amarim* [Messianism and Eschatology: A Collection of Articles] ed. Zvi Baras (Jerusalem: Merkaz Zalman Shazar 1983–1984), pp. 253–279.

19. Ibn Gabirol, *Shire haqodesh* 2:485 (poem 158); *Shire sh^elomo teen y^ehuda ibn gabirol* 2:59; commentary section, p. 33.

20. This usage derives from Ps. 22:21 and 35:17. It is explained by Abraham Ibn Ezra in his commentary to 22:22 as follows: "The reason [the soul is called] 'my Only One' is that every person's soul is individual, separated with its body from the universal soul, and when it separates from its body it then is joined to the universal [soul]." Saadia explains the word differently: "It is called 'Only One' . . . because there exists nothing comparable to it among all creatures, either celestial or terrestrial." Saadia Gaon, *The Book of Beliefs and Opinions*, trans. Samuel Rosenblatt (New Haven and London: Yale University Press, 1948), p. 244

21. Moses Ibn Ezra, *Shire qodesh*, p. 46 (poem 45, lines 17–18).

22. Ibn Gabirol, *Shire haqodesh* 1:42 (no. 22, lines 3–7); idem, *Selected Religious Poems*, pp. 86–87; Schirmann, *Hashira ha'ivrit* 1:261. See above, Introduction, n. 20.

23. I thus take issue with R. Loewe's interpretation of these lines in his otherwise excellent article "Ibn Gabirol's Treatment of Sources in the *Kether Malkhuth*," in *Studies in Jewish Religious and Intellectual History*, ed. S. Stein and R. Loewe (University, Alabama: University of Alabama Press, 1979), pp. 183–195. After convincingly pointing to the similarity in the first part of the quotation between Ibn Gabirol's thought and the ideas of the Brethren of Purity, Loewe explains the "clear-eyed servants" in the second part as referring to Israel, declaring the passage a retreat from the universalism of the first part. But neither does the language require nor the context permit such an interpretation. There can be no reason to attribute such inconsistency to Ibn Gabirol when the consistent interpretation, that the "clear-eyed servants" are the philosophers of all religions, is so close at hand.

24. Moses Ibn Ezra, *Shire qodesh*, pp. 68–70 (poem 62); idem, *Selected Poems*, pp. 148–151 (poem 63). In the first two lines I follow the reading adopted by Bernstein. The last line of the first stanza is a quotation from Exod. 13:21.

25. The phrases from Lamentations are: "She lowers her . . . to the ground" (Lam. 2:10); "tears on her cheek" (Lam. 1:2); "She weeps at night" (Lam. 1:2). Other phrases associated with national suffering are: "She goes in darkness" (Ps. 42:10), and "She lowers her ornaments" (Exod. 33:5). The apparent shifting back and forth between national and individual language confused Solis-Cohen in his attempt to translate the poem; see his note in Moses Ibn Ezra, *Selected Poems*, p. 386.

26. See poem 1, n. 1, and the discussion of poem 3.

27. See Abraham Ibn Ezra, *Shire haqodesh* 1:171 (poem 91, lines 22–23).

28. Judah Halevi, *Shirc haqodesh* 3:714 (poem 294, lines 23ff.).

29. Jarden's commentary misses the point, glossing the vine as a symbol for Israel.

30. Ibn Gabirol, *Shire haqodesh* 2:555 (poem 203). The "land of beauty" is of course Palestine; cf. Ezra 20:6, and especially Jer. 3:19. Incidentally, the word translated "beauty" is *ṣ^evi*, a homonym of the usual word for "gazelle."

31. Attributed to Halevi in his *Shire haqodesh* 1:251–252 (poem 108). Jarden identifies this poem as intended for the Sabbath before Purim but fails to explain whether this identification is a surmise based only on the internal reference to Amalek or whether it is supported by manuscript evidence of a liturgical tradition.

32. *Zohar* 3:281b.

33. Ibn Gabirol, *Shire haqodesh* 2:537 (poem 193); cf. Songs 6:2. Brody, as reported in Ibn Gabirol, *Shire sh^elomo ibn gabirol* 3:52, commentary section, explained the reference to the spheres as the flaming doom of the wicked threatened in Mal. 3:19.

34. Ibn Gabirol, *Shire haqodesh* 2:573 (poem 215); cf. Songs 1:4.

35. Ibn 'Aquin's Arabic commentary on the Song of Songs, *Inkishāf al-asrār wa-ẓhūr al-anwār* [*The revelation of the mysteries and the appearance of the lights*], was published with a Hebrew translation by Abraham S. Halkin (Jerusalem: Mekize Nirdamim, 1964). For allegorical love stories, see, for example, Yonah David, "The First Chapter of the Book of Fables by R. Jacob b. Eleazar" (Hebrew) in *Sefer avraham even-shoshan*, ed. Ben Tsiyon Luria (Jerusalem: Kiryat Sefer, 1985), pp. 139–155; Schirmann, *Shirim*, pp. 385–388.

36. See the articles mentioned in poem 27, n. 11.

37. Ibn Gabirol, *Fons vitae* 5:32.

38. Commentary on Ecclesiastes, incorrectly attributed to Saadia, in Y. Kafiḥ, ed., *Ḥamesh m^egilot* (Jerusalem: Hoṣa'at ha'aguda l^ehaṢalat ginze teman, 1961–1962), p. 179 or 181.

39. For "hewn" meaning "built," see Prov. 9:1. As for the speech of the heavens, medieval commentators assumed that Ps. 19:2 reflected the Greek idea that the spheres emit harmonious sounds as they rotate: they identified this idea with the rabbinic notion that the angels constantly sing God's praises.

40. Ibn Gabirol, *Shite haqodesh* 1:245 (poem 76).

41. Abraham Ibn Ezra, *Shire haqodesh* 1:71–74 (poem 41). This and the following example were identified by Vajda, *L'amour*, p. 114.

42. Abraham Ibn Ezra, *Shire haqodesh* 1:131–132 (poem 72): see Levin's commentary for an explanation of the enigmatic third and founh lines of the quotation.

43. On the complementary character of the themes, see Vajda, *L'amour*, p. 91; ". . . au grand désarroi des amateurs des situations nettes."

Poem 1

Sources:
 Schirmann. *Hashira ha'ivrit* 1:466.
 Judah Halevi, *Shire haqodesh* 3:775.
Translation:
 Carmi, *Penguin Book*, p. 335.

. 1. See above, pp. 36–37, and *Wine, Women, and Death*, p. 79. The word *ma'on* (abode) in verse 1 is the Hebrew equivalent of the *aṭlāl* and *diyār* of the erotic prelude to the Arabic desert ode. These words denote the ruins of the desert camp where the poet weeps as he recalls his beloved, whose tribe once encamped there. The image is discussed more fully, with an example from Arabic poetry, below in connection with poem 3. For a Hebrew example, see Moses Ibn Ezra, *Shire haḥol* 1:9 (poem 7). Incidentally, the Arabic terms ordinarily used in poetry are *aṭlāl* and *diyār*, not *mawāḍi' al-ḥubb*, as stated by Yisrael Levin in "*Biqashti*," p. 118 n. 2. The latter simply means "site of love" and is not a technical term.

2. Songs 3:6 and Targum; Songs 8:5. This translation of the unusual word *mitrapeqet* accords with the way the word was probably understood in Halevi's circle, to judge from Abraham Ibn Ezra's commentary. He explains it by its Arabic cognate, presumably *raf īq*, a traveling companion. This derivation was, incidentally, known to Rashi, who, though he did not know Arabic, actually cites the Arabic word.

3. In poems 9 and 10 it refers specifically to the Arabs.

4. C. H. Becker, "Ubi sunt qui ante nos in mundo fuere," in *Aufsätze zur Kultur- und Sprachgeschichte, vornehmlich des Orients, Ernst Kuhn zum 70. Geburtstag 7.II.1916 gewidmet* (Breslau: Verlag von M. & H. Marcus, 1916); Nehemya Allony, "*Nusaḥ aye b'shirat s'farad*," *Oṣar y'hude s'farad* 2 (1959): 16–28.

5. *Wine, Women, and Death*, pp. 106–107; the Hebrew there reads *esh ahavim nis'qa*, as compared with *v'hi esh nis'qa* here.

6. Songs 8:6–7.

Poem 2

Source:
 Schirmann, *Hashira ha'ivrit* 1:405–406.
Translation:
 Moses Ibn Ezra, *Selected Poems*, p. 101.

1. See *Wine, Women, and Death*, pp. 90–91 (poem 11), and the discussion on pp. 92–95.

2. *Wine, Women, and Death*, p. 97 and also pp. 74–75; for another occurrence of the verb *qṭl* in the same context, see ibid., p. 130. For another example of Job 13:15 in a liturgical context, see Moses Ibn Ezra in Schirmann, *Hashira ha'ivrit* 1:404. For the overall theme, see especially the discussion of poem 5, below.

3. This is a literal translation of the verse in *Wine, Women, and Death*, p. 128.

4. Arabic: Ibn Zaidūn, *Dīwān*, ed. 'Alī 'Abd al-'Aẓīm (Cairo: Maktabat Nahḍa, 1957), p. 165: "Ask for my life, and I'll give it; I am not capable of refusing you. / Time was my slave, until I became—through love—your slave." Hebrew: Samuel the Nagid in *Diwan:Ben t'hilim*, ed. Dov Jarden (Jerusalem: Hebrew Union College Press, 1966), p. 296: " . . . why have you treated your servant badly?"

5. On this subject, see poem 12.

Poem 3

Sources:
 Schirmann, *Hashira ha'ivrit* 1:405.
 Moses Ibn Ezra, *Shire qodesh*, p. 38.

Translation:
Moses Ibn Ezra, *Selected Porms*, p. 102.
Discussion:
Yisra'el Levin, *"'Biqashti et she'ahava nafshi:' l*^e*heqer hahashpa'a shel shirat haḥesheq haḥilonit 'al hashira hadatit ha'ivrit bime habenayim."* Hasifrut 3 (1970–1971): 116–149, especially p. 123.

Idem, *"Hab*^e*khi 'al ḥorvot hame'onot v*^e*had*^e*mut halelit ham*^e*shoṭeṭ,"* Tarbiz 36 (1966–1967): 278–296, especially pp. 289–290.

1. Labīd ibn Rabī'a, in Michael A. Sells, trans., *Desert Tracings: Six Classic Arabian Odes* (Middletown, Conn.: Wesleyan University Press, 1989), pp. 35–36. For an exploration of many conventions adopted by Hebrew poets from the pre-lslamic desert ode, see Nehemya Allony, *"Haṣ*^e*vi v*^e*hagamal b*^e*shirat s*^e*farad,"* Oṣar y*^e*hude s*^e*farad 4(1961): 16f., and Levin's articles cited above.

2. Levin, *"Hab*^e*khi,"* for the inventory of occurrences of this theme in Moses Ibn Ezra and others.

3. It is cited here according to Makkot 24b. It is also found in *Sifre* Deuteronomy 43; *Ekha raba* 5:18 (ed. Buber, p. 80a).

4. Celestial: Deut. 26:15; mundane: Ps. 26:8: lair of wild beasts: Jer. 10:22.

5. As interpreted by Shimeon Bemstein, in his Moses Ibn Ezra, *Shire qodesh*.

6. Poems 9, 10, 11.

7. Songs 2:5.

8. This interpretation, found in the third version of his commentary, the allegorical one, is the basis of a reference to the verse in one of his own poems; see Abraham Ibn Ezra, *Shire haqodesh* 1:186 (poem 99, line 8). Incidentally, the translation of *rap*^e*duni* is based on Abraham Ibn Ezra's first commentary, the philological one. The word is used with the same meaning by Joseph Ibn Ṣadiq, in *The Poems of Joseph Ibn Saddik* (Hebrew), ed. Yonah David (New York: American Academy for Jewish Research, 1982), p. 46 (poem 12, line 19).

9. See S. M. Stern, *Hispano-Arabic Strophic Poetry*, ed. L. P. Harvey (Oxford: Clarendon Press, 1974), p. 59.

Poem 4

Source:
Schirmann, *Hashira ha'ivrit* 1:471.
Translation:
Judah Halevi, *Selected Poems*, p. 118.
Note:
In line 14, I have translated *ṣa'ara* as if it were related to *ṣa'ar* (pain): but since it is contrasted with *kav*^e*da* (to be important, weighty), the main meaning in the poet's mind was probably "to be small, insignificant," a loan-translation from the cognate Arabic root *ṣghr*. Of course, the other interpretation is not excluded by this observation.

1. Ibn Ḥazm, *The Ring of the Dove*, trans. A. J. Arberry (London: Luzac & Co., 1953).

2. *Wine, Women, and Death*, pp. 72–73.

3. Songs 2:14, 5:2, 6:9; see also 1:15, 4:1.

4. Isa. 38:14: Ps. 55:7–8; Hos. 11:11 and Isa. 60:8; Gen. 8:9; Lev. 5:7, 12:8; Songs R. on 1:15.

5. The Hebrew is obscure. My translation reflects the Targum, but other interpretations were current in the Middle Ages.

6. Other examples in Halevi: Schirmann, *Hashira ha'ivrit* 1:455 (poem 183, verse 3); 1:504 (poem 4, verse 3).

7. Moses Ibn Ezra, *'Anaq* 4:20 in *Shire haḥol* 1:347.

8. Jer. 20:7–9.

9. Cf. Abraham Ibn Ezra, Ps. 50:3: "These are the words of the righteous hoping that He will destroy those who rebel against Him. This is the meaning of 'Fire consumes before Him.'"

10. Schirmann, *Hashira ha'ivrit* 1:475 (poem 198, line 5). For further discussion of messianic calculations, see below on poem 11. Halevi refers several times to the frustrated hope that the messianic redemption would occur at the millennium of the destruction of the Temple, i.e., c. 1068 (according to the Jewish reckoning the destruction occurred in 68 instead of 70). See Judah Halevi, *Shire haqodesh* 2:599 (poem 246, verse 5); 3:650 (poem 266, verse 3); 3:671; see also 4:1168 (poem 274, verse 8); 3:766 (poem 326, verse 5). For other evidence of messianic expectations for 1068, see Abba Hillel Silver, *History of Messianic Speculation in Israel*, (Boston: Beacon Press, 1959), pp. 67–69.

In the course of the discussion, Silver cites our poem, dating it to the year 1132. This dating derives from an improbable *gemaṭria* proposed by Abraham Harkavi in the notes to his edition of Halevi's poems (*Rabi y'huda halevi: qoveṣ shirav um'liṣotav* [Warsaw: Aḥiasaf, 1893], p. 60).

Poem 5

Sources:
   Schirmann, *Hashira ha'ivrit* 1:467.
   Judah Halevi, *Shire haqodesh* 3:778–779.
Translations:
   Carmi, *Penguin Book*, p. 333.
   A free translation by me of this poem and the one referred to in note 8 below was set for baritone and orchestra by Hugo Weisgall under the title "Love's Wounded" and performed by the Baltimore Symphony Orchestra on September 18 and 19, 1986.
Discussion:
   Yisra'el Levin, "Biqashti et she'ahava nafshi," *Hasifrut* 3 (1971): 116–119.
   Arye L. Strauss, *B'darkhe hasifrut* (Jerusalem: Mosad Bialik, 1959), pp. 95–104.

1. Ibn Ḥazm, *The Ring of the Dove*, p. 120.

2. *Kuzari* 1:113; trans. Hartwig Hirschfeld (London: M. L. Cailingold, 1931), pp. 68–69.

3. Schirmann, *Hashira ha'ivrit* 1:324; Ibn Ghiyath, *Shire ibn giyat*, pp. 182–183 (poem 98). Y. Levin considers the Ibn Ghiyath poem as identical to our poem in theme, differing only in the form of expression. But Halevi's poem is not simply more decorated than that of Ibn Ghiyath, as claimed by Levin; in fact it is *less* decorated. And more important, it is about a more profound idea.

4. Abraham Ibn Ezra, *Shire haqodesh* 1:268 (poem 144, line 8).

5. S. D. Luzzatto (*Diwan R. Judah Halevi* [Lyck: M'kize Nirdamim 1864], pp. 21–22), quoted by Levin, pointed out as another index of the radical character of

Halevi's poem the fact that verse 3b alludes unmistakably to Ps. 69:27–29, which reads: "For they persecute those You have struck; . . . add that to their guilt; let them have no share of Your beneficence; may they be erased from the book of life." The Psalmist urges vengeance against the enemies, though in their mistreatment of Israel they have only been doing God's will. By alluding to the psalm, Halevi seems to underline his own quite different attitude.

6. Translation by Sir Thomas Wyatt in *Five Courtier Poets of the English Renaissance* (New York: Washington Square Press, 1967), p. 24. For a more literal translation, see Robert M. Durling, ed. and trans., *Petrarch's Lyric Poems: The Rime Sparse and Other Lyrics* (Cambridge: Harvard University Press, 1976), p. 318 (poem 172).

7. See Durling, *Petrarch's Lyric Poems*, p. 272 (poem 134) and p. 56 (poem 21). The Job allusion is to Job 13:15, used by Moses Ibn Ezra in poem 2, above.

8. Schirmann, *Hashira ha'ivrit* 1:439. Levin, "*Biqashti*."

9. David, *Ibn Ṣadiq*, pp. 45–46 (poem 12, verse 4); Levin, "Biqashti." For yet another example, cf. the anonymous verse in Schirmann, *Shirim*, p. 310.

10. The quotations from Ibn Zaidūn are from his *Dīwān*, pp. 181 and 166. It was Y. Levin's stunning discovery, published in "*Biqashti*," p. 118, that our poem is actually a Hebrew translation, with the addition of one verse, of an Arabic love poem by abū al-Shīṣ (eighth–ninth century). Further, I have now discovered that the poem was already used by Muslim mystics, who gave it religious meaning. It is quoted by an Andalusian Sufi, Ibn al-ʿArif, a contemporary of Halevi, in his *Maḥāsin al-majalis*, edited and translated by Miguel Asín Palacios (Paris, 1933), pp. 50, 91.

11. *Le Dīwān d'al Hallāj*, ed. Louis Massignon (Paris: Librairie orientaliste Paul Geuthner, 1955), pp. 59–60.

12. Abū ʿAbd al-Raḥmān Muḥammad al-Sulamī, *Kitāb ṭabaqāt al-ṣūfiyya*, ed. Johannes Pedersen (Leiden: E. J. Brill, 1960), p. 174.

13. Pace Levin ("*Biqashti*," pp. 117–118), who inexplicably states that the poem is richer in imagery than the one by Ibn Ghiyath.

14. *Ḥalal* ordinarily means corpse, which obviously is not appropriate in the context of pursuit. But in the passage in Psalm 69, the word seems to be used to mean "wounded"; see Kimḥi *ad loc*. I owe the observation and the reference to Dr. Menaḥem Schmelzer.

Poem 6

Sources:

Schirmann, *Hashira ha'ivrit* 1:483.

Judah Halevi, *Shire haqodesh* 2:419.

Translation:

Carmi, *Penguin Book*, p. 334.

Note:

The Hebrew verb in line 10 of the translation derives from Hos. 14:1, where the plain meaning is "Zion is guilty." Several commentators of the period, however, explain it as meaning "Zion will be ruined." The translation attempts to incorporate both interpretations.

1. See *Wine, Women, and Death*, pp. 139–140.

2. I have identified only one other possible example by Halevi, in his *Shire haqodesh* 3:828 (poem 358).

3. *Kuzari* 2:24 (trans. Hirschfeld, p. 88).

4. Num. 24:17, which the Targum renders, "A king will arise from Jacob, a Messiah will be anointed from among Israel."

5. Judg. 16:20.

6. Other biblical quotations, less densely packed, are in verse 3b–c of the Hebrew text (Hos. 14:1); 3d (I Kings 9:3 and elsewhere): 4c–d (Mal. 3:17).

7. *Kuzari* 2:14 (trans. Hirschfeld, p. 79); 4:3 (Hirschfeld, p. 185).

8. Ḥ. Schirmann, "*Ḥaye yᵉhuda halevi*" and "*Hashlamot lᵉḥaye yᵉhuda halevi*," in *'Al hashira vᵉhadrama* (Jerusalem: Mossad Bialik, 1979), 1:302–303 and 1:336, respectively.

9. Sanhedrin 98a; L. Ginzberg, *Legends of the Jews* (7 vols.: Philadelphia: Jewish Publication Society of America, 1913–1946) 6:426.

10. Ps. 44:24, 78:65.

11. Ibn Gabirol, *Shire haqodesh* 1:177. The Hebrew phrase is *ṣaʿir rodem*, meaning "the youth who rules them" but used by Gabirol as if *rodem* were derived from *rdm* (to slumber) instead of *rdy* (to rule). Isaac Ibn Ghiyath has a similar usage, but referring to Israel rather than to the Messiah; see Ibn Ghiyath, *Shire ibn giyat*, p. 348 (poem 243, line 1).

Poem 7

Sources:

Schirmann, *Hashira haʿivrit* 1:240.

Ibn Gabirol, *Shire haqodesh* 2:468.

Translation:

Carmi, *Penguin Book*, p. 314.

Discussion:

Shalom Luria, *Shire ahava ben qodesh lᵉḥol*, in Zvi Malachi and Hanna David, *Studies in the Work of Shlomo Ibn Gabirol* (Hebrew) (Tel Aviv: Katz Research Institute for Hebrew Literature, 1985), pp. 113–125.

Z. Krol, "*Haʾahava bᵉshire r. shᵉlomo ibn gabirol*," *Mizraḥ umaʿarav* 2 (1928–1929?): 275ff.

N. Roth, "Sacred and Secular in the Poetry of Ibn Gabirol," *Hebrew Studies* 20–21 (1979–1980): 78.

Dreyer, *Religiöse Gedankenwelt*, pp. 66–74.

1. Ibn Gabirol, *Shire haqodesh*, poems 95, 96, 103, 105, 123, 131, 133, 136, 137, 144, 145, 148, and 223. All except 105, 123, and 137 have four lines, have the acrostic *Shᵉlomo* (Solomon), and are in the meter called *mitpasheṭ*. The problem poems are 95, 96, 131 (poem 9 in this book), 133 (here, poem 8), and 144 (the present poem). They appear together in Bialik and Ravnitzky, *Shire shᵉlomo ibn gabirol* 2:35–37. The difficulty of identifying the personae in these poems seems to have first been noted by Dreyer in his *Religiöse Gedankenwelt* (p. 72) and then blithely ignored by all subsequent editors and commentators. Dreyer's attempt to resolve the problem by reference to the history of the messianic idea is unsuccessful, but his sensitivity to its existence should have been a stimulus to later students of these poems.

Also unclear is the original liturgical function of these poems. Several, like the one under discussion and number 10 in this collection, open with a call for a gate to be opened. This image could hint at a liturgical context, for in the later practice of the North African congregations poems called "The Opening of the Gate" were recited between *Nishmat* and *Kaddish*. It has been conjectured that the ark was opened at this point in the service. Since the liturgical practice of the North African communities was heavily influenced by that of Spain, the North African poems may be a survival of a practice dating from the Golden Age, and poems like those under discussion may have been intended for this point in the service. See Ephraim Ḥazan, "*Suge hashir bashira haʿivrit biṣ*fon afriqa*," *S*funot* 17 (1983): 358–359.

2. I Sam. 16:11–12

3. See Yoma 54a, Rashi, and Ibn Ezra (third commentary) on the passage from Song of Songs. The Talmud imagines these cherubim themselves as having been sculpted in an erotic attitude.

4. *Wine, Women, and Death*, pp. 68–71 (poem 8); Schirmann, *Shirim*, p. 158. On the homosexual theme, see *Wine, Women, and Death*, pp. 82–89. As mentioned earlier, David, or the person of the Messiah, plays a role in Ibn Gabirol that is completely unknown in the poetry on redemption of other Golden Age poets. Passages in his secular poetry also contain unexpected references to incidents or persons connected with David. This is a topic deserving further research and reflection.

5. The question is raised by Luria in the article listed above.

6. E.g., Isa. 26:2, 60:11.

7. Isa. 45:1.

Poem 8

Source:

Schirmann, *Hashira haʿivrit* 1:241.

Translation:

Ibn Gabirol, *Selected Religious Poems*, p. 4.

Discussion:

Dreyer, *Religiöse Gedankenwelt*, p. 70.

Norman Roth, "'Sacred' and 'Secular' in the Poetry of Ibn Gabirol," *Hebrew Studies* 20–21 (1979–1980): 78.

1. Both verses seem to be alluded to here: Pss. 42:3 and 63:2.

2. Ezek. 23:41; Prov. 9:2.

3. Ps. 23:5, explicitly titled "A Psalm of David."

4. Sacrifice, Lev. 1:8; the table of the sanctuary, Exod. 40:4; the shewbread, Exod. 40:23; prayer, Ps. 5:4.

5. The Targum on Ps. 132:3 puts David's vow into plain words by translating *in e*ol ʿal iteti* (I shall not have congress with my wife); II Sam. 11:11 shows that this sort of abstinence was practiced in ancient Israel in connection with war. For David's intention to build a Temple, see II Sam. 7:1–3; I Chron. 22:7–8.

6. Cf., for example, Yoma 54a.

Poem 9

Sources:

Schirmann, *Hashira haʿivrit* 1:241.

Ibn Gabirol, *Shire haqodesh* 2:457.

Translations:
    Carmi, *Penguin Book*, p. 314.
    Ibn Gabirol, *Selected Religious Poems*, p. 3.
Discussion:
    Dreyer, *Religiöse Gedankenwelt*, pp. 68–69.
    1. E.g., *Wine, Women, and Death*, pp. 40–45. An English example deriving from Eastern models is the opening of Edward Fitzgerald's *Rubá'iyát of Omar Khayyam*.
    2. See Songs 5:1. Though the list in our poem is not taken verbatim from the verse, it is in that spirit. All the items mentioned in the poem do occur in the book.
    3. For the golden cherubim, see discussion on poem 7. On the celestial Jerusalem, see A. Aptowitzer, "The Heavenly Temple in the Agada" (Hebrew), *Tarbiz* 2 (1930–1931): 137–153; 257–287.

Poem 10

Sources:
    Schirmann, *Hashira ha'ivrit* 1:242.
    Ibn Gabirol, *Shire haqodesh* 2:469.
Translations:
    Carmi, *Penguin Book*, p. 313.
    Ibn Gabirol, *Selected Religious Poems*, p. 7.
    1. Gen. 21:1–21, especially verse 17.
    2. Gen. 16:6–12. See above on poem 1.
    3. See poems 1 and 9.
    4. A large number of homilies identifying biblical animals with the nations who subjugated Israel (including the above-mentioned interpretation of Ps. 80:14) may be read in Lev. R. 13:5. The perspective there is, however, pre-Islamic.
    5. See Abraham Ibn Ezra on Dan. 11:30.
    6. Abraham bar Ḥiyya used both methods in his eschatological work *M'gilat ham'gale*. See Silver, *A History of Messianic Speculation*, pp. 69–74.
    7. Gen. 14:15; Exod. 12:29; Ruth 3:8. Cf. also the liturgical poem by Yannai beginning "Then You performed wondrously many miracles at night," in Zvi Meir Rabinovitz, *The Liturgical Poems of Rabbi Yannai according to the Triennial Cycle of the Pentateuch and the Holidays* (Hebrew) (Jerusalem: Bialik Institute, 1985), 1:302–303. The poem also appears in most editions of the Passover *Haggadah*.
    8. The poem is linked verbally to the verse from Daniel by several Hebrew words characteristic of that book, including *mevin* used in the sense of "explain" rather than "understand," as in Dan. 8:27.
    9. Schirmann, *Hashira ha'ivrit* 1:243 (poem 8).

Poem 11

Sources:
    Schirmann, *Hashira ha'ivrit* 1:480.
    Judah Halevi, *Dīwān* 2:302.
    1. Dan. 2:3. Most medieval commentators, including Abraham Ibn Ezra, hold that Nebuchadnezzar had actually forgotten his dream. The other possibility is that he was simply testing the wizards by demanding that they tell him both the dream and its interpretation.

2. Dan. 7:25, 8:14, 9:24, 12:7, 11–12. For similar concern with the dating of redemption, see above, poem 4, and perhaps poem 10.

3. Jer. 1:10. But the use of the number 890 as the basis for the calculation of the messianic era arose independently of and prior to Halevi. There is a source that dates the beginning of the messianic era 890 years after the destruction; see *Pirqe hekhalot rabati* 40:1, in Shᵉlomo Aharon Wertheimer, *Bate midrashot*, ed. A. J. Wertheimer, 2d ed. (Jerusalem: Kᵉtav vasefer, 1967–1968), p. 133, and the discussion in Alexander Marx, "Studies in Gaonic History and Literature," *Jewish Quarterly Review*, n.s., 1 (1910–1911): 76. For this number in Abraham bar Ḥiyya's calculations, see Joseph Sarachek, *The Doctrine of the Messiah in Medieval Jewish Literature* (New York: Jewish Theological Seminary of America, 1932), pp. 320–321. It should also be noted that the earliest possible date projected by Abraham bar Ḥiyya for the beginning of the messianic era is 1135/1136, a scant six years after the date of Halevi's dream; see *Mᵉgilat hamᵉgale*, ed. Adolf Poznanski (Berlin: Druck von H. Itzkowski, 1924), p. 36.

4. The identification of the four beasts has of course changed with the changing political fortunes of Israel.

5. My translation from the Arabic text of Maimonides' *Epistle to Yemen*, ed. A. S. Halkin (New York: American Academy for Jewish Research, 1952), pp. 96f. See Lewis, *Jews of Islam*, p. 102. For an equally bitter remark by one of Maimonides' contemporaries, see Ibn ʿAqnin, *Inkishāf al-asrār*, p. 38.

6. The fragility of the Jews' position and Maimonides' point about even the young needing to be constantly on their guard is brought home in an amusing but sobering fiction contained in Chapter 22 of the *Taḥkemoni* by Judah al-Ḥarizi (c. 1235), ed. Y. Toporowski (Tel Aviv: Maḥbarot lᵉsifrut, 1952), pp. 213–217; Schirmann, *Hashira haʿivrit* 2:156–161.

7. See Yitzhak Baer, *A History of the Jews in Christian Spain* (Philadelphia: Jewish Publication Society of America, 1961), 1:59–77. Note Baer's suggestion of a possible historical occasion for the composition of our poem (p. 71).

Poem 12

Sources:

Schirmann, *Hashira haʿivrit* 1:464.

Judah Halevi, *Shire haqodesh* 3:797.

Translations:

Judah Halevi, *Selected Poems*, p. 109.

Goldstein, *Hebrew Poems*, p. 95.

1. The equivalent in Hebrew is *biṭaḥon*. For a definition, see Schimmel, *Mystical Dimensions*, p. 117. Baḥya Ibn Paquda devotes to this important theme the whole of Chapter 4 of his *al-Hidāya ilā farāʾiḍ al-qulūb* [Guidance to the duties of the hearts]. See the translation by Menahem Mansoor et al., *The Book of Direction to the Duties of the Heart* (London: Routledge and Kegan Paul, 1973), pp. 221–272. See also R. J. Zwi Werblowsky, "Faith, Hope, and Trust: A Study in the Concept of Bittahon," Papers of the Institute of Jewish Studies I (1964), 95–139.

2. This consonant, which in most modern Hebrew pronunciations has been reduced to a glottal stop where not completely elided was still pronounced in medieval Spain as a voiced pharyngeal fricative, a harsh sound common in Arabic and still heard in Yemenite Hebrew. Its association with sobbing is used with remarkable effect in Ibn Gabirol's secular poem in his *Shire haḥol*, ed. Dov Jarden

(Jerusalem: Dov Yarden, 1975), pp. 284–285: for other examples, see Mirsky, *Mashma'ut heḥaruz*, pp. 192–295. See also below, poem 18, n. 1.

3. Ibn Gabirol, *Shire haqodesh* 2:538 (poem 194). The word derives its messianic associations from many passages in Daniel, especially in Chapter 12.

4. The epithet derives from Ps. 80:16: the same psalm provided the image of Israel as a vine in a passage quoted above. Incidentally, in his commentary on this word, Abraham Ibn Ezra happens to cite Judah Halevi's opinion on its meaning, an interpretation at variance with Halevi's own use of it here.

Poem 13

Sources:
> Schirmann, *Hashira ha'ivrit* 1:412–413.
> Moses Ibn Ezra, *Shire haqodesh*, p. 8.

Translations:
> Moses Ibn Ezra, *Selected Poems*, pp. 124–125.
> Carmi, *Penguin Book*, p. 330.

Discussion:
> Vajda, *L'amour*, p. 101.

1. Jer. 8:22.

2. As in Yerushalmi B⁽ᵉ⁾rakhot 5:1 (8d); Bava Batra 14b. Other references in David de Sola Pool, *The Kaddish* (New York: Bloch Publishing Company, 1929), pp. 64–65.

3. Jer. 31:19–20.

4. On the expression "the heart's eye," see below, poem 19.

5. See Aaron Mirsky, "The Significance of Rhyme in Girdle Poems" (Hebrew), in *Shai l⁽ᵉ⁾heman*, ed. Zvi Malachi (Tel Aviv: Katz Research Institute for Hebrew Literature, 1976–1977), pp. 202–203.

6. Abraham, Gen. 17:1: Noah, Gen. 6:9: Enoch, Gen. 5:22: God, Gen. 3:8.

7. See *Wine, Women, and Death*, pp. 3–4 and index, s.v. gardens.

8. See Abraham Ibn Ezra on Eccles. 1:5.

9. It is understood as meaning "birthstool" in Exod. 1:16.

10. I differ with Aharon Mirsky's interpretation of this passage in his article "Poems of the Spaniards from Chapter III of 'The Duties of the Heart' by R. Baḥya Ibn Paquda" (Hebrew), *Tarbiz* 50 (1980–1981): 307–308. He sees it as reflecting Baḥya's description of the location of the element earth with respect to the other three elements (*The Book of Direction*, p. 158). The other poem by Moses Ibn Ezra cited by Mirsky in support of this interpretation also seems to me, as it did to Abudarham, to refer more naturally to the place of the earth among the spheres. See Moses Ibn Ezra, *Shire qodesh*, pp. 130–133 and Bernstein's commentary. In fact, the passage in Baḥya itself seems to me to have the same meaning, rather than that attributed to it by Mirsky. The difference as to the interpretation of the Baḥya passage does not in itself contradict Mirsky's main thesis, that Ibn Ezra's language reflects that of Bahya. That the earth stands in the center of the spheres is, however, commonplace: cf. Abraham Ibn Ezra on Eccles. 1:7 and Job 26:7: Isaac Ibn Ghiyath on Eccles. 1:5–7 in *Ḥamesh m⁽ᵉ⁾gilot*, ed. Yosef Kafiḥ (Jerusalem: Ha'agada l⁽ᵉ⁾haṣalal ginze teman, 1962–1963), p. 179. Professor Schmelzer calls my attention to the same idea in a poem by Ibn Ghiyath, *Shire ibn giyat*, p. 70, ll. 21–35.

11. For this idea, see above, pp. 49–50.

NOTES

Poem 14

Sources:

Abraham Ibn Ezra, *Shire haqodesh* 1:200–201.

1. For examples, see *Wine, Women, and Death*, pp. 90–106.

2. Other allusions: line 1, to Songs 6:4, 10, 7:7; line 3, to Ezek. 16: 12; line 6, to Jer. 31:3 and Songs 7:8–9; line 8, to Songs 1:8, 5:9, 6:1; line 9, to Songs 6:10; line 13, to Jer. 31:3. For "awesome one," see p. 44.

3. The Hebrew actually has "mountain goats," another animal term often used to denote the beloved; see Prov. 5: 19. As mentioned in the Introduction, I translate all animal terms of endearment as "gazelle" or "fawn."

4. Isa. 60:7.

5. See above, pp. 48–49 and n. 36 for references.

Poem 15

Sources:

Schirmann, *Hashira ha'ivrit* 1:465.

Judah Halevi, *Shire haqodesh* 4:1172.

Translations:

Judah Goldin in *The Menorah Journal* 33 (1945): 196.

Nina Davis, *Songs of Exile* (Philadelphia: Jewish Publication Society of America, 1901), p. 51.

Note:

The idea of rendering the word *emet* in the poem's opening "O Truth" (i.e., O God) instead of the ordinary "truly" is borrowed from Franz Rosenzweig; see his *Jehuda Halevi*, p. 183; it was adopted by Goldin in his translation.

1. The suffix that ends verse 2, though not pronominal, happens to be identical to the suffix of the first person possessive and could be construed as such.

2. Deut. 6:4–9. The poem focuses on Deut. 6:5–7.

3. Baḥya himself correlates the two pairs of terms in his introduction to *Book of Direction*, pp. 87ff. Islamic sources are listed by A. S. Yahuda in the introduction to his edition of the Arabic original, *Al-Hidāja ilā farā'iḍ al-qulūb des Baḥja ibn Josef ibn Paquda aus Andalusien* (Leiden: E. J. Brill, 1912), pp. 59–60. Baḥya's work, in its medieval Hebrew translation, became one of the most popular Jewish books ever written.

4. Ps. 16:8.

5. Ibn Gabirol, *Shire haqodesh* 2:530 (poem 187). For "only one," see introduction to Chapter I, n. 20.

2 · GOD AND THE SOUL

Introduction

1. Ibn al-Tabbān, pp. 126–127 (poem 48); see his appendix.

2. *Ibid.*, pp. 175–178 and the later sources cited by Pagis.

3. Abraham Ibn Ezra, *Shire haqodesh* 1:26 (poem 2, line 3). The "heart's eye" = reason. See poem 24.

4. *Siddur Rav Saadia Gaon*, ed. Israel Davidson, S. Assaf, and B. I. Joel (2nd ed.; Jerusalem: M*e*qiṣe nirdamim, 1963), p. 48, line 18 f.

5. *Al-hidāja*, ed. Yahuda, p. 401. For the image, see Hab. 2:11.

6. Abraham Ibn Ezra, *Shire haqodesh* 1:25 (poem 1).

7. See above, pp. 12, 45.

8. For the same theme treated more concisely and from a particular point of view, see poem 26.

9. Joseph Ibn Ṣadiq was the author of a treatise on metaphysics and an excellent poet (d. 1149). Unfortunately, little of his poetry has been preserved. This passage is found in David, *Poems of Ibn Ṣadiq*, pp. 55–56 (poem 17); Schirmann, *Hashira Ha'ivrit* 1:552–553 (poem 245). "Where," "how," and "why" stand for philosophical inquiry into the nature of a thing. See S. Horowitz, *Der Mikrokosmos des Josef Ibn Ṣaddik* (Breslau: Druck von Th. Schatzky, 1903), p. 48.

10. Cf. the ancient preface to the liturgical poetry of the *'Amida*, found in most rites, "From the counsel of the wise and understanding" in Philip Birnbaum, *High Holiday Prayer Book* (New York: Hebrew Publishing Company, 1951), p. 210; Morris Silverman, *High Holiday Prayer Book* (Hartford, Conn.: Prayer Book Press, 1951), p. 77; or "I am fearful as I open my mouth to draw forth speech," the introduction to the *piyyuṭ* of the first day of the New Year in the Ashkenazic rite in Birnbaum, pp. 211–212; Silverman, pp. 77–78.

11. Buried in *Nishmat* is a single passing reference to a specifically Jewish event, the Exodus from Egypt. The authenticity of the passage is suspect (see Daniel Goldschmidt, *The Passover Haggadah: Its Sources and History* [Hebrew] [Jerusalem: Bialik Institute, 1960], p. 68); but it is found already in Saadia's prayer book, and so was probably present in the text used in Golden Age Spain.

Although the *Kaddish* (the second of the two following quotations) is an eschatological prayer, it does not refer explicitly to the redemption of Israel. Rather, it prays for the universal recognition of God and is thus an extension of the theme of universal praise begun in *Nishmat*. It does refer to Israel when it asks that the eschaton arrive in the lifetime of the members of the worshiping community, but this does not much weaken the prayer's overall universal bent.

12. The underlined words are identical in Hebrew: *nishmat*.

13. The roots of the underlined words are the same in the Hebrew: *gdl*.

14. Again, the underlined words are almost identical in the Hebrew: *bar*e*khi . . .adonai* and *bar*e*khu et adonai*.

15. See *Wine, Women, and Death*, pp. 85–86.

16. See Afterword, n. 3.

Poem 16

Source:

   Ibn al-Tabbān, p. 58.

1. The verb *l*e*zamer* (to sing) is frequently construed with the object of the song in the accusative. Thus we find in a single biblical verse, Ps. 47:7, *zam*e*ru elohim* (sing [to] God) alongside *zam*e*ru l*e*malkenu* (sing to our king).

2. Examples are legion. One that may be familiar because it is still found in

the standard liturgy is *Oḥila la'el* (I hope in the Lord), the precentor's prayer preceding the poem describing the Temple service on the Day of Atonement. See Philip Birnbaum, *High Holiday Prayer Book* (New York: Hebrew Publishing Company, 1951), p. 809; Morris Silverman, *High Holiday Prayer Book* (Hartford, Conn.: Prayer Book Press, 1951), p. 367; Jules Harlow, ed., *Maḥzor for Rosh Hashana and Yom Kippur* (New York: Rabbinical Assembly, 1972), p. 254.

3. So the liturgical tradition understood Exod. 34:5–7. See *Rosh Hashana* 17b and Elbogen, *Hat'fila b'yisra'el*, p. 166. The picture of God teaching Moses the words of the prayer for atonement is of course a survival of the pagan notion that the god teaches man magic.

4. The classic study of the "decorated speech" doctrine in medieval Hebrew poetry is Dan Pagis, *Shirat haḥol v'torat hashir l'moshe ibn ezra uv'ne doro* (Jerusalem: Bialik Institute, 1970), especially pp. 35–54. For the idea—often implied but never, as far as I know, articulated by the tradition—that prayer consists in a returning to God of His own words, see above, p. 17 and poem 22, n. 10.

Poem 17

Sources:
> Schirmann, *Hashira ha'ivrit* 1:514.
> Judah Halevi, *Shire haqodesh* 1:213.

Translation:
> Judah Halevi, *Selected Poems*, 114.

1. The last verse contains allusions to both prayers. The poem is usually considered to have been intended for *Nishmat*.

2. This usage of the word *yeḥida*, literally "only one," has been explained above, Chapter I, n. 20.

3. See *Wine, Women, and Death*, p. 139.

4. This form cannot possibly derive from early Sufi poetry, as asserted by Y. Levin, "*Hab'riḥa*," p. 178.

5. Various Arabic and Hebrew sources on Time are assembled by Yisra'el Levin in "*Z'man v'tevel b'shirat haḥol ha'ivrit bis'farad*," *Oṣar y'hude s'farad* 5 (1961–1962), 68–79, and in "*Hab'riḥa*," pp. 149–184.

6. Quran 15:39, where the Devil says, "I shall adorn the path of error for them [i.e., for mankind] in the earth" (Pickthall translation, p. 192).

7. *Wine, Women, and Death*, p. 143. See the discussion there for an explanation of the anagram in the Hebrew words represented by the "poison" and "honey."

8. The biblical source of the verb is Jer. 2:36. Most medieval grammarians derived it from the root *'zl* (to go), but it could also be explained as deriving from the root *zll* (to be worthless, to squander). Somewhere in the semantic ambience is a third root, *nzl* (to flow), with its connotations of the instability of water (Menaḥem ben Saruq, *Maḥberet*, ed. Herschell E. Filipowski (London: Ḥevrat m'̔or'̔re y'̔shenim, 1854), p. 79.

Poem 18

Sources:
> Schirmann, *Hashira ha'ivrit*, 1:513.
> Judah Halevi, *Shire haqodesh* 1:25.

Translations:
    Carmi, *Penguin Book*, p. 335.
    Judah Halevi, *Selected Poems*, p. 93.
Discussion:
    Zur, *ʿIyunim*, pp. 17–23.
    A. L. Strauss, *Bᵉdarkhe hasifrut*, pp. 102–104.
    1. Readers familiar with modern Hebrew must bear in mind that the letter *ʿayin* (here represented by ʿ) was not elided or reduced to schwa as in most modern Hebrew dialects but, rather, had a distinctive pharyngeal articulation. See above, poem 12, n. 2.
    The ordinary Hebrew word for "awake" is *ʿer*. Several medieval commentators saw a connection between *lᵉnaʿer* (to shake off) and *naʿar* (youth). See David Kimḥi on I Sam. 1:24 and Ibn Janāḥ, *Kitāb al-Uṣūl* [The book of Hebrew roots], ed. Adolf Neubauer, with additions and corrections by Wilhelm Bacher (reprint; Amsterdam: Philo Press, 1968), s.v. *nʿr*.
    2. The paradox of youth being linked to night because of its dark hair and old age being linked to dawn because of gray hair is a topos of Arabic and Hebrew.
    3. Halevi turned this into a triple pun in his poem in Schirmann, *Hashira haʿivrit* 1:504, using a third meaning of this versatile group of sounds, "myrrh."
    4. Jer. 31:12 (11).

Poem 19

Sources:
    Schirmann, *Hashira haʿivrit* 1:516.
    Judah Halevi, *Shire haqodesh* 2:417.
Translation:
    Solomon Solis-Cohen, in Shalom Spiegel, "On Medieval Hebrew Poetry," in Louis Finkelstein, ed. *The Jews: Their History, Culture, and Religion*, 3d Ed. (New York: Harper & Brothers, 1960), p. 857.
    1. Halevi's wording is slightly closer to Ps. 118:23 ("This is the Lord's doing; it is marvelous in our sight"), but his train of thought is clearly more inward than that of that verse, which is part of a public celebration. Seeking the biblical allusions in medieval Hebrew poems is not simply a matter of locating the nearest verbal match; the overall theme and mood are sometimes more important, a point often overlooked by commentators. Jarden, for example, cites only Ps. 118:23.
    But Ps. 118:23 is not irrelevant. By combining the theme of Ps. 139 with the words of Ps. 118, Halevi was able to include the connection between "wonders" and "eyes," the latter standing for the intellect, as in the common expression "the heart's eye," which we shall soon encounter again.
    My translation is based on Halevi's own interpretation of Ps. 139:14, which happens to be preserved in Abraham Ibn Ezra's commentary: "'I know it very well' in the opinion of Rabbi Judah Halevi (who rests in glory!) means, 'Your works are too wonderful for me [i.e., beyond me], even though my soul is very aware.'"
    2. See Abraham Ibn Ezra on verse 1. "This Psalm is very weighty in the ways of the Lord; in these five books [= the five books of the Psalms] there is none like it. Its meaning can be penetrated only to the extent of one's understanding of the ways of God and the ways of the soul." The verse figures prominently in Ibn

Gabirol's *The Kingly Crown* and in Isaac Ibn Ghiyath's cycle for the Day of Atonement referred to above, p. 241, n. 29.

3. Baḥya, *Book of Direction*, pp. 160–173; Alexander Altmann, "The Delphic Maxim in Medieval Islam and Judaism,"; his *Studies in Religious Philosophy and Mysticism* (London: Routledge and Kegan Paul, 1969), pp. 24, 36.

4. Exod. 19:16ff., 33:22, 34:6.

5. For this rendering, see Hermann Greive, *Studien zum Jüdischen Neuplatonismus* (Berlin: Walter de Gruyter, 1973), p. 83 n. 42.

6. His comment on Ps. 17:15 embedded in his comment on 139:18.

7. For the interpretation of the ascent of Moses as ecstatic union with the upper worlds, see the fragment of the commentary of Dunash Ibn Tamim on *Sefer yeṣira*, published by Georges Vajda, "Nouveau fragments arabes du commentaire du Dunash b. Tamim sur le *Livre de la Création*," in *Revue des Etudes Juifs* 113 (1954): 193–194. For Abraham Ibn Ezra's interpretation, see Greive, *Studien*, pp. 73–84.

8. I am aware that this interpretation is contrary to the tenor of Halevi's way of thinking in the *Kuzari*, where the literal historical truth of Israelite history is central to the argument. But as long as the literal meaning was not rejected, it is not necessary to assume that Halevi would have rejected the principle of allegorization. Moreover, Halevi's thinking was not necessarily completely consistent throughout his career.

Poem 20

Sources:

Schirmann, *Hashira haʿivrit* 1:238.
Ibn Gabirol, *Shire haqodesh* 1:79.

Translations:

Ibn Gabirol, *Selected Religious Poems*, page 2.
Goldstein, *Hebrew Poems*, p. 69.
Nina Davis, *Songs of Exile*, p. 29.
See also the prayer books listed in note 1.

Discussion:

Aaron Mirsky, "Poems of the Spaniards," 335–336.

1. Though found even in some older versions of the Ashkenazic rite, it seems to have become especially popular in modernized prayer books. See Jules Harlow, ed., *Siddur sim shalom: A Prayerbook for Shabbat, Festivals, and Weekdays* (New York: The Rabbinical Assembly and The United Synagogue of America, 1985), p. 334; Morris Silverman, ed., *The Sabbath and Festival Prayer Book* (New York: The Rabbinical Assembly of America and the United Synagogue of America, 1946), p. 371 (translation by Nina Salaman [Davis]); *The Union Prayerbook for Jewish Worship*, 2 vols. (Cincinnati: Central Conference of American Rabbis, 1947), 1:103; *Gates of Prayer: The New Union Prayerbook* (New York: Central Conference of American Rabbis, 1975), p. 332; *Sabbath Prayer Book*, ed. Mordecai M. Kaplan and Eugene Kohn (New York: The Jewish Reconstructionist Foundation, 1945), pp. 74–75 (translation by Eugene Kohn).

2. For the dynamics of Arabic prosody, see my *Form and Structure in the Poetry of al-Muʿtamid Ibn ʿAbbād* (Leiden: E. J. Brill, 1974). Particularly relevant in connection with this remark are the discussions of opening pairs of lines (pp. 102–103; 147–148). I believe that the study of poems in Hebrew quantitative verse

would benefit from the application of the principles worked out in this book in connection with Arabic poetry, published in 1975.

3. Pointed out by Mirsky, "*Shire hasᵉfaradim,*" in p. 336.

4. Also by Mirsky; the source is Baḥya, *Hidāya*, p. 113: *innamā 'l-insān / al-qalb wa-'l-lisān; Book of Direction*, p. 167. But there is no reason to suppose with Mirsky that Ibn Gabirol got the phrase from Baḥya. For one thing, Baḥya probably wrote later than Ibn Gabirol; his dates are now generally agreed to be c. 1050–c. 1090. For another, Baḥya is now known to have copied the passage almost verbatim from an earlier work, a non-Jewish one at that; see above, p. 9 and n. 12.

Poem 21

Sources:

Schirmann, *Hashira haᶜivrit* 1:235.

Ibn Gabirol, *Shire haqodesh* 1:20.

Translation:

Ibn Gabirol, *Selected Religious Poems*, p. 14.

Notes:

In verse 1 I have translated *aqademkha* as meaning "to come bringing a gift," in accordance with the usage in Mic. 6:6.

In some versions of our poem the last line reads

אֲשַׁחֵר אֵל בְּרֵאשִׁית רַעְיוֹנִי \ אֲשֶׁר לִשְׁמוֹ תְּהַלֵּל כָּל נְשָׁמָה

(I seek God early, with the first of my thoughts, / To whom every soul gives praise).

1. Berakhot 33b.

2. I Kings 8:27.

3. This analysis is based on a principle first established for medieval Hebrew poetry by Mirsky in his seminal article, "*Mashmaᶜut heḥaruz,*" already referred to more than once. A poem's rhyme syllable, by dint of repetition, may contribute to its semantic content over and above its function as part of the word to which it belongs. Every monorhymed poem must be examined to see if this principle applies, and to what extent.

4. "Prayer (I)," in Mario Di Cesare, ed., *George Herbert and the Seventeenth Century Religious Poets* (New York: W. W. Norton & Company, Inc., 1978), p. 21.

Poem 22

Sources:

Schirmann, *Hashira haᶜivrit* 1:236.

Ibn Gabirol, *Shire haqodesh* 2:461–462.

Translations:

Carmi, *Penguin Book*, p. 316.

Ibn Gabirol, *Selected Religious Poems*, p. 13.

Discussion:

Zur, *ᶜIyunim*, pp. 24–33, 145–153.

Vajda, *L'amour*, p. 90.

Dreyer, *Religiöse Gedankenwelt*, pp. 148ff.

1. I Kings 8:27; Gen. R. 68:11 (ed. J. Theodor and Ch. Albeck, 2d ed. [Jerusalem: Wahrmann Books, 1965], 2:777).

2. Reynold A. Nicholson, *The Mystics of Islam* (London: G. Bell and Sons, 1914), p. 68: Schimmel, *Mystical Dimensions*, p. 190.

3. A. Aptowitzer, "The Heavenly Temple in the Agada" (Hebrew), *Tarbiz* 2 (1930–1931): 137–153: 257–287.

4. Repeatedly in I Kings, but elsewhere, too.

5. Abraham Ibn Ezra, *Shire haqodrsh* 1:31. For another use of this image by Abraham Ibn Ezra, see poem 29.

6. Ibn Gabirol, *Shire haqodesh* 2:529. "Bound" represents *ʿaqod*, which means "bound like a sacrificial lamb," as in Mishna Tamid 4:1.

7. Jer. 20:9. The verb *gavar* is associated with water in Gen. 7, where it is used repeatedly in connection with the flood.

8. For another occurrence of this idea, see Ibn Gabirol in *Shire haqodesh* 2:465: "My heart loves You very much, it cannot hide it; it reveals my love in my speech." For a more lighthearted version of the same idea in Ibn Gabirol, see his epigram in *Shire haqodesh* 2:593 (poem 230):

> When God appears within my heart
> —for nowhere does Your like exist—
> My lips pronounce Your name; were I
> To muzzle them they'd not desist.

9. *Wine, Women, and Death*, p. 102. The idea is related to the theme of the lover's delight in his beloved's name, which we have seen above in poem 5. Cf. Ibn Ḥazm, *The Ring of the Dove*, pp. 76–86.

10. Above, p. 17 and poem 16, n. 4.

Poem 23

Sources:
Schirmann, *Hashira haʿivrit*, 1:237.
Ibn Gabirol, *Shire haqodesh* 2:464.
Translations:
Ibn Gabirol, *Selected Religious Poetry*, p. 5.
Eugene Kohn, in *Sabbath Prayer Book* (New York: Jewish Reconstructionist Foundation, 1945), pp. 110–111.
Discussion:
Binyamin Bar Tiqva, *Hagut vᵉhavaya barᵉshut "shᵉlosha nosᵉdu" lᵉr. shᵉlomo ibn gabirol*, in *Talpiyot* (1984–1985): 39–43.

1. See Baḥya, *Book of Direction*, Chapter II.

2. See poems 13, 19, and 24.

3. See the discussion of poem 3.

4. I owe this observation to Bar Tiqva's article cited above, p. 40, though I interpret it differently.

5. Sachs, quoted by Bar Tiqva.

Poem 24

Sources:
Schirmann, *Hashira haʿivrit* 1:304.
Ibn Ghiyath, *Shire ibn giyat*, p. 248.

Translation:

Goldstein, *Hebrew Poems*, p. 73.

1. See the discussion of poem 19.

2. That the allusion to Ps. 139 is not accidental is confirmed in verse 2 by the words *da'at nisg'va* and *niflet*, which occur together in a single verse in the psalm.

3. Exod. 33:12.

4. *Midrash t'hilim* 103:4 (ed. Buber, 217a); for more on this midrash, see poem 26.

Poem 25

Sources:

Schirmann, *Hashira ha'ivrit* 1:516.

Judah Halevi, *Dīwān* 2:296.

Translation:

Nina Davis, *Songs of Exile*, p. 52.

1. Schimmel, *Gärten der Erkenntnis* (Düsseldorf: Eugen Diedericks Verlag, 1985), p. 28.

2. Schimmel, *Mystical Dimensions*, p. 39.

Poem 26

Sources:

Schirmann, *Hashira ha'ivrit*, 1:237.

Ibn Gabirol, *Shire haqodesh* 1:80.

Translations:

Carmi, *Penguin Book*, p. 315.

Ibn Gabirol, *Selected Religious Poems*, p. 41.

Discussion:

Zur, *'Iyunim*, pp. 41, 44, 50–51.

Jonathan Wittenberg, "A Reshut to *Nishmat*," *Prooftexts* 8 (1988): 340–345.

1. For a complete list of rabbinic sources, see *Midrash Wayyikra Rabbah*, ed. Mordecai Margulies (Jerusalem: Ministry of Education and Culture of Israel and the American Academy for Jewish Research, 1953), 1:96. Altmann, "Delphic Maxim," p. 6 n. 33. The theme was versified by Yannai, *Maḥzor piyuṭe rabi yanai latora v'lamo'adim*, ed. Zvi M. Rabinovitz (Jerusalem: Bialik Institute, 1985–87), 1:371, and by Saadia in a *rahiṭ* published by Menahem Zulay, *Ha'askhola hapay'ṭanit shel r. sa'adya ga'on* (Jerusalem: Schocken Institute for Jewish Research of the Jewish Theological Seminary of America, 1964), p. 111. It is also echoed in Abraham Ibn Ezra's commentary on Gen. 1:26.

2. The term has been more fully explained above in the introduction to Chapter I, n. 20. As will be presently shown, "uniqueness" is also one of the points of comparison between God and the soul in several rabbinic sources.

3. Gen. R. 2:3, ed. J. Theodor and Ch. Albeck, 2d ed. (Jerusalem: Wahrmann Books, 1965), pp. 15–16, and the references in the notes.

4. See Wittenberg, "A Reshut to *Nishmat*," p. 344. The applicability of the question "why" to simple substances is treated by Ibn Gabirol in *M'qor ḥayim* 5:24 (Bluwstein, pp. 197–198).

5. *'Olam* with no qualification was often used as the Hebrew equivalent of the Arabic *dunyā*, the mundane (literally lower) world; for an example, see Halevi in

Schirmann, *Hashira ha'ivrit* 1:522 (poem 228, line 13). The usage derives from Eccles. 3:11; cf. the last two comments by Abraham Ibn Ezra and the very interesting remarks of Ibn Ghiyath (ed. Kafiḥ, p. 204). For the usage here, compare the rabbinic sources cited by Wittenberg. On the interpretation of the verse, see also Zur, *'Iyunim*, p. 42.

    6. Ps. 103:1.

Poem 27

Sources:
    Schirmann, *Hashira ha'ivrit* 1:236.
    Ibn Gabirol, *Shire haqodesh* 2:451.
Discussion:
    A. Mirsky, *Mashma'ut heḥaruz*, pp. 172ff.
    Idem, "*Shire has'faradim*," *Tarbiz* 50 (1980–1981): 315ff., 324.

    1. A number of Golden Age poems employ this device. Most are *baqashot*, petitions for forgiveness couched in very personal language and addressed directly to God. Isaac Ibn Mar Saul (tenth century) seems to have originated the genre, or at least his is the earliest metrical *baqasha* to come down to us. His poem was imitated by many poets, notably by Halevi in his famous *adonai negd'kha kol ta'avati* (famous in the sense that it is found in the prayer rites of nearly every Jewish community except that of the Ashkenazim). Ibn Gabirol's poem is markedly different in tone and content from the other examples of the genre. As Schirmann points out, we do not know the poem's original function.

    2. In his illuminating article "*Shire has'faradim*," Mirsky has demonstrated a close relationship between the sequence of ideas, and even the language, in this poem and in Baḥya's *Book of Direction*, pp. 158–159. Impressive as these parallels are, they cannot be permitted to govern the interpretation of the poem in the face of the details of the poem's wording. Baḥya's intention is to urge his reader to pious humility and gratitude. Ibn Gabirol's poem, though addressed to God in ostensibly pious language, reflects quite a different frame of mind, as will appear from the discussion.

    Furthermore, it is improbable on chronological grounds that Ibn Gabirol modeled his poem on Baḥya's work. See poem 20, n. 4.

    3. This confusion has been confirmed by actual classroom experience in teaching the poem. In the first interpretation the syntactic relationship of the two objects is determined by the word order, while the preposition *l'* is understood as being a marker of the the direct object, as in rabbinic Hebrew; in the second, it is determined by the preposition *l'*, taken in its usual meaning in the expression *sam x l'y* (to make *x* into *y*), and the word order is considered to be inverted.

    For a similar ambiguity, cf. Ibn Gabirol's enigmatic philosophical poem, *Ahavtikha*, in *Sh'lomo ibn Gabirol: shire ha-ḥol*, ed. H. Brody and H. Schirmann (Jerusalem: Schocken Institute for Jewish Research, 1974), p. 17, in which the following line appears: "He longs to make being like-being." For entry into the fairly extensive literature on this poem, see the essays collected by Zvi Malachi and Hanna David, *Studies in the Work of Shlomo Ibn-Gabirol* (Hebrew) (Tel Aviv: Tel Aviv University, 1985).

    4. Ps. 139 and Job 10:10.
    5. Gen. 2:7.

NOTES

6. Whether Jonah's prayer of thanksgiving was composed by the book's author or by someone else and simply inserted into the book by an editor makes no difference: the expression is an excellent metaphor for Jonah's predicament, and there is no way to connect it to the womb, as Schirmann (*Hashira ha'ivrit*) attempts to do in his notes to the poem.

7. As noted by Mirsky, *Mashma'ut heḥaruz*, p. 174. Here is yet another case where the idea rather than the exact wording is the point of a biblical allusion. Commentators on medieval Hebrew poetry are not always on the lookout for such allusions, which cannot be concretely verified.

8. In translating "wove," I have given preference to a meaning attested in some rabbinic sources (e.g., *Yoma* 72b) because it yields a vivid image. Other rabbinic sources, e.g.. Mishna *Ḥulin* 9:6, use the word in connection with an embryo, in the sense "to form." Maimonides, in his commentary on that passage, explains it by reference to Ps. 139:15, which, as we have seen, was on Ibn Gabirol's mind in composing the poem. The passages cited by Mirsky to support his explanation of the word as "drawn" seem less relevant.

9. Moses Ibn Chiquitilla, as quoted in Abraham Ibn Ezra's commentary, but not Ibn Ezra himself. I disagree with Mirsky, who bases his interpretation on the Targum, supported by other medieval commentators on the psalm.

10. From the conclusion to his tirade against the Jews of Saragossa, *Niḥar b'qor'i g'roni* in Schirmann, *Hashira ha'ivrit*, I, verses 47–49.

11. Helen Waddell, *Medieval Latin Lyrics* (New York: W. W. Norton & Co. Inc., 1977), p. 330. For a similar idea, see George Herbert's poem "Judgement" in Di Cesare, *George Herbert*, p. 68.

12. David Kaufmann, "Salomo Ibn Gabirols Philosophische Allegorese," in his *Stüdien uber Salomon Ibn Gabirol* (reprint; Jerusalem: Makor Publishing Ltd., 1971), pp. 63–79, especially pp. 70–71: Julius Gutmann, "*Zu Gabirol's allegorischer Deutung der Erzählung vom Paradies,*" *Monatschrift für Geschichte und Wissenschaft des Jüdenthums* 80 (1936): 180ff.

Poem 28

Sources:
    Schirmann, *Hashira ha'ivrit* 1:523.
    Judah Halevi, *Shire haqodesh* 1:169.
Note:
    Verse 2 has a curious parallel in a secular love poem by Samuel the Nagid in *Diwan Sh'muel hanagid* (Jerusalem: Hebrew Union College Press, 1966), p. 299, poem 166: "Is my wound fatal, if you are the healer? / Is my pain eternal if you are the doctor?" The rhythm is very similar (though not identical), as is the sentence structure. Our poet's affirmation in verse 2 seems rather tentative by comparison.

Poem 29

Sources:
    Abraham Ibn Ezra, *Shire haqodesh* 1:107.
    Schirmann, *Hashira ha'ivrit* 1:604–605.
Discussion:
    Levin, "*Biqashti,*" p. 139.

1. See especially Ps. 119:35,125. Like our poet, the author of the psalm frequently calls himself "Your servant," and one of his preeminent themes is love (though in the psalm it is love of God's commandments that is stressed, and though the psalm does not use the particular Hebrew word for love found in verse 2 of the poem).

2. In passages such as Num. 6:26 or Ps. 4:7.

3. On Exod. 33:23; see Greive, *Studien*, pp. 77ff.

4. Perhaps another allusion to Moses, Exod. 2:12.

5. For example, Ibn Gabirol, *The Kingly Crown* (*Shire haqodesh* 1:66, section 38, lines 2–3), trans. Lewis, p. 62: "And if Thou search out my sin, I shall flee from Thee to Thee, and hide from Thy wrath in Thy shadow." For a list of Hebrew sources, see Dov Sadan, *"Mim*ᵉ*kha elekha*: *ᶜim midrash ᶜaseret hadib*ᵉ*rot,"* in his collection *Galgal hamo*ᶜ*adim* (Tel Aviv: Masada, 1964), pp. 121–148. I wish to thank my colleague Professor Menahem Schmelzer for calling my attention to this article.

6. Here translated, "Your folk"; for the justification, see Abraham Ibn Ezra's commentary on Ps. 80:18.

Poem 30

Source:
Schirmann, *Hashira ha*ᶜ*ivrit* 1:527.
Translations:
Judah Halevi, *Selected Poems*, p. 119.
Goldstein, *Hebrew Poems*, p. 99.

1. Noted by Schirmann, *Hashira ha*ᶜ*ivrit* 1:532, on a more elaborate poem by Halevi dividing the cosmos into three parts. See Abraham Ibn Ezra's commentary on Ps. 103:20–22 and Dan. 10:21. Schirmann also refers to *Sefer habahir*, a contemporary work from a different cultural sphere that employs a similar division of the cosmos.

AFTERWORD

1. For a convenient summary, see Ivan G. Marcus, "Beyond the Sephardic Mystic," *Orim* 1 (1985): 35–53.

2. Ismar Schorsch, "The Myth of Sephardic Supremacy," *Leo Baeck Institute Year Book* 34 (1989): 47–66.

3. Ezra Fleischer, *"Hirhurim bid*ᵉ*var ofyah shel shirat yisra*ʾ*el bis*ᵉ*farad,"* P*ᵉᶜamim* 4 (1979): 15–20; for the typology of the two communities (without the retrospective judgment), see Gerson D. Cohen, "Messianic Postures of Ashkenazim and Sephardim," *Leo Baeck Memorial Lecture Number 9* (New York: Leo Baeck Institute, 1967).

Technical Terms

adab	(Arabic), p. 7
adīb	(Arabic), p. 7
ʿAmida	(Hebrew), pp. 15, 144
ahᵃva	(Hebrew; pl. *ahᵃvot*), pp. 35, 36
baqasha	(Hebrew), p. 262n.
Barᵉkhu	(Hebrew), pp. 144, 145
bᵉrakha	(Hebrew), p. 14
dīn	(Arabic), p. 12
dunyā	(Arabic), p. 12
gᵉʾula	(Hebrew), pp. 35, 36
ghazal	(Arabic), pp. 37, 140
Kaddish	(Hebrew), pp. 144, 145, 157, 250n., 255n.
kalām	(Arabic), p. 10
kharja	(Arabic), p. 19
midrash	(Hebrew), p. 20
muwashshaḥ	(Arabic), pp. 18, 19, 20, 26, 36, 69, 128
nᵉshama	(Hebrew), pp. 179, 180
Nishmat	(Hebrew), pp. 144, 145, 146, 152, 157, 173, 250n., 255n., 256n.
piyyuṭ	(Hebrew; pl. *piyyuṭim*), pp. 13, 15, 16, 17, 22, 23, 24, 41, 44, 45, 152, 240n.
qaṣīda	(Arabic), p. 66
qiṭʿa	(Arabic), p. 18

rᵉshut	(Hebrew; pl. *rᵉshuyot*), pp. 145, 146, 147, 148, 153
Shᵉma	(Hebrew), pp. 14, 35, 36, 133, 134, 144
Taḥanun	(Hebrew), p. 15
tawakkul	(Arabic), pp. 63, 117, 216
Tᵉfila	(Hebrew), p. 15
tokheḥa	(Hebrew), pp. 21, 87, 157
ʿulamāʾ	(Arabic), p. 11
yoṣer	(Hebrew), p. 15
zuhd	(Arabic), pp. 21, 22, 239n.
ẓaby	(Arabic), p. 37
zuhdīyāt	(Arabic), pp. 7, 157

Index

See also Technical Terms, *page 265.*

Ibn Ḥazm, 73, 79
Ibn Tibbon, 231
Ibn Zaidūn, 81
Ideas, children of, in Arabic
    idiom, 163
Illusions of time, 158
Individualism, 23–25, 41, 118,
    133, 145, 147–148, 153,
    233–234
Intellect
  as divine reflection, 167–168
  knowledge of God via, 123,
    140–144, 173–175,
    191–193, 196–197
Intimacy, with God, 94–95, 216
Isaac Ibn Ghiyath, 26, 49–50
  poetry of, 80, 195–197, 201
Isaac Ibn Mar Saul, 95
Isaiah, 179
Ishmael, 106, 110, 111
Islam. See also *Arabic.*
  in Andulusia, 11
  Arabic poetry and, 7–9
  devotional poetry of, 40–41
  pietistic literature of, 133
  prophecy concerning, 111–113
  socioreligious contradictions in,
    11
  tolerance of Jews by, 112–113
  wild ass symbolizing, 55, 106
Israel
  gazelle symbolizing, 37, 55
  God's love for, 36, 38, 94–95,
    228–229
  redemption of. See *Redemption.*
  special status of, 228–229
  subjugation of
    paradox of, 33–36, 80–81
    passivity and, 74–75
    self-hatred and, 79–81

Jeremiah, 74–75, 187, 216
Jews
  abandonment of, 74–75

ambivalence of, 74–75
assimilation of, 5–6, 10–12, 74
Islamic tolerance of, 112–113
marginality of, 33–34,
    112–113, 228–229
persecution of, 113, 228–229,
    231, 232
redemption of. See *Redemption.*
self-hatred of, 79–81
Joseph Ibn Ṣadiq, 81, 143
Judah Halevi, 27, 33, 40
  poetry of, 46–48, 52–57,
    70–89, 81–82, 108–119,
    131–135, 154–169,
    198–201, 214–217,
    226–229, 227–229
Judaism, Islamic influences on,
    10–12
Judeo-Arabic duality, 3–6

Kaddish, 265
Kallir, 17
Kallirian style, 19
Khazars, 79
Kimḥis, 231
King, sleeping, 88–89
King David. See *David.*
Kingly Crown, The (Ibn Gabirol),
    12, 21–22, 44–45
Kuzari (Judah Halevi), 27, 42, 79,
    87, 88, 110, 228

Lamentations, 45–46
Levi Ibn al-Tabban, 27, 140
  poetry of, 150–153
Liturgical poetry, 13–25. See also
    Religious poetry, Hebrew.
  admonitory, 157
  ambivalence in, 74–75
  Arabic love poetry's
    incorporation into, 36–41
  artistic principles of, 16–17

Quantitative metrics, 184
Quran, 8, 9, 158

Rabbinic eschatology, 106–107
Rabbis. See *Courtier-rabbis*.
Rābiʿa, 200–201
Rationality. See *Intellect*.
Redemption
    benediction of, 35–36
    dating of, 107, 111
    erotic vision of, 90–103
    exile and, 43
    gate of, 95, 106, 122, 125
    national vs. personal, 43–49,
        125, 129
    site of, 98
Redemption poetry, 36, 128
Religious persecution, 113,
        228–229, 231, 232
Religious poetry
    Hebrew
        Arabic influences in, 8–9,
            11–12
        Christian influences in, 8–9
        liturgical, 13–25. See also
            Liturgical poetry.
        love. See *Love poetry*.
        Midrash and, 16–17
        piyyuṭ tradition in, 13–18, 22
    Islamic, 40–41
    Sufi, 41
Religious universalism, 12, 23,
        34, 142, 143–144,
        228–229
Rhetorical effects, 27, 56
Romance love poetry, 68–69

Saadia Gaon, 10, 21, 41, 140,
        142, 223
Salvation. See *Redemption*.
Samuel the Nagid, 57, 61, 95,
        113

Schirmann, Ḥayim, 29, 79
Scientific data, incorporation of in
        poetry, 21–22
Secular poetry
    Arabic. See *Arabic poetry*.
    Hebrew. See *Hebrew poetry*.
Self-denial, 79–83
Self-hatred, 79–83
Shᵉma, 265
Sheol, 211
Sleeping, 162–163
Sleeping king, 88–89
Solomon, 179, 185
Solomon Ibn Gabirol, 12, 21, 26,
        37, 39–40, 41–45, 49, 89,
        205, 206, 223
    poetry of, 39, 43–45, 47, 48,
        50, 91–107, 118, 134–135,
        170–175, 202–213
Song of Songs, 20–21, 43, 44, 55,
        128
    allegorical character of, 38, 49,
        88
    Arabic love poetry and, 37–41
    exegesis of, 36, 40, 48–49, 93
Soul
    cerebrating, 204
    concept of, 22–23
    development of, 42
    divinity of, 152–153, 175,
        179–181, 185–187, 196,
        205, 206, 216
    love and, 41–49
    national vs. personal
        redemption and, 43–49
    philosophical concepts of,
        139–144. See also
        Philosophical concepts.
    as poetic theme, 22–23, 42–49,
        142–144
    three types of, 204
    uniqueness of, 43, 205–206
    universal, 204
Soul-body conflict, 134–135